圖書館學的世界觀

1963-1989論文選集

李華偉　著

俄亥俄大學圖書館

1991

臺灣學生書局印行

LIBRARIANSHIP

IN WORLD PERSPECTIVE

Selected Writings, 1963 - 1989

by

Hwa-Wei Lee

Ohio University Libraries

1991

STUDENT BOOK CO., LTD.

TABLE OF CONTENTS

Foreword

I.   Area Studies Collections

    1.   Africana -- A Special Collection at Duquesne University (1963)   3

    2.   International Information Exchange and Southeast Asia Collections: A View from the U. S (1980); Co-authors: K. Mulliner and Lian The-Mulliner. 7

    3.   Library Acquisitions From the Third World: An Introduction (1982); Co-author: K. Mulliner 19

    4.   Funding for the Southeast Asia Collection and Research Resources at Ohio University (1986); Co-author: K. Mulliner . . 29

II.   Bibliographic Control

    1.   Scholarly Publications: Considerations on Bibliographic Control and Dissemination (1975); Co-author: Stephen W. Massil 49

    2.   International Standard Numbering for Books and Serials and the Standardization of Bibliographic Descriptions (In Chinese) (1975); Co-author: Jane C. Yang 55

    3.   Co-operative Regional Bibliographic Projects in South-East Asia (1977) 63

III. International Cooperation

    1.   An Approach to Regional Cooperation in Scientific and Technical Information Services for Southeast Asia (1972) 77

    2.   Regional Cooperation for ISDS (1977) 91

    3.   Educating for International Interdependence: The Role of the Academic Library -- Ohio University and Malaysia (1985); Co-author: K. Mulliner 101

IV. International Exchanges and Internships

    1.   International Exchange of Librarians and the Ohio
        University Internship Program (1982); Co-author:
        K. Mulliner   111

    2.   International Library Internships: An Effective Approach
        to Cooperation (1985)   117

V. Library and Information Services

    1.   User and Use Analysis: A Case Study of the Information
        Utility by Geotechnical Engineers in Asian Countries
        (1974)   127

    2.   The Application of Information Technology to Close the
        Information Gap (1974)   137

    3.   The Experience of a Specialized Information Service in Asia --
        AGE (1975)   149

    4.   Approaches to Development of Water Resources Scientific
        Information Systems (1978); Co-author: Marjorie H. Rhodes . .   157

    5.   Challenges for the Library and Information Profession (1983) .   171

VI. Library Automation

    1.   The Information Technology -- New Tools and New Possibilities
        for Information Storage, Retrieval and Dissemination (1973) . .   187

    2.   Recent Breakthroughs in Library Automation in Taiwan (1981)   199

    3.   ALICE at One: Candid Reflections on the Adoption,
        Installation, and Use of the Virginia Tech Library System
        (VTLS) at Ohio University (1984); Co-authors: K. Mulliner,
        E. Hoffmann-Pinther, and Hannah McCauley   211

    4.   Trends in Automation in American Academic Libraries:
        Ohio University's Experiences (1989)   225

VII. Library Development

1. Fragmentation of Academic Library Resources in Thai
    University Libraries (1971) 243

2. A New Engineering Library Emerging in Asia (1971) 257

3. Principles of National Library and Information Policy (1986) .. 261

VIII. Library Networking

1. Proposal for the Establishment of a National Library and
    Information Network (In Chinese) (1974) 275

2. Sharing Information Resources Through Computer-Assisted
    Systems and Networking (1978) 281

3. A Sketch for a Computerized National Library and Information
    Network (1981) 289

4. Planning Process and Considerations for a State-wide
    Academic Libraries Information System in Ohio (1989) 297

Bibliography 309

Index 317

FOREWORD

During my thirty-one year library career--beginning at the University of Pittsburgh in 1959, including seven years in Bangkok, Thailand, 1968 to 1975, under the sponsorship of the United States Agency for International Development, and through the present directorship of the Ohio University Libraries since 1978, I have been fortunate to have many opportunities to write for professional journals and to present papers at conferences. Additionally, I have served on several editorial boards for library journals, written many book reviews, and co-edited two conference proceedings. Despite my heavy administrative responsibilities, the writings and accompanying research have enriched my professional knowledge and served to broaden my understanding in many areas of librarianship. I can well remember the many evenings, weekends, holidays, and vacations spent, instead of with my family or friends, in my study reading, researching, thinking, and writing. These have become my prime hobbies.

Because of my Chinese origin and years of library work in the United States and Asia, I long have been interested in international librarianship and have had opportunities to cultivate a world perspective in my professional outlook. This is reflected in my writings. I fortuitously have been privileged to be involved in or be witness to the development of library and information services in the many Asian countries with which I have had the honor to be associated.

At the suggestion of many friends and associates--and especially with the encouragement of the Library Association of China in Taiwan which is publishing this collection of my professional writings--I have selected twenty eight papers published between 1963 to 1989 as representative of my professional interests and concerns. These papers are grouped under eight topics: Area Studies Collections, Bibliographic Control, International Cooperation, International Exchanges and Internships, Library and Information Services, Library Automation, Library Development, and Library Networking. Two are written in Chinese and the remainder in English. Within each group, papers are arranged in chronological order. The British spelling in some of the papers published in journals using that form has been preserved.

Throughout my years of writing, I have been indebted to many former and current colleagues and friends with whom I have collaborated in writing. Each is acknowledged in the Table of Contents and in the Bibliography. I am especially grateful to Kent Mulliner, my close colleague at Ohio University, for his most valuable assistance in preparing this final form for publication.

In reviewing the papers, I realize that many tend more to reportage than scholarly work; nevertheless, they fairly represent my feelings and thoughts on issues confronting librarianship around the world. Some earlier papers now are dated but serve as records of the past, providing a historical perspective on more recent developments.

This collection of my writings could not have been published without the encouragements and sponsorship of the Library Association of the Republic of China. Ms. Teresa Y. Wang Chang, Professor Margaret Chang Fung, Mr. Karl Min Ku, Professor Lucy Te-Chu Lee, Professor Harris B. H. Seng, and Professor Chen-Ku Wang, among others, all deserve special and heartfelt thanks for making this publication possible. I sincerely and humbly invite the comments and advice of all readers and will accept all criticisms and responsibility for any shortcomings of this book.

Finally, I must single out my wife, Mary, for my profound gratitude for her continuing support, tolerance and understanding of my "workaholic" life style. In many of my writings, she was the very first reader and constructive critic. To my late parents, I would like to dedicate this book as a memorial to their love.

Hwa-Wei Lee
Ohio University Libraries
Athens, Ohio 45701
U.S.A.

December 1990

Section I

Area Studies Collections

Africana -- A Special Collection at Duquesne University (1963) 3

International Information Exchange and Southeast Asia
Collections: A View from the U. S. (1980); Co-authors: K.
Mulliner and Lian The-Mulliner 7

Library Acquisitions from the Third World: An Introduction (1982);
Co-author: K. Mulliner 19

Funding for the Southeast Asia Collection and Research Resources
at Ohio University (1986); Co-author: K. Mulliner 29

AFRICANA -- A SPECIAL COLLECTION AT DUQUESNE UNIVERSITY

The rapidly expanding African Collection at Duquesne was first inspired by the work of the Holy Ghost Fathers who were the founders of Duquesne. Their missionary zeal has for many years penetrated deep into the African Continent. The interest they have always held in the civilization and Christianization of Africa[1] was the prime source of inspiration for the establishment of an African Collection at Duquesne.

History

In the early years, the book budget of the collection was far from sufficient and the importance of such a collection still far from being properly recognized. Pioneer efforts sought to enlist the help of missionaries stationed in Africa. It was not surprising that many warm responses were received. From knowledgeable persons such as the Reverends Constantine Conan, Stephen J. Lasko and Anton Morgenroth, all of whom have had long careers as devoted missionary workers in Africa, many valuable materials and suggestions were obtained. Father Morgenroth later joined the faculty of the Institute of African Affairs at Duquesne where he now also serves as Consultant for the African Collection.

The founding of the Institute of African Affairs in 1956 made Duquesne the fifth university in this country and the first Catholic university to offer an organized African program of studies.[2] Under the directorship of Dr. Geza Grosschmid, the Institute has acquired nation-wide recognition. This is evident from the annual grant begun in 1960 from the United States Office of Education to establish within the Institute an "African Language and Area Center." The Federal Government has thus provided part of the much needed book funds for the collection. Since then the collection has been growing steadily. As of July 1963, the total volume of book materials and periodicals almost trebled the 1960 figures.

---

[1]Henry J. Koren, *The Spiritans; A History of the Congregation of the Holy Ghost* (Pittsburgh: Duquesne University, 1958) p. 440.

[2]Thomas Patrick Melady, "A Suggestion for the Establishment of the Institute of African Affairs at Duquesne University." (Pittsburgh: Duquesne University, 1955?) p. 2. (Mimeographed)

Scope

At present there are nearly 4,500 volumes in the collection. The number of periodicals in the stacks amounts to 217 titles, more than two thirds of which are current subscriptions. Pamphlets number nearly 1,000. There are also 74 reels of microfilms, most of which are made from the archives of the Missionnaires de la congregation du Saint-Esprit et du Saint-Coeur de Marie in Paris, 18 records of linguistics and music, 19 reels of tapes recording the complete lessons of language instruction in Swahili and Gio. The former was made under the direction of Father A. Loogman assisted by Mr. Peter Kyara; the latter was made by Kenneth E. Griffes and William E. Welmers to accompany their language text. The collection also includes a small number of manuscripts including scripts such as the *English-Idoma Dictionary by Rev. John M. Schreier, Nomen und Verbum in Afrikanischen Sprachen; Eine Strukturstudie* by Robert Laessig, etc., and some 200 photographs on North Africa, especially Algeria, collected by Mrs. L. E. Hubbell.

Staff

The collection is housed in a well equipped room separate from the general collection of the University Library. A professional librarian from the Reference Department spends half of his time in the collection and has the assistance of a half-time secretary who is proficient in German and French, a part-time cataloger, and two graduate assistants assigned to work for the collection by the Institute of African Affairs. Both the assistants have had extensive training in Swahili and possess a general knowledge of African matters.

Specialization

The collection originally had its special concentrations. Geographically, its interest was mainly on East Africa. Topically, its emphasis was centered on linguistics, history, anthropology, sociology, economics and missionary works. During recent years as more funds were made available, it no longer limited itself to the above areas. A broadened acquisition program was adopted to include the whole continent and works of various subject areas.

The expansion of the African program in the Institute of African Affairs has been responsible for the expansion of the African library collection. In addition to the teaching of the Swahili Language, a *lingua franca* in central Africa spoken by nearly 13 million people, Classical Arabic and Hausa are to be added this fall. The

4

latter is also widely spoken by more than 9 million people in northern Nigeria and the Sudan.[3]

For interested scholars and African specialists, the following specialties of the collection are worth noting.

Linguistic works

There are some 96 African languages represented in the collection. About 20 of these are spoken by more than one million people--Arabic, Swahili, Hausa, Amharic, Fula, Ibo, Malagasy, Yoruba, Luba, Somali, Sotho, Zulu, Kanuri, Moundu, Shona, Xhosa, Fang-Bulu, Ganda, Kongo and Nyamwesi-Sukuma. Most of the books in these languages are grammars, bilingual dictionaries, readers and religious teachings.

Studies on the Former Belgian Congo

The collection possesses an almost complete set of the publications (nearly 400 titles) by the Academie Royale des Sciences d'Outre-mer in Brussels. It includes the *Biographie Coloniale Belge, Bulletin des Seances,* and the *Memoires* which are in three classes: The *sciences morales et politiques*; the *sciences naturelles et medicales*; and *sciences techniques.* Many of these *Memoires* begin with Tome I, fasc. 1 which were published as early as 1930 and present a most thorough study of that region.

Bibliographies and Catalogs

To assist scholarly research, various bibliographical works are indispensable. The collection has a good collection of bibliographies and catalogs. The notable ones include those on official publications of various countries or regions by the Library of Congress and the *Catalog of African Government Documents and African Area Index* by Boston University. For national bibliographies, there are *Nigerian Publications, Bibliographie du Congo Belge et du Ruanda-Urundi,* and *South Africa Bibliography,* etc. The International African Institute's *Africa Bibliography Series* provides good bibliographic information on ethnography, sociology and linguistics. In the missionary field, there are two important bibliographies: the *Bibliotheca Missionum* by Robert Streit and the *Bibliografia Missionaria.* Perhaps the most up-to-date bibliography indexing books and periodical articles of social and economic interest is the *Fiches Bibliographiques* of the Centre

---

[3]C.F. and F.M. Voegelin, ed., "Languages Now Spoken By Over a Million Speakers," *Anthropological Linguistics,* III, no. 8 (Nov. 1961), pp. 15-18.

de Documentation Economique et Sociale at Brussels. It is arranged on 3" x 5" cards. Some 1,500 items are indexed each year with full bibliographic information.

The published Catalogs of the African Collections of both Northwestern University Library and Howard University Library are also sources of information to supplement the National Union Catalog for locating rare items in Africana.

There are also a few periodicals in the collection which regularly feature book reviews and abstracts. They include: *Africa, African Abstracts, African Affairs, African Studies, African Ecclesiastical Review, Africana Nova, Bibliographie Courante, Current Bibliography on African Affairs, Bulletin of the Institute Francais d'Afrique Noire, Journal of African History, Journal of Modern African Studies, Bulletin of the School of Oriental and African Studies of London University* and *The Rhodes-Livingstone Journal.*

Publications

In addition to contributing regularly to the *Joint Acquisitions List of Africana* compiled by the African Department of the Northwestern University Library, the collection also publishes a monthly acquisitions list of its own which is distributed free upon request. Publication of a printed catalog of the collection is being considered and it is hoped that it will provide needed bibliographic assistance to scholars and specialists who are interested in such information.

INTERNATIONAL INFORMATION EXCHANGE AND SOUTHEAST ASIA COLLECTIONS: A VIEW FROM THE U.S.*

Co-authors: K. Mulliner and Lian The-Mulliner

Historical Summary

Southeast Asia as a focus of academic concentration is a relatively recent arrival on the American academic scene. Even Cornell University's internationally acclaimed Echols (formerly part of Wason) Collection dates only after World War II. In the 1960s, interest in Southeast Asia Studies (and supporting library holdings) as a legitimate academic endeavor increased (probably as much from the efforts of graduates of the existing centers [Yale and Hawaii as well as Cornell] as from increasing military involvement in Indochina. But even with expansion, there are fewer than ten major collections focusing on Southeast Asia--although a number of additional libraries afford access to significant materials on the region, especially with regard to the Philippines as a former colony. Today these include (in alphabetical order to avoid offense) California at Berkeley, Cornell, Hawaii, Michigan, Northern Illinois, Ohio, Wisconsin, and Yale as well as the Library of Congress.

Such a small number of collections, in comparison even to major collections on other parts of Asia (37 on East Asia and 20 on South Asia),[1] has contributed to cooperation among the collections. This is best reflected in the Committee on Research Materials on Southeast Asia (CORMOSEA); a committee of the Southeast Asia Council of the Association of Asian Studies). Founded in 1967, this committee-- with a membership of scholars and librarians--has provided focus for information exchange both within and outside the United States. By obtaining financial assistance, it was able to commission the publication of a large number of reference aids on the area at minimal cost.[2] Most recently, it has successfully sponsored (under the direction of Shiro Saito of Hawaii, financially supported by the National Endowment for the Humanities, NEH) a survey of existing and needed research tools

---

*This joint paper was presented by Hwa-Wei Lee at the Meeting of the International Association of Orientalist Librarians, August 19, 1980; held concurrently with the 46th General Conference of IFLA in Manila, August 18-23, 1980.

[1]Extracted from Lee Ash, *Subject Collections: A Guide to Special Book Collections and Subject Emphases* (5th ed.; New York: Bowker, 1978).

[2]A list of projects supported and a summary of the most recent report on efforts at publication of the projects can be found in the *CORMOSEA Bulletin*, Vol. 9, No. 3 (Nov. 1977), p. 9-13.

on each Southeast Asian nation and the region as a whole.[3] Having identified existing weaknesses and needs, it is currently seeking financial support for production of these bibliographies, directories, dictionaries, etc.[4]

CORMOSEA's other apparent accomplishment has been the publication of the *CORMOSEA Bulletin* (formerly *Newsletter*) which has featured articles on important sources of information, reviews, reprints, news, and announcements relevant to scholars and librarians with Southeast Asian interests. Despite lapses in its frequency of issue, its past editors have provided a valuable reference tool and an important medium for disseminating and sharing information on the region internationally.[5]

CORMOSEA, which meets at least annually, serves as a forum in which inter-institutional competition can give way to exchanges of information, sharing of experiences, and cooperation in projects of import to the international research community.

One major obstacle to international information exchange has been the absence of agreed upon standards of bibliographic reference. International efforts, such as the ISBD and the ISDS, have provided overall guidance in addressing this problem, but inconsistencies in orthography, forms of reference, and local usages (not to mention personal preferences) can only be addressed by those concerned. In this regard, CORMOSEA has served as an umbrella organization for dedicated librarians from the United States who have worked with librarians within the nations concerned and in Europe in an attempt to alleviate this situation.[6]

---

[3]Three surveys, identified collectively as Southeast Asia Paper No. 16--*Southeast Asian Research Tools* (Honolulu: Southeast Asia Studies, University of Hawaii, 1979), were issued separately as: Part I, *Summary and Needs* by Shiro Saito; Part II, *Indonesia* by Lan Hiang Char; Part III, *Burma* by Michael Aung Thwin; Part IV, *Malaysia* by William R. Roff; Part V, *The Philippines* by Edita Baradi; Part VI *Thailand* by Charles F. Keyes; and Part IX, *Vietnam* by Michael G. Cotter. The final part, covering Southeast Asia as a region by Pat Lim Pui Huen will be published by the Institute of Southeast Asian Studies in Singapore

[4]A report on this new effort will appear in a forthcoming issue of *CORMOSEA Bulletin*. Editor's note, 1991: That effort proved unsuccessful.

[5]A brief summary of the *Bulletin*'s publishing history is provided by the current editor, Joyce Wright, in Vol. 9, No. 3 (Nov. 1977), p. 34. Beginning with Vol. 11 (late 1980/early 1981, *Insya Allah*, two of the authors of this paper, Lian The-Mulliner and K. Mulliner, have been named as editors.

[6]Noteworthy examples include the efforts of Abdul Kohar Rony, J. N. B. Tairas, and others in the Library of Congress meeting with Indonesian librarians to standardize entry elements and forms of entry for personal and corporate Indonesian authors, described in J. N. B. Tairas, "Some Aspects of Descriptive Cataloguing standardization in Indonesia," in International Congress of Orientalists, 1971 *International Co-operation in Orientalist Librarianship* (Canberra: National Library

The other national medium of exchange of import has been the Library of Congress, particularly through the Southeast Asia Field Office of its Cooperative Acquisitions Program (CAP), headquartered in Jakarta, Indonesia. This program has provided materials and preliminary descriptive cataloging for publications from Brunei, Indonesia, Malaysia, and Singapore to participating collections. While the primary beneficiaries have been the cooperating libraries in the United States, the program has dramatically increased the accessibility of information produced in Southeast Asia for users in the United States and abroad.[7]

While national efforts have yielded the most dramatic results, the major burden in information exchange has been carried by individual institutions and, more correctly, by active and concerned Southeast Asian Studies librarians within those institutions (most of whom comprise the librarian membership of CORMOSEA). Of greatest importance have been the exchange programs which have provided Southeast Asian institutions with materials of interest published in the United States in return, in most cases, for materials from Southeast Asia. In addition to increasing resources in the United States, these programs have helped overcome the complaints of academic exploitation in which researchers have availed themselves of hospitality--yet have neglected to share their research with the scholars and libraries of the host nation.

Appropriately for the Asian context, much of the international exchange of information in the past has been through personal contacts and consultations.[8] These have included exchanges of visits and conference attendance by American and Southeast Asian librarians, attendance at American universities and library schools by would-be librarians from the region, and secondment through AID, Fulbright, Peace Corps, and other agencies of practicing American librarians to work for periods of a few months to several years in Southeast Asian libraries and with the librarians serving those bodies.

---

of Australia for the Library Seminars Planning Committee, 1972), pp. 58-82, and Lian Tie Kho, with regard to Burmese, described most recently in *CORMOSEA Bulletin*, Vol. 10, No. 1 (Dec. 1979), pp. 21-23.

[7]Recently the descriptive cataloging, if not the Cooperative Acquisitions Program has been expanded to include materials from Burma and Thailand. [By 1990, The Philippines has also been added and a Cooperative Acquisitions Program has been established for Thailand with the intent to expand it to other countries in mainland Southeast Asia.] These can be found in the Library of Congress, *Accessions List, Southeast Asia.*

[8]The early efforts of Cecil Hobbs of the Library of Congress are noteworthy in this regard. See his *An Account of an Acquisition Trip in the Countries of Southeast Asia* (Ithaca, NY: Southeast Asia Program, Cornell University); reports on subsequent trips appeared in Cornell's Southeast Asia Data Paper Series Nos. 11, 40, 67, and 85.

Because of the topic of this paper, the foregoing discussion has omitted the significant role of individual scholars and librarians in the U.S. outside the major research centers in contributing to international information exchange. Even more importantly, it has not touched upon the substantial efforts of librarians in Southeast Asia in intra- and extra-regional cooperation and the development and production of needed research aids.[9] The increasingly dominant role of Southeast Asians, scholars and institutions, in facilitating exchange of information about the region in the past decade has been a welcome development. It should also be noted that omission of British, Canadian, European, Australian, and Japanese contributions to information exchange does not indicate a lack of appreciation of the substantive gains provided by their efforts.

Current Assessment

This short historical sketch was intended to provide a basis for assessment of the current role of Southeast Asia Collections in the United States in international information exchanges as a prelude to projecting future possibilities.

Having highlighted cooperative efforts among collections in the United States, it is appropriate to note one at least temporarily divisive element accompanying automated library systems and networks. These have been well-developed and widely accepted in U.S. libraries. The overall result has been the effective emergence of a national online union catalog among the networks serving 2,000 libraries nationally as part of the OCLC system.[10] In 1979 this was augmented by an online interlibrary loan subsystem which enhanced the value of the online union catalog. Since that point, OCLC's monopoly has been challenged by the RLIN system which serves many

---

[9]Some of the important efforts in this direction were featured in Hwa-Wei Lee, "Co-operative Regional Bibliographic Projects in South-East Asia," *UNESCO Bulletin for Libraries*, Vol 31, No. 6 (nov.-Dec. 1977), pp. 344-351 & 370. Particularly noteworthy since that summation has been the appearance through the efforts of the Southeast Asia Branch of the International Council on Archives (SARBICA) and the Congress of Southeast Asian Librarians (CONSAL), under the editorship of the late Winardi Partaningrat, of *Masterlist of Southeast Asia Microforms* (Singapore: Singapore University Press, 1978). The UNESCO-supported project originally known as the "UNESCO Study of Malay Culture" and now the "Study of South East Asian Cultures" is another potentially important effort which has, however, suffered from funding problems. See P. Lim Pui Huen, "Bibliography on Malay Culture (UNESCO Study of Malay Culture)," *CORMOSEA Bulletin*, Vol. 10, No. 1 (Dec. 1979), p. 10, and addendum on p. 12.

[10]The growth and refinement of OCLC as a national library utility has been well documented in Susan K. Martin, *Library Networks* (White Plains, NY: Knowledge Industry Publications, Inc., 1978), esp. pp. 35-42, but the entire volume is of interest to consideration of online systems development.

of the major research libraries.[11] The intricacies of the current situation lie beyond our scope and interest here, but it is important to note that the division into two major information utilities has split the Southeast Asia Collections which effectively reduces accessibility and understanding regarding each other's holdings.[12] With efforts currently underway to interface the two major systems as well as the Library of Congress system, it is hoped that the gap can at least be bridged. With such a small number of important collections, intra-national communication is vital and a necessary prelude to future trends in facilitating international information exchange.[13]

Individual and collective efforts in such projects as exchanges and research tools have been successful in the past and should continue. There is a need for greater efforts in this direction and, hopefully, greater cooperation between Southeast Asian Institutions and those outside the region, as exemplified in CORMOSEA's Research Tools Project (see Endnote 3). In this regard, there should be an important role for organizations such as this [International Association of Orientalist Librarians] and other librarians' organizations to encourage greater international cooperation. Although exchanges have been mutually beneficial in the past, there is still considerable need for extending these efforts, particularly to include the younger universities in Southeast Asia as well as the major research institutions in each nation. Intra-national and intra-regional cooperation can address some of this need, but it is important for Southeast Asia Collections and Programs in the United States and the rest of the world to recognize the explosion in higher education in Southeast Asia as these nations strive to meet their internal technological and manpower needs.

---

[11]RLIN also cooperates with the WLN (Washington [State] Library Network), CLASS (California Library Authority for Systems and Services), and the Library of Congress in projects. Its vision of its role and relation to OCLC is well presented in Richard DeGennaro, "Research Libraries Enter the Information Age," *Library Journal*, Vol. 104, No. 20 (Nov. 1979), pp. 2405-2410.

[12]The University of Hawaii, Northern Illinois University, Ohio University, and the University of Wisconsin are served by OCLC while the University of California at Berkeley, Cornell University, the University of Michigan, and Yale University are participants in RLIN.

[13]The impact of this division extends far beyond the Southeast Asia Collections, and its alleviation has been recognized as an important task. The Council on Library Resources, Inc. (One Dupont Circle, N.W., Suite 620, Washington, D.C. 20036) is just now (mid-August 1980) receiving a study from Battelle Columbus Laboratories on interfacing these systems. This paper will probably be published by the Council in September 1980 and hopefully will provide ways of overcoming the current impasse. The findings and recommendations should be of interest internationally in terms of interfacing as well as of national importance in the U.S. [1990: This was the basis of the Linked Systems Project (LSP) which is still underway.]

Accompanying the expansion of higher education in Southeast Asia has been the growth and maturation of academic libraries and library schools in the region to meet internal informational needs. While this growth may continue to require international personnel (of whom many will be those with a Southeast Asia focus or at least interest) to contribute to libraries and library instruction, there is an increasing body of trained personnel with most of the nations which can respond to these needs. This will require some reassessment of the role of American and other international institutions in meeting the technical requirements of Southeast Asia as well as the personal and professional preferences of those librarians who in the past have welcomed an opportunity to live and work in the region.

In this regard, the Ohio University Library has recently been pioneering an internship program for librarians from Southeast Asia. The goal is to offer hands-on experience working with the technological tools and systems which are transforming our profession. Southeast Asia Collections are in a unique position to offer such experience for, in addition to the technological facilities, they are able to offer an intern an opportunity to work with the same types of materials (and languages) with which they will have to deal in their home institutions. Although still in its nascent phase (initially, participants have come only from Chulalongkorn University), the program has been discussed with UNESCO, which has indicated an interest in exploring such an offering library school faculty members from the region to enhance their abilities to serve as cadre in preparing Southeast Asian libraries for technological innovation. A complementary program is also being initiated to more-senior library administrators (initial participants are from Taiwan).

While this approach is only a small beginning, we do think that it affords an indication of the types of programs that will be needed in the future, especially if some of the developments which will be discussed in the following section are realized. Special note should be made that this is not a simple donor-donee program, but, in affording interns an opportunity to work with Southeast Asian materials, the internees are also providing the host library and Southeast Asia Collection with language as well as other professional skills which are in rather short supply in the U.S.--and which are likely to remain so, if institutions seek to avoid contributing to the brain drain from the Southeast Asian nations.

The Future: Some Projections

Despite identification of favorable activities by American Southeast Asia Collections and libraries in Southeast Asia, one must concur with the 1969 assessment by a member of the Library of Congress staff that the international transfer of information "is still in a relatively primitive state of development."[14] That progress is being made is evidenced in the preceding, but real international information exchange is yet to be realized.

In this section we will attempt some crystal ball gazing to identify what appear to be likely developments and the role of Southeast Asia Collections in facilitating and perhaps cushioning these developments.

Underlying this analysis is the belief that information is the property of no individual, institution, or nation and that its accession and dissemination is the goal of librarianship. Yet we must also recognize that political, economic, ideological, and belief systems are often major obstacles in disseminating information. The following projections are primarily directed toward the member-nations of the Association of Southeast Asian Nations (ASEAN), not because of any desire to discriminate against the other nations of the region but simply because those nations presently have the most developed information systems on which to base projections.

It seems likely that the most dramatic changes in international information exchange for the region will be technologically driven. In part, these will probably follow the trends in other parts of the world where networking and automation are rapidly transforming our profession.[15] The seeds of cooperation and online systems are evident in the area of bibliographic searches.[16]

Probably more important than the automation systems--which will have the greatest impact on the internal operation of libraries and the domestic services provided within each nation--are the potentialities offered by satellite communications. Previously, many of the innovations in information technology have been inappropriate to Southeast Asia because of the distances separating the research

---

[14]John G. Lorentz, "International Transfer of Information," *Annual Review of Information Science and Technology, 1969* (White Plains, NY: Knowledge Industry Publications, Inc., 1969), p. 398.

[15]These have been well summarized in John J. Eyre, "The Impact of Automation on Libraries--A Review," *Journal of Library and Information Science*, Vol. 5, No. 1 (Apr. 1979), pp. 1-15.

[16]An excellent discussion of prospects and proposals can be found in Lim Huck Tee, "The Southeast Asia University Library Network (SAULNET): A Proposal and a Model for Resource Sharing in ASEAN Countries," in IFLA/UNESCO Pre-session Seminar for Libraries from Developing Countries, *Resource Sharing of Libraries in Developing Countries* (IFLA Publications 14; Munchen: K.G. Saur, 1979), pp. 217-233. A very elaborate model can be found in the work prepared for the UNESCO/UNISIST Programme by Bo Karlander and Sverre Sem-Sandberg, *Information Networks for Online Bibliographic Retrieval* (Paris: UNESCO, 1977).

facilities in the many nations, a problem compounded by sometimes unreliable telephone line communications and the costs associated with such systems.

But satellite systems virtually eliminate geographical distance as a factor. In considering this development we are not so naive as to believe that research libraries much less Southeast Asia Collections will be in the vanguard of this process. A recent article in *Asiaweek* focusing on the online business office in Southeast Asia is one indication of the direction from which major innovations are likely to come.[17] In her seminal article on telelibraries, Rosa Liu, Librarian for INTELSAT indicated that the special libraries associated with corporate communications systems are likely to derive the earliest benefits arising from advances in transmission and transcription technology.[18] And, based on current developments in Europe and North America, other early applications of the system will be for technical and medical information. Because at least some this data is so time-sensitive, one can hardly fault such a development.

But this technology should also offer new opportunities to area studies collections (Southeast Asia in this case) and to the libraries in Southeast Asia. For example, our library is currently linked by landline to the OCLC database in Columbus, Ohio (a distance of 75 miles). Yet if satellite transmission were used, the difference in contacting Malaysia rather than Columbus would be negligible (at least theoretically, depending on usage charges). Particularly encouraging are the cost possibilities. The trend (as well as the increasing sophistication) is well demonstrated in the appended charts from Ms. Liu's paper.

While the declining cost of a unit of service is documented, equally exciting are the developments which will determine just what such a unit includes. A recent library test of facsimile transmission systems sponsored by the U. S. Department of Health, Education, and Welfare compared two major types of systems as well as slow-scan television (which was considered generally unacceptable). One was a system requiring six minutes per page and the other 35 seconds (90 seconds for very high resolution work).[19] Even as this paper was being written, we learned of a new system which will reduce this to under one second.[20] The combination on non-real time satellite transmission of facsimiles greatly expands the possibilities for meaningful international exchange of information.

---

[17]*Asiaweek*, 20 June 1980, pp. 52-54.

[18]Rosa Liu, "Telelibrary, Library Services Via Satellite," *Special Libraries*, Vol. 70, No. 9 (Sept. 1979), pp. 363-372.

[19]*Telefax Library Information Network (TALINET). Final Report* (New Grant 032A-7804-P4041; Denver: Graduate School of Librarianship and Information Management, University of Denver, 1979).

[20]"Satellite Business Systems and AM International Demonstrate World's First Communicating Copier," joint press release, May 14, 1980.

While we are hardly prepared to deal with the technical intricacies of these developments (and it is disappointing how few librarians are), it is clear that the information explosion will soon be taking on megaton dimensions for librarians. It is in meeting this exponential challenge that area collection librarians can provide major services. If the innovators in this new information barrage are the businesses, the sciences, engineering and medicine, it is likely that much of this information will be in non-Southeast Asian languages. It will fall to the librarians in Southeast Asia and those concerned with Southeast Asia in other countries to assure that information-handling systems are compatible with Southeast Asian languages and that Southeast Asian materials are available in machine-readable format and are in an accessible form.

Essentially these exciting developments should provide additional emphasis on the role of the area collections, in conjunction with librarians in the region as mediators between the technology and the region. Their combination of professional skills, language competence, experience, and cultural sensitivity, if augmented by awareness of technological developments and implications, will qualify them to recommend gates and parameters which must be considered in preparing systems for international exchange. Complementary to this is the potential role of area collections in providing the practical exposure to the new technology for Southeast Asia librarians in a context familiar to the librarians. Our university's efforts in this direction were indicated in the earlier section.

Stimulating as it is to consider the benefits arising from overnight, if not instantaneous, transmission of information between America (for example) and Southeast Asia libraries, no one can believe that the contact through a terminal can compare with the opportunity to meet socially and professionally with one's counterparts in the other parts of the world. Area collections are likely to remain potential homes away from home for visiting professionals from Southeast Asia and, similarly, the area bibliographers will continue to treasure the opportunities to visit their colleagues in Southeast Asia. For this we can be grateful, especially for an opportunity such as afforded by this conference to meet jointly with colleagues with shared interests from throughout the world.

Acknowledgements

Special thanks for assistance in preparing this final section are due to Rosa Liu (INTELSAT Library, Washington, D.C.), Mary Diebler (Public Service Satellite Consortium, Denver, Colorado), and John J. Welsh and Joan Maier (U.S. National Oceanic and Atmospheric Administration Library, Boulder, Colorado), all of whom were most generous in sharing their knowledge and resources which they had available. Thanks also to Dennis Rose (Satellite Business Systems, Washington, D.C./McLean, Virginia) for timely assistance.

15

Appendix A

Five Generations of INTELSAT Satellites Showing Increased Circuit Capacity and Decreased Cost

Intelsat Satellites

	I	II	III	IV	IVA	V
Year of First Launch	1965	1967	1968	1971	1975	1979
Dimensions						
Diameter (m)	0.72	1.42	1.42	2.38	2.38	2.0
Height (m)	0.60	0.673	1.04	5.28	5.90	15.7
In-Orbit Mass (kg)	38	67.3	152	700	790	967
Launch Vehicle	——— Thor-Delta ———			—Atlas-Centaur—		Atlas-Centaur or Shuttle
Primary Power (watts)	40	75	120	400	500	1200
Number of Transponders	2	1	2	12	20	27
Total Usable Bandwidth (MHz)	50	130	500	500	800	2300
eirp/Beam (dBW)	11.5	15.5	23	22.5 global 32.7 spot beam	22 global 29 HEMI	22.29 at 4GHz 44 at 11 GHz
Two-Way Telephone Circuits	240	240	1200	4000	6000	12,500
Design Lifetime (years)	15	3	5	7	7	7
Cost/Circuit Year ($K)	30	10	2	1	1	0.7

Appendix B

Comparison of INTELSAT Charges to the Consumer Price Index

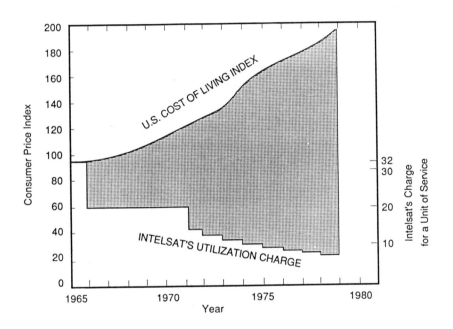

LIBRARY ACQUISITIONS FROM THE THIRD WORLD: AN INTRODUCTION*

Co-Author: K. Mulliner

Before discussing the contents of this issue, consideration must be given to the title and scope of the contents. As a first defense, the editors aver that the title was inherited rather than chosen by them. This comment is necessary as a number of contributors questioned the validity or content of the term "Third World". Yet the experience of compiling and editing this issue has forced the recognition that this term, whatever its limitations, is among if not the most appropriate to identify those countries other than the OECD member nations (the Organization for Economic Cooperation and Development, which includes the nations of Western Europe as well as the United States, Canada, and Japan) or the Soviet Union and its allies in Eastern Europe.

As becomes evident in the following articles, the term is most easily defined by what it is not rather than what it is. To refer to many of the same countries, the Library of Congress uses "developing nations," a not altogether pleasing alternative to the pejorative "underdeveloped." Those interested in rationales for grouping the nations included should consult the Library of Congress Acquisitions Policy Statement no. 30, summarized by Mulliner in this issue[1], The case is further elaborated in the Samore article[2] which follows it.

With the acknowledgement that there are criteria for grouping these nations, the editors are sympathetic with observers such as Maureen Patterson (South Asian Bibliographer, University of Chicago Library) who felt that the industrial capacity as well as the level of literacy and enormous book trade in a country such as India preclude meaningful comparisons with some of the poorer nations of the world. This argument is further amplified when applied to a nation such as Singapore where the per capital GNP is expected to surpass that of Great Britain next year. Unlike some

---

*This article introduced a special thematic issue (Vol. 6, Number 2, 1982) of the *Library Acquisitions: Practice and Theory*, on acquisitions from Third World Countries. Subsequent references in this article refer to this issue, identified as *LAPT*, unless noted otherwise. So many excellent articles were received that a number of articles were carried over to Vol. 6, No. 4.

[1]K. Mulliner, "Library of Congress Acquisitions Policies: Synopsis Covering Developing Countries," *LAPT*, pp. 103-106.

[2]Theodore Samore, "Acquisitions of Materials from Third World Countries for U.S. Libraries," *LAPT*, pp. 107-112.

OPEC states, this wealth is based on a diverse industrial and trading base. Additionally, Singapore would fail to qualify under virtually any of the criteria established by the Library of Congress.

The editors have become doubly aware of the problems involved in the term as they have been asked by the British Library (engaged in the preparation of an article to appear in a supplementary issue) to specify countries to be included or excluded. Thus, while denying any claims to scientific rigor, the editors have used the term Third World to refer to the nations covered by the exclusionary definition given at the end of the opening paragraph.

The term is further justified by its currency in library literature. Based on a conference of the Ligue des Bibliotheque Europeennes de Recherche (LIBER) at the University of Sussex in 1973 on the same theme as this special issue, the proceedings were reported under the title, *Acquisitions from the Third World*.[3] This conference and its proceedings represented a marked departure from two efforts which immediately preceded it. In 1971 the Institute on the Acquisition of Foreign Materials at the University of Wisconsin--Milwaukee presented a 2-week program on acquiring foreign materials.[4] Demonstrating the synchronicity which often characterizes important intellectual concerns (as well as the importance of the issue for librarians and scholars), the Librarian of the School of Oriental and African Studies, B.C. Bloomfield, was also organizing a session on the same theme for the University, College and Research Section for the Annual Conference of the Library Association.[5] Both of these efforts shared the characteristic of addressing the problem from a particular national perspective (the U.S., for the Institute and the United Kingdom for Bloomfield) and the problem of attempting to treat acquisitions from the rest of the world. Before returning to the LIBER Conference, mention should also be made of the 1965 conference of the Graduate Library School at the University of Chicago[6] which addressed much the same theme and which Bloomfield credited with inspiring the Library Association program.[7]

---

[3]D. A. Clarke, ed. *Acquisitions from the Third World*, Papers of Ligue des Bibliotheque Europeennes de Recherche seminar, 17-19 September 1973 (London: Mansell, 1975).

[4]Theodore Samore, ed. *Acquisitions of Foreign Materials for U.S. Libraries*, 2nd rev. ed. (Metuchen, N.J.: The Scarecrow Press, Inc., 1983).

[5]B. C. Bloomfield, *Acquisition and Provision of Foreign Books by National and University Libraries in the University Libraries in the United Kingdom: Papers of the Morecambe Conference, 16 April 1972* (London: Mansell, 1972).

[6]Tsuen-hsuin Tsien and Howard Winger, eds. *Area Studies and the Library*, Proceedings of the 30th annual conference of the University of Chicago Graduate Library School, May 20-22, 1965 (Chicago: University of Chicago, 1966).

[7]Bloomfield, *Acquisition and Provision*, p. ix.

In several regards, the LIBER conference was able to go beyond the earlier efforts because of its narrower focus (the Third World) and because of the larger number of nations represented by participants (including France, West Germany, Nigeria, Finland, and Australia in addition to the U.S. and the U.K.). The resulting publication has guided the editors in attempting to develop the articles which follow (and those which will be included in a supplement). There is one major distinction. The articles in this special issue were solicited especially for this publication rather than growing out of a conference. This has permitted a (minimal) degree of editorial guidance but has precluded the cross-fertilization and exchanges possible in a conference. It has further necessitated considerable international correspondence and accompanying mail delays (including a postal strike in Australia).

In citing the illustrious forebears, one additional note on content is in order. Specifically missing from this issue are historical discussions of Third World acquisitions. These are certainly important to understanding the field (and the fact that *plus ca change, plus c'est la meme chose*) but the above volumes and citations therein provide sufficient background as to make additional treatment redundant. Thus the articles herein focus largely on the present and the future.

Since the LIBER Conference, much of the collective effort at addressing problems of Third World acquisitions has focused on specific geographical/cultural regions.[8] Articles in this issue refer to several of these, such as the Seminar on the Acquisition of Latin American Library Materials, and others which operate in cooperation with or as part of library professional or area studies organizations. Additionally, cooperative efforts have been increasing (primarily as the magnitude of materials published in the Third World and the costs of obtaining them have soared) both at national and international levels (as reflected in the introduction of international participation in Library of Congress programs and in the international membership of some of the microform programs of the Center for Research Libraries).

Concern with acquisitions particularly in Third World nations has also received the attention of international organizations and related bodies. As a result, there has

---

[8]One notable exception to this trend was the 1977 Library of Congress workshop on "Acquisitions and the Third World," which included presentations on the Middle East (by George Atiyeh), Africa (by Hans Panofsky), and Latin America (by John Hebert) as well as a presentation on U.S. Government Documents (by Merwin C, Phelps). The proceedings and discussion were summarized and edited by Janice Carroll and James Thompson, "Workshop on Acquisitions from the Third World: Proceedings." In: *Library Acquisitions: Practice and Theory*, 1(2), pp.117-133. The inclusion of U.S. Documents, justified because "problems in acquiring [them] present many of the same difficulties, and do so for (in many ways) analogous reasons" (p.117), certainly extended the definition of Third World well beyond that used in this issue.

been a burgeoning of the literature on books and publishing in the Third World.[9] Even while preparing this introduction the editors chanced across two recent major works on the book industry in Africa, one from UNESCO and one from a monographic series at the editors' home institution.[10] An additional factor of relevance to the discussion is the growing concern within the Third World of access to materials published within each of the nations and, increasingly, from nearby nations and other regions. As evidenced by the Unesco discussions on a new world information order, Third World nations are increasingly unwilling to learn about each other through the media of non-Third World sources.[11] Without digressing to that issue, it must be recognized that citizens, scholars, and librarians of Third World nations usually share the same difficulties as described by the contributors here, even within their own nations.[12]

Further contributing to expanded concern regarding acquisitions of Third World materials has been the international spread of information and bibliographic databases.[13] A number of these offer document delivery[14] as well as bibliographic

---

[9]These are discussed and identified in Philip G. Altbach and Eva-Maria Rathgeber, *Publishing in the Third World: Trend Report and Bibliography* (New York: Praeger, 1980).

[10]S. I. A. Kotei, *The Book Today in Africa* (Paris: UNESCO, 1981). *Mazungumzo: Interviews with East African Writers, Publishers, Editors and Scholars*, edited and compiled by Bernth Lindfors. Papers in International Studies, Africa Series No. 41 (Athens: Ohio University Center for International Studies, 1980).

[11]International Commission for the Study of Communication Problems. *Many Voices One World: Towards a New More Just and More Efficient World Information and Communication Order* (London/New York: Kogan Page/Unipub, 1980).

[12]In a recent bibliographic compilation, a librarian with the Malaysian National University [University Kebangsaan Malaysia] Library succinctly presented the problems encountered "by libraries in Malaysia" in collecting Malaysiana. Ding Choo Ming, *A Bibliographies of Bibliographies on Malaysia* (Petaling Jaya, Malaysia: Hexagon Elite Publications, 1981) pp. vii-ix. These remarks, which parallel comments found in the Acquisition from Regions section of this issue, were initially aired as the first section of a paper by the same author, "Problems in Acquiring Malaysiana Materials and Prospects for Resource Sharing in the 1980s" presented to the International Association of Orientalist Librarians meeting in Manila, August 19, 1980.

[13]An excellent but not exhaustive summary of these can be found in *International Cooperative Information Systems*. Proceedings of a seminar held in Vienna, Austria, 9-13 July 1979 (Ottawa: International Development Research Centre, 1980).

[14]The article by Maureen Sly, "Improving Accessibility to Development Literature: Some Activities of the International Development Research Centre (IDRC)," pp. 117-122, in this issue presents information on the programs of the International Development Research Centre (IDRC) which has been particularly active and effective

entries, but even in these cases the acquisition of one article or document frequently leads to the identification of a further dozen titles of relevance. As a result, questions regarding access to Third World publications are becoming as important to Third World institutions as they have been to research libraries elsewhere. Cooperation both in acquisitions and in sharing materials from the Third World is now significant not only for the traditional research centers, which have had to face a Malthusian dilemma in which the growth in published materials has far outpaced funding for acquisitions, but also for universities and agencies in the Third World which have recognized that many of the problems of development are not unique to each individual nation.[15] This is an important issue for achieving IFLA's medium-term programme for Universal Availability of Publications (UAP).[16]

Turning then to the contents of this special issue, contributions are divided into three: those discussing cross-regional patterns, those focusing on collection materials from a specific region, and those focusing on cooperative efforts. Before considering these, be advised that the articles are only a partial reporting. Because of the press schedule for this volume, a number of anticipated articles have had to be deferred to a subsequent issue. This is most important for consideration of the role and practices of British institutions (specifically the British Library[17] and the Library of the School of Oriental and African Studies[18]) in acquisitions from the Third World. Their omission represents only a deferral of their contributions, not a slight of their pioneering efforts and substantial contributions.

The emergence of the Library of Congress as a major force in Third World acquisitions is a post-World War II phenomenon; in fact, that this year marks the

---

in this arena. Cf., Thorpe, Peter. "Third World Agricultural Information," *Agricultural Information Development Bulletin*, III, 2 (June 1981), 3-7.

[15]H.D.L. Vervliet, *Resource Sharing of Libraries in Developing Countries*, Proceedings of the 1977 IFLA/UNESCO Pre-Session Seminar for Librarians from Developing Countries, Antwerp University, August 30-September 4, 1977. IFLA Publications 14 (Munich et al.: K.G. Saur, 1979).

[16]Approaches to UAP for the Third World are discussed in M.B. Line. "Universal Availability of Publications and developing countries," ibid., 162-169. Although much of the emphases in UAP is on interlibrary loan, loans depend on availability. The importance of acquisitions, and retention, to an effective interlibrary loan system is made in M.B. Line et al., *National Interlending Systems: a Comparative Study of Existing Systems and Possible Models* (Paris: UNESCO General Information Programme, 1978), p.ix; cf. ERIC ED188611.

[17]Diana Grimwood-Jones, "British Library Acquisition of Material from the Third World," *LAPT*, VII, 1 (1983), pp. 71-80.

[18]Rosemary Stevens, "Acquisition of Serials from Asia and Africa at the School of Oriental and African Studies (SOAS) Library," *LAPT*, VII, 1 (1983), pp. 59-70.

twentieth anniversary of its field office in New Delhi attests to its recency. Today, it not only provides information to the libraries of the world on what is available through its regional Accessions Lists but also oversees the actual acquisition of a significant quantity of materials, through its PL 480 and CAP (Cooperative Acquisitions) programs, for libraries in the United States. In discussing the Overseas Operations Division (of which she is Assistant to the Chief), Alice Kniskern describes the current plans for international participation in these acquisitions programs[19] (in Egypt initially) as well as provides details on the related microfilming programs which, through the Photoduplication Service of LC, now provide relatively inexpensive copies to libraries anywhere in the world of materials which previously would have existed in only one or two institutions.

In contrast to this sprawling effort which serves a multitude of institutions as well as governmental users is the activity of a special agency library, such as that of the International Labor Organization described by Aileen Ng[20]. At this level, the need for information is practical, directly related programs and policies. The acquisitions problems are the same as those faced by LC, but with only a fraction of the staff. Yet both LC and the ILO Library find that reliable information on what is available and acquisition thereof depends on having a knowledgeable and dedicated person present in the region--even if, in the case of the ILO, this may be someone not specifically responsible for acquisitions. Akin to the mission of the ILO Library in providing useful information when needed are the programs of the International Development Research Centre (IDRC) to identify and deliver, through international cooperation and databases, information to meet the needs of government agencies and others involved in development. Maureen Sly outlines the growth of the service. Allowing that "the medium is the message," the IDRC deserves special recognition for its introduction of online searching and databases (with software such as MINISIS which is adaptable to a number of library functions) to many Third World nations. The information and document delivery services of SALUS and DEVSIS are valuable sources but are probably outweighed by the significance of the introduction of automation to Third World librarians and information specialists.

The Acquisitions from Regions section addressees the specific acquisitions problems for each of the major Third World areas. Contrasting experiences are offered as acquisitions problems not only vary from region to region but also considerably within a region and frequently depend as much on the acquiring institution as on the

---

[19]Alice Kniskern, "Library of Congress Overseas Offices: Acquistion Programs in the Third World," *LAPT*, pp. 87-102.

[20]Aileen W. K. Ng, "Coping with Collection Building of Third World Material in an International Organisation Library," *LAPT*, pp. 113-116.

supplier. In considering African materials, the articles by Panofsky and Rathgeber[21] cite many of the same source materials but with distinct evaluations of the contributions of each. In this instance there is the added benefit of comparing the perspectives of the doyen in the field and of an active and published post-doctoral fellow. On Asia, the article from the Australian National University[22] cites materials from Taiwan (Republic of China) as presenting problems while for the People's Republic of China today it is more a question of selectivity in avoiding duplication. In contrast, William Wong (Assistant Director for Technical Services [for the Asian Library], University of Illinois) in an article that will appear in the supplement[23] concentrates on the PRC since there are few problems in acquiring Taiwan materials. Disparities within a region are apparent in the article by Laura Gutierrez-Witt and Donald L.Gibbs[24] compared with that of Salvador Miranda.[25] An issue not considered here, since it has become largely academic, is the very definition of a region. In many cases, geographic proximity offers little indication of linguistic, economic, or cultural affinities, but, even for the Middle East, which shares a common religion in Islam and a common basic language in Arabic (not to neglect Persian-speaking peoples), political strife is perhaps an even greater problem for acquisitions efforts than in more heterogeneous regions.

The two contributions by Directors of LC Field Offices, Gene Smith[26] and Michael Albin,[27] deserve special comment. A theme explicit or implicit in most of the articles is the value of the field acquisitions trip to identify available materials, suppliers, and ways of surmounting difficulties. The Field Office Directors are talented individuals on extended or semi-permanent acquisitions trips. They are intimately involved in the regions for which they are responsible and daily must cope not only with the vagaries of dealers and government agencies but also with the insatiable demands of researchers and libraries as well as the LC Washington staff,

---

[21]Hans E. Panofsky, "Acquisitions of Africana," *LAPT*, pp. 123-128; Eva-Maria Rathgeber, "Africana Acquisitions Problems: The View from Both Sides," *LAPT*, pp. 137-148.

[22]Enid Bishop, Y. S. Chan, and W. G. Miller, "Recent Australian Experience with China and Southeast Asia," *LAPT*, pp. 149-160.

[23]William Sheh Wong, "Acquiring Library Materials from the People's Republic of China," *LAPT*, VII, 1 (1983), pp. 47-58.

[24]Laura Guutiérrez-Witt and Donald L. Gibbs, "Acquiring Latin American Books," *LAPT*, pp. 167-176.

[25]Salvador Miranda, "Library Matierals from Latin American and the Caribbean: Problems and Approaches in Acquisitions," *LAPT*, pp. 177-184.

[26]E. Gene Smith, "The New Delhi Office of the Library of Congress at Twenty: Changing Acquisition Parameters," *LAPT*, pp. 161-166.

[27]Michael W. Albin, "Acquisition of Conference Proceedings from the Arab World," *LAPT*, pp. 201-211.

all of whom want everything that has never been published on a topic and want it yesterday. The articles by the two Directors are valuable in themselves but their inclusion here should also be considered a salute to the services provided by all of the Field Office Directors. One testament to the value of these services was the creation of similar offices in Indonesia by the Dutch and the Australians. Gene Smith's article is additionally important as, on its twentieth anniversary, the New Delhi office must devise a dollar-based cooperative program for the first time, Michael Albin affords insights into an area seldom trod by Field Office Directors, and excluded from LC acquisitions for the most part, conference proceedings. His article documents the immensity of the task of attempting to acquire proceedings,[28] but also whets the appetite of the researcher for these largely inaccessible "publications." Note should be made that efforts such as those of the IDRC index are beginning to bridge the inaccessibility chasm--presumably to the chagrin of catalogers using different systems.

Despite the contrasts, an overriding impression from this section is that the problems are largely similar, while the languages, cultural, and economic practices may vary from region to region (and within a region), many of the difficulties transcend national and regional delineations (giving credence to the consideration of Third World acquisitions as a theme). This results in a certain repetitiveness but a repetition which should encourage the individual concerned with a particular region to consider what is being attempted and achieved in other regions. One constant in Third World acquisition is that solutions are seldom transplantable. What works in one cultural-economic milieu is likely to remain fruitless in another. But an idea or an approach translated to meet socio-political realities can afford new avenues for exploring possibilities. Robert Theobald has cogently phrased the choice: a situation can be approached as a problem or as a possibility.[29]

Evidence of the possibilities of cross-fertilization can be found in the section on cooperation. Waxing publishing industries in Third World nations, static acquisitions budgets elsewhere, and inflation everywhere are combining to greatly reduce the number of institutions attempting, or even claiming to attempt, comprehensive collecting for one or more Third World region. While the less well off are likely to take satisfaction in seeing the mighty humbled, no one can celebrate the demise or even the decline of a major collection on the Third World. As on occasion in the past, cooperation is an obvious alternative. Perhaps now economic realities have caught up with idealistic platitudes.

---

[28]This point is reinforced by the forthcoming publication of the estimated 12,550 listings in the *Africana Conference Paper Index*, prepared by the Melville J. Herskovits Library of African Studies, Northwestern University, (Boston: G.K. Hall, November 1982).

[29]RobertTheobald, *Teg's 1994; An Anticipation of the Near Future* (Chicago: Swallow Press, 1972).

One working example in the U.S. for cooperation can be found in the area microform programs administered by the Center for Research Libraries (CRL). While these are hardly of the magnitude required to meet more than a very selective need, they do present an approach to the acquisition and retention of valuable research materials which would otherwise be largely unavailable. Additionally, as described by Boylan and Shores[30], the program for each region has maintained a distinct operational character. One of the characteristics of area or Third World studies is that the participants, scholars and librarians alike, assume many of the patterns of interpersonal and organizational interaction found among the peoples and nations which they study. In part this is commendable and in part quaint. But it is a reality which must be considered in cooperative undertakings. Many of the same sensitivities that are required in Third World areas are needed in organizing even mutually beneficial efforts. If meaningful cooperation is achieved, it is unlikely to resemble Western concepts of organizational structure. Nor, as cited by Boylan and Shore, are the decisions likely to be arrived at in uniform fashion. One additional characteristic of these programs is some provision for international participation, a theme which is echoed in the opening of LC CAP programs to participating institutions outside the United States.

Lessons there are in the CRL experience but--with its concentration on centralized holdings--the microform projects are not the seeds of future amplified cooperation. Libraries in the U.S., at least, are unlikely to commit substantial financing for an area collection which will be stored 1,000 miles away. Thus, the reports by Cason et al.[31] and by Lesnik[32] indicate a more likely avenue of distributed acquisitions foci (shades of the Farmington Plan). The two articles also afford a view of the two approaches to cooperation found in the U.S.: through professional area studies organizations and through professional library organizations. The paper by Cason, Easterbrook, and Scheven was originally three papers presented to the annual meeting of the African Studies Association. While such an organization assures a vitally concerned constituency, it also is a constituency with a limited voice in library decisions. The Research Libraries Group (RLG) is the parent body of the Research Libraries Information Network (RLIN) utility. Within this group, the problem of Third World Collections is reversed. Decisions are likely to have greater impact on policies in participating institutions but the support for Third World collections is greatly diluted and the priority which they receive reduced accordingly. Completing this bleak

---

[30]Ray Boylan and Cecelia L. Shores, "Collecting Retrospective Materials from Developing Nations: A Cooperative Approach Through Microforms," *LAPT*, pp. 211-220.

[31]Maidel Cason, David L. Easterbrook, and Yvette Scheven, "Cooperative Acquisitions of Africana: Past Performance and Future Directions," *LAPT*, pp. 211-232.

[32]Pauline Tina Lesnik, " The Research Libraries Group's Cooperative Acquisitions Program for South Asia," *LAPT*, pp. 233-238.

picture for the U.S. are the federal budget cuts anticipated for area studies and Title II-C (Strengthening Research Library Resources Program) of the Higher Education Act, both of which have provided substantial funding for Third World collections.

Despite these problems, the approaches described and proposed in the papers of Cason et al. and Lesnick are a glimmer of hope. Realistically, their papers do not propose a comprehensive solution to the need for cooperation. But they do describe current steps toward increasing cooperation. Unfortunately (from the editors' perspective), both approaches are located within RLG and will rely on RLIN for sharing. While meaningful cooperation is to be applauded, siting such activities within RLIN excludes the larger number of libraries in the United States which participate in OCLC. During preparation of this issue, the research library organization in OCLC was queried as to possible plans for cooperation or even study groups of Third World collections held by participants. The response was negative and the indication was that no need was seen for such. Given this atmosphere, librarians and scholars in the U.S. must support the cooperative undertakings described for RLG and hope that the example set will stimulate greater consideration of additional avenues for other libraries and other Third World areas.

One of the goals prompting this issue was the wish to reestablish and enlarge the international approach to Third World acquisitions provided by the LIBER conference. Yet it has concluded with a discussion on cooperation in the U.S. No justification is given beyond the necessity to place one's own house in order before asking the neighborhood to improve. The article from the Australian National University provides information on cooperative efforts there. What is missing in all of this, and what is needed, is a concentrated consideration of international cooperation to address the difficulties described in the articles of this issue. Particular attention must be given to increasing concern for the question among Third World nations and for increasing understanding among Third World peoples through access to the intellectual and cultural products of each society, rather than just news stories-- whether of the great accomplishment or the great failure type.

International bodies such as Unesco and IFLA have substantially contributed to increasing awareness of the value of information among Third World nations. IDRC and some other national aid agencies have provided practical assistance in information sharing and in modern information technology. But, too often, questions such as technology transfer focus on the flow of information to the Third World. What needs to be considered, and what is the vital question of this issue, is the flow of information from the Third World. To this should be added the flow of information among Third World countries. Some indications of the problems and approaches have been given here. Whether these will continue for another decade, as has been the case since the LIBER conference, will depend on international concern and, of course, funding.

28

FUNDING FOR
THE SOUTHEAST ASIA COLLECTION
AND RESEARCH RESOURCES
AT OHIO UNIVERSITY

Co-Author: K. Mulliner

As our topic requires a historical background, it is appropriate that we offer a historical prologue regarding the panel. Of the Southeast Asia Collections and study programs in the United States, that at Ohio University is the youngest, looking forward to its 20th anniversary next year. It is particularly appropriate that Professor Varner, our fellow contributor, and Dr. Provencher, the Chair, are from Northern Illinois University, also one of the younger Southeast Asia programs in the U.S. In tracing the genealogy of Southeast Asian Studies at Ohio University, the common ancestor is Cornell University but the immediate parentage is from Northern Illinois University.

When Ohio University's activist president, Vernon R. Alden, decided that, if Ohio University was going to be active in Southeast Asia (operating a model high school in Vietnam for U.S. AID), it was appropriate to learn and teach more about the area, a search for staff was begun in 1967. The leader selected to build the program was one of the founders of Northern Illinois University's Southeast Asia Program, Professor J Norman Parmer (now a professor of History at Trinity University), who was hired as Assistant Dean of Arts and Sciences for International Studies. Professor Parmer asked one of his colleagues at N.I.U., Professor Paul W. van der Veur, to join him as the Director of Southeast Asian Studies. To add just one more, of many, connections, in that year Northern Illinois University was seeking a librarian for its Southeast Asia Collection to replace Donald Clay Johnson, who had accepted a position at Yale University.   One of the candidates that was interviewed was an Indonesia-born cataloger at Cornell University, Ms. Lian The (now Lian The-Mulliner). Following her interview in DeKalb, she was interviewed in Chicago by Professors Parmer and van der Veur. The upshot was that she accepted the position at Ohio University and has overseen the development of one of the major research collections on Southeast Asia in the U.S.

Others, particularly in history, have given attention to the development of Southeast Asian Studies in the U.S.[1] (although with less attention to genealogy). Our

---

[1]The 1981 Annual Meeting of the American Historical Association in Los Angeles had a program on "Southeast Asia History R.I.P.?" with papers presented by William Frederick (Ohio University) and Craig Lockard (University of Wisconsin--Green Bay) and comments by Bruce Cruikshank and Bob van Niel. A decade earlier, the late Jay

purpose is not to add to that effort but to focus on a micro study of a specific institution. Before that, however, it is perhaps appropriate to observe one significant similarity between Ohio University and Northern Illinois University, that is the stature of Southeast Asian Studies within the institution. At both universities, Southeast Asian Studies has emerged as the major area studies program and the Southeast Asian library collection at each is the major research collection in the university library. To this I would add that the University Presidents have also demonstrated a commitment to each university's involvement in the region. While we are loath to comment on other institutions, I believe that many of you can envy the primacy which Southeast Asia studies and research enjoy within the two institutions.

Southeast Asia Studies at Ohio University -- Historical Highlights

To turn our gaze from descent to ascent, we return to Ohio University and the establishment of Southeast Asian Studies in the fall of 1967. Although now Distinguished Professor Emeritus John Cady had taught at Ohio University for several years and other faculty occasionally offered courses treating the region, there was nothing resembling a program of study and the library resources were hardly adequate to support even that relative neglect. While Professor van der Veur has since indicated that he regrets not having asked the University for greater assured funding for Southeast Asian materials, it is demonstrative of the development of Southeast Asian Studies at Ohio University that the Librarian was hired at the same time as the leadership of the program.

One other important trend which has shaped the direction of Southeast Asian Studies at Ohio University also dates from this early period. This has come to be known on campus as "the Malaysia Connection."[2] In 1968, six Malaysian students enrolled at Ohio University under a tripartite agreement among the Mara Institute of Technology (ITM), the Asia Foundation, and Ohio University. These were the first of thousands of Malaysians who have studied at Ohio University since, under a variety of sponsorships, and Ohio University offers its degrees in selected programs on the ITM campus. In recent years, students from ASEAN countries account for about 1/3 of the University's international student population (which comprises about 10% of the student body).

Maryanov provided a broad assessment: Gerald S. Maryanov, *The Condition of Southeast Asian Studies in the United States: 1972* (Occasional Papers No. 3; DeKalb: Center for Southeast Asian Studies, 1974).

[2]Felix Gagliano, "The Malaysian Connection: Ohio University's Link to the World's Other Side is a Decade Old," *The Ohio University Alumnus Magazine*, March 1977, pp. 8-13.

During this period, Ms. The was responsible for building an appropriate collection almost from scratch, but she also divided her time between work within the library and work in the Center for International Studies, establishing the close ties between the Southeast Asia Studies program and the library which continue to this day. She was also able to demonstrate the interrelationship between the library and research in the major works which she compiled jointly with the Director of Southeast Asia Studies.[3]

The next significant developments were in the 1970s. Emerging from its infancy, the Ohio University Library was able to join the Library of Congress administered Cooperative Acquisitions Program (CAP) in 1970, just as that program was expanding to cover materials from Malaysia and Singapore as well as Indonesia. Ohio University was partially able to capitalize on its relatively late membership as a result of Indiana University transferring uncataloged materials which it had received during participation in the 1960s (giving us a backlog almost from the beginning). Ohio University also took over Indiana's slot on the priority list.

It is difficult to overemphasize how important the CAP program has been to the growth of the Southeast Asia Collection at Ohio University but a review of our records also reveals how demanding it was in terms of budget. The history of the programs of the Jakarta Field Office is deserving of a separate treatment in the history of Southeast Asian Studies in the U.S. Suffice it to say that the doubling in cost of even partial participation in the program after only one year was traumatic for the then library administration. Unfortunately, that trauma has only slightly abated.

Offsetting the influx of materials (and bills) from CAP was the success of the Southeast Asia Program in gaining federal support from a grant under the National Defense Education Act (NDEA). The importance of that grant support, which continued for about 8 years, cannot be over-stated. Indeed, without that federal support, Southeast Asian Studies likely would have withered at Ohio University, especially as those years of support fell during a time that the University and the Library faced sharp enrollment drops accompanied by slashed budgets. The present stature of our Southeast Asia Collection owes much to that funding but even more so to the concern of the faculty associated with Southeast Asian Studies at Ohio University who were perceptive enough to recognize that of all of the things for which the grants might be used that library resources would yield the greatest benefits over the longest period. That this awareness was not unique to Ohio University was

---

[3]Lian The and Paul W. van der Veur, *Treasures and Trivia: Doctoral Dissertations Accepted by Universities in the United States* (Papers in International Studies, Southeast Asia Series No. 1; Athens: Ohio University Center for International Studies, 1968) and Lian The with Paul W. van der Veur, *The Verhandelingen van het Bataviaasch Genootschap: An Annotated Content Analysis* (Papers in International Studies, Southeast Asia Series No. 26; Athens: Ohio University Center for International Studies, 1973).

evident in a study of NDEA Centers for 1978-79 which found that Southeast Asia Centers expended 21.7% of their budgets on library acquisitions compared to an average of 11.1% for all Centers.[4]

While this funding was crucial, we would also emphasize an additional consideration, one which was occasionally the subject of criticism in grant competitions: the decision to focus efforts on those parts of Southeast Asia most consistent with the foci of the Southeast Asia Program and the University, rather than inadequately attempt to blanket the region. This is not to ignore particular countries in Southeast Asia or to claim that some are more important than others. Rather it was and is a recognition that comprehensive collecting on the ten countries of the region is prohibitively expensive for any institution. Further it recognizes that researchers nationally are better served by the availability of research collections concentrating on specific countries, particularly if some coordinated distribution of collection development could be implemented, than by a number of collections ranging from moderate to mediocre.[5]

While there have been various attempts at distributed collection development among the fewer than ten collections in the U.S. that focus on Southeast Asia, these remain in the exploratory phase. This is in rather marked contrast to the success achieved with SEASSI (Southeast Asian Studies Summer Institute) in cooperative summer language programs. In the meantime, each collection, depending on its budgetary resources, has been forced to emphasize some materials and areas and to neglect others. Lacking central coordination, Ohio University assayed the strengths of various collections in the U.S. and identified the countries of Brunei, Malaysia, and Singapore as unserved by a comprehensive research collection. Having identified this niche, the basis for a rational collection development policy was laid. Beyond seeking comprehensive coverage on these three countries, materials on Indonesia, the Philippines, and Thailand are collected (forming the core of an ASEAN focus) in decreasing priority and on the rest of Southeast Asia, with increasingly largely western language materials.

The budgetary rationale is obvious, but this concentration also facilitates the cultivation of relationships with librarians, scholars, and others concerned with the

---

[4]Ann I. Schneider, "NDEA Centers: How They Use Their Federal Money," in *President's Commission on Foreign Language and International Studies: Background Papers and Studies* (Washington, D.C.: U.S. Department of Health, Education, and Welfare, 1979), p. 174.

[5]The importance of distributed collection development is cited from a number of sources in William E. Carter, "International Studies and Research Library Needs," *President's Commission on Foreign Language and Area Studies: Background Papers and Studies* (Washington, D.C.: Department of Health, Education and Welfare, 1979), pp. 177-178. While the citations are concentrated on East Asian collections, they are equally applicable to Southeast Asia.

area and greater familiarity with research needs and interests. It has also evolved into the compilation of a bibliography of new materials on and from Brunei, Singapore, and Malaysia which appears regularly in *Berita,* the newsletter of the national Malaysia/Singapore/Brunei Studies Group.

The discussion of this collection development policy, which evolved over a number of years, marks an appropriate transition from history to the subject at hand, funding at Ohio University for the Southeast Asia Collection and research programs. Funding such as from federal grants is commonly referred to as "soft money," in contrast to regular operating allocations which are called "hard money." One of the lessons learned at Ohio University, during the budget and enrollment crises of the mid-1970s, alluded to above, was just how "soft" that hard money could be. In fact during one year the library, but not the Southeast Asia Collection which enjoyed grant support, was forced to forego the purchase of monographs. When revisions for the regulations covering NDEA centers resulted in the loss of federal funding, that source of support also disappeared. It is relevant to note that, just as the library identified a niche to serve national scholarship and research, the Southeast Asia Studies Program had similarly emphasized its unique capacities to provide well prepared students with masters degrees to other institutions, to provide strong background at the masters level for those seeking to work in Southeast Asia, and to stimulating awareness of Southeast Asia outside the centers (what is commonly termed outreach). While Southeast Asian foci were available in a few doctoral areas, there seemed no overwhelming demand for additional doctoral programs. Unfortunately for the university, the new federal regulations indicated that doctoral programs were to be the basis in identifying centers.

Having been spared much of the crisis of the mid-1970s that shook the rest of the university, failure to continue federal funding shocked the Southeast Asia Studies program and the library. While care had been taken, as far as possible, to transfer positions from soft funding to regular university positions, it was recognized among the faculty that the greatest threat was to the library. If the Collection, which had emerged as a major resource under federal funding, were not to be severely crippled, alternative funding would be needed. This was especially true for continued meaningful participation in CAP where reducing or halting acquisitions for a year can result in the loss of irreplaceable resources.

Ohio University Responses

It was at this point that the strong support of the President and senior administrators, alluded to in our opening, became crucial. Interim emergency funding was approved to cover the cost of CAP participation and for retention of a Southeast Asia Cataloging position through a competitive internal program of project grants.

It was also at this time that the pioneering "Tun Abdul Razak Chair in Southeast Asian Studies" was created. Through matching funding from the Malaysian

Government and American corporations doing business in Malaysia, earnings provide for the presence of a distinguished Malaysian professor on our campus each year. This year we have been very pleased that the Tun Razak Chair holder is Professor Zainal Abidin bin Abdul Wahid of the History Department of the National University of Malaysia. In addition to the usual provisions in an endowed Chair, this also provides a special allocation each year for library acquisitions.

Challenges & Responses

With this historical introduction, we now will expand our view while retaining a local focus consonant with our theme. Our rationale is that, with so few collections offering any depth on Southeast Asia, each of the collections is de facto a national resource center. Moreover, to continue to grow, each must consider the national community of users to justify such growth.

In describing funding, we will focus on funding for libraries as the basis for most research activity. This reflects our area of greatest experience but it also, we believe, targets the area of greatest neglect.[6] While funding for research from various sources (SSRC, ACLS, Fulbright, etc.), the major continuing external source of funding for library collections in the U.S. has been for National Centers under Title VI of the Higher Education Act. We will return to this point later.

Before discussing approaches to funding for library collections, two points should be emphasized. The first is that in discussing funding, we do not necessarily mean money, that is, gifts in kind can be an important means of building and maintaining collections. Depending on the nature of such gifts, they can contribute to the growth of the collection with little or minimal acquisitions cost to the collection and thus free money for other purposes.

The second point, partially the antithesis of the first, is that the cost of acquiring materials is of secondary importance to collection growth. It is a rule of thumb in libraries that acquisitions budgets account for 30 to 35% of a library budget. To be of use to researchers the materials must be made available, preferably easily accessible via national bibliographic utilities such as RLIN or OCLC. Even more striking in this

---

[6]An indication of the neglect is evident in the study by Robert A. McCaughey, *International Studies and Academic Enterprise: A Chapter in the Enclosure of American Learning* (New York: Columbia University Press, 1984) which concentrates on international expertise and the production of graduates with Ph.D.s but ignores the resources on which research, Ph.D. or otherwise depend. There is no entry for libraries in the detailed index to the volume. This may partially explain why the Head of Ohio University's Southeast Asia Collection entitled her bibliography of dissertations on Southeast Asia *Treasures and Trivia* (see fn. 3 above), to the chagrin of some reviewers.

regard, a single title acquired under CAP may cost $4 or $5 but the processing costs will be many times that figure ($100 per title was the figure given for the Library of Congress a few years ago). In addressing funding, consideration must be given to processing and servicing the materials as well as simply acquiring them. Discussions among Southeast Asia collection curators and librarians at the eight universities with identified collections indicate that significant cataloging and processing backlogs, especially of vernacular materials, are the rule rather than the exception. The result, for the research community, is that the materials may be no more accessible than if they had not been acquired.[7]

1. Local Support. Although funding will be addressed from a number of perspectives, the local situation is the most critical. Without the support of the library and the university administration as well as the faculty, the other approaches to funding which we will discuss will be unlikely. At the same time, it is at the local university level that a collection is likely to be most directly challenged. To the extent that it depends on operating funds and even undesignated non-operating funds, it is in competition with most other academic areas and programs. Without regard to the size of a particular institution's budget, an area collection, in this case a Southeast Asia Collection, must be able to justify its slice of that particular pie. Moreover, with considerable institutional variation, there will be ongoing challenges to the size of that slice, no matter how great or small.

Translating this discussion to Ohio University, we have prepared graphs, focusing on the current acquisitions budget, which indicates how that budget is spent (Figure 1) and how it is financed (Figure 2). We have mentioned our collection development foci (Brunei, Singapore, and Malaysia) and as a result acquisitions through the Southeast Asia Cooperative Acquisitions Program in Jakarta (referred to simply as CAP in this paper, although we recognize that there are many other CAP programs). Within that program, the acquisitions money divides 2:1 for Brunei, Singapore, and Malaysia materials compared to Indonesian materials. Yet Indonesia is the next most important area of focus. That so many Indonesian materials are now microfiched in New Delhi, subscription to the Library of Congress Photoduplication offering of Southeast Asia microfiche is a significant adjunct to our CAP participation. And the Southeast Asia Microform project (SEAM) is important in obtaining and preserving rare research materials but also in supporting doctoral research. As was evident in the historical discussion, the remainder of the money is spent for current western language materials on the area (many of these materials are acquired also from the disciplinary allocations but identifying a specific amount was not possible) and for some retrospective buying and research collections in microformat as well as news-

---

[7]The most recent assessment of area studies collections is the chapter, "Library and Information Resources" in Richard D. Lambert *et al. Beyond Growth: The Next Stage in Language and Area Studies* (Washington, D.C.: Association of American Universities, 1984), pp. 232-259. Pages 244-247 specifically address staffing and cataloging backlogs.

Figure 1
Ohio University Southeast Asia Collection
1985-86 Acquisitions Budget

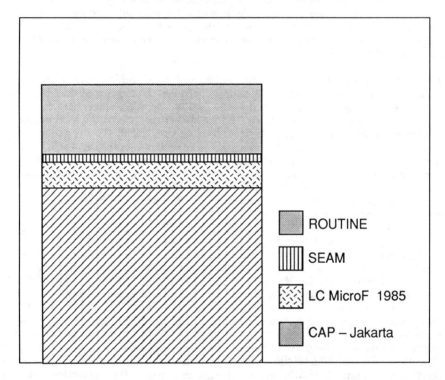

papers (a not insignificant expense) and other materials from other countries in the region. Also, these graphs reflect expenditures and not the value of gifts in kind.

Dollar figures for the expenditures are omitted as these change substantially from year to year (generally upward, with the exception of SEAM) but the proportions are illustrative. Implicit in the graph is that the first three expenses (are basically fixed costs) while expansions and contractions in budgets mostly affect the "routine" portion, increasing or decreasing the ability to buy retrospective materials and vernacular materials from other areas.

As Figure 2 evidences, meeting the cost of the expenditures in Figure 1 requires a blending of funding sources. The routine allocation is the share of operating funding for acquisitions identified for the Southeast Asia Collection (about 1.1%). The special allocation is also from the operating budget (about 1% of the 1985/86 budget)

Figure 2
Ohio University Southeast Asia Collection
Funding for 1985-86 Acquisitions

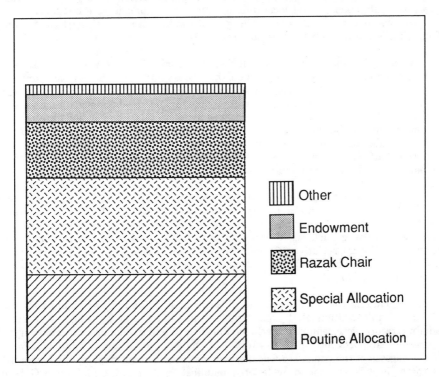

to assure continuation in the CAP programs. The funding from Razak Chair is based on endowment earnings. As it is subject to variation, it is shown at its minimum level. Depending on other needs of the Tun Razak Professor, it can increase 50% or more from that illustrated. These funds are used to intensify our efforts at comprehensive collecting on Malaysia and to support special research efforts of the Tun Razak Professor. The endowment earnings reflect our current fund raising campaign (discussed below). The proportion reflects the current year allocation but actually would be over twice the level shown when the endowment has been invested for the full earning period. The small "other" reflects private gifts to support the collection.

As noted, other operating funds are used to acquire Southeast Asian materials from disciplinary allocations,[8] library-wide endowment funding for special collections, and one-time money for research collections.

Without dwelling on these graphs, which are simply selective snapshots of a single year, it should be clear that local funding can require considerable imagination. It is also obvious that what we are calling local funding is not entirely local funding. This affords a transition to other funding areas.

2. Private, Corporate, and Foundation Support. Having experienced how "soft" both grant and operating funding can be, the Library and the University are currently engaged in a campaign to raise a substantial endowment for the Southeast Asia Collection, the earnings from which will provide for the acquisition and processing of materials. It would be premature to report in detail on this effort at this time. As was evident in the last graph on local funding, earnings from this campaign have begun to be available to support the acquisitions effort, but the goal of the campaign is to generate sufficient earnings to contribute to the cost of processing and bringing researchers and research materials together as well.

Figure 2 also indicates the role of the endowment for the Tun Abdul Razak Chair for Southeast Asian Studies in supporting the Collection. While the Malaysian Government played a key role in developing and supporting the Chair, American corporations doing business in Malaysia provided two-thirds of the funding. We continue to be appreciative of their contributions which continue to support the activities of the Chair and the Collection in perpetuity (see acknowledgement of donors in Appendix A).

In concluding the brief discussion of this source of funding, we would be remiss if we did not caution that considerable time and travel by senior University administrators were required to achieve the goal. While the donors indicated varying degrees of support, both in their efforts and the amounts given, a significant factor in the success of the campaign was the demonstrated commitment by the University at the highest levels, not to neglect the manifest support of the Malaysian Government, which convinced donors of the importance of the Tun Razak Chair.

It is also important to note that the beneficiaries of these donations have been scholars and researchers throughout the nation, the thousands of Malaysian students studying in North America, and the members of the Ohio University community who have had the opportunity to consult with the distinguished Malaysian professors who have been named to the Chair to date or have used the materials acquired by the Southeast Asia Collection (at Ohio University) through interlibrary loan, or, as not

---

[8]Ohio University's approach to allocating acquisitions funds in general is described in K. Mulliner, "The Acquisitions Allocation Formula at Ohio University," *Library Acquisitions: Practice and Theory*, Vol. X, 4 (1986), pp. 315-327.

infrequently occurs, through urgent telephone requests to the Collection for information.

3. Southeast Asia. The Malaysian Government was particularly farsighted in its support for the Tun Razak Chair. But this is not the only example of how governments, organizations, and individuals can support Southeast Asia Collections. In recent years the Malaysian Government has also recognized that it is important to provide the thousands of students which it sends to North America with authoritative information on what is happening in Malaysia. As American newspapers (even the best) are most likely to provide regular reports on Southeast Asia only when there is a particular crisis--and that in a manner aimed at the American reader, Malaysia has provided for regular air mail subscriptions to Malaysian newspapers for universities with sufficient Malaysian students enrolled. This, of course, provides the students with a basis to interpret the crisis news which they receive in American newspapers and to help the students remain in touch. From a library perspective, in which air-mailed newspapers can be a substantial expense, even through CAP, the newspapers are a valuable addition. The Indonesian Government, through the Embassy, has also provided special gifts to Southeast Asia Collections of special series on Indonesian and local language literature.

These are but examples of the potential for mutually beneficial cooperation between Southeast Asian individuals, groups and governments. An even more important effort may be the creation last May of the Malaysian Resource Center at Ohio University, which was dedicated by Minister of Education Abdullah Ahmad Badawi. The Resource Center represents a further stage of cooperation between the Collection and Malaysian agencies and organizations. The goal, approved at several levels but difficult to implement (librarians will appreciate that government officials and diplomats do not always understand the needs of a library, especially for continuity), is to have Ohio University as a depository in the U.S. for government publications. News of the Center has also attracted deposits from a number of non-governmental organizations. Of particular note was the deposit of a number of historic films from the Malaysian Embassy which otherwise would have been discarded. These have since been transferred to videotape. In moving to assure accessibility of Southeast Asian resources in the U.S., we think this is a fertile field for exploration.

Having identified some of the possibilities, we would be remiss if we did not also mention an important hazard. Despite some concerns expressed at the time of its establishment by informed scholars, the Tun Razak Chair has provided benefits to Malaysia and to Ohio University without compromising the integrity of either (see description in Appendix B). Similarly, the Malaysian Resource Center receives valuable support in kind from the Malaysian Government but it is not a governmental information agency but a research and media resource of and about the people and nation of Malaysia. While we have not been troubled by financing or associations which would compromise Ohio University, the library or the Southeast Asia Collection, it is always a concern.

4. International. We use this term to refer to non-Southeast Asia funding and to international agencies. We have little to say about it beyond noting that Southeast Asia nations are not the only nations that rely on the U.S. to educate their scholars and researchers. It remains to be seen whether the governments, organizations, and corporations in these other nations will realize that investing in the research resources that these students and researchers use in the U.S. is an investment in their future. At the international level, UNESCO was instrumental in helping Ohio University to develop and refine a pioneering internship program[9] for library science faculty from Southeast Asia which continues to serve professional librarians from the region and other parts of Asia as well as to provide contacts and expertise in processing and handling Southeast Asia materials. Such funding is no longer available but it remains an area that cannot be ignored.

5. Federal. At a time when Gramm-Rudmann-Hollings has precipitated virtual panic, we are contrarians in discussing the present and potential federal support of Southeast Asian resources and research. In the first place, we unlikely would be here today were it not for past federal support as an NDEA/FLAS center, as apparent in the history section of this paper. Also, we are presently in the midst of a cataloging project supported under Title II-C of the Higher Education Act which will both greatly alleviate our backlog and will provide the basis for national online access to the wealth of information in the Southeast Asia microfiche produced in New Delhi. Our project focuses on the pre-AACR2 fiche[10] and was intended to provide access to the fiche that Delhi could not. Whether scholars will receive access to the remainder (those produced since 1982) is reportedly threatened by present and pending forced budget reductions.

---

[9]Described in Hwa-Wei Lee and K. Mulliner, "International Exchange of Librarians and the Ohio University Internship Program," *College & Research Libraries News*, Vol. X (November 1982), pp. 345-348; and Hwa-Wei Lee, "International Library Internships: An Effective Approach to Co-operation," *International Library Review*, Vol. XVII (1985), pp. 17-25, which is also available as "Library Internships: A New Approach to Cooperation," in *Areas of Cooperation in Library Development in Asian and Pacific Regions*, (Athens, Ohio: Chinese-American Librarians Association, 1985), pp. 21-27.

[10]About one-half of the activity in Ohio University's present HEA Title II-C Grant is aimed at providing full AACR2 cataloging in machine readable form for Southeast Asia microfiche produced in New Delhi prior to the implementation of AACR2 by the Library of Congress. This is being done as a Major Microform Project through OCLC, which permits other institutions with the fiche to add holdings at a fraction of the cost of separate cataloging. It also provides a tape which can be loaded into RLIN for institutions using that utility. "AACR2" stand for the Second Edition of the Anglo American Cataloging Rules, which made substantial changes in the way information is entered in machine- readable format. With machine-readable records, consistency in entries is essential to assure fullest retrieval of information sought.

Without entering into partisan issues, one of the international areas reportedly least threatened is the Caribbean Initiative, yet when this thrust was announced it was likened to creating Singapores in Central America. That, of course, was before the present economic slump in Singapore. The allusion was evidence of a lack of understanding of Southeast Asia in general and Singapore in particular. Without belaboring it, the previous identification of international programs as "National Defense Education" was not entirely inappropriate. We share the contention of many of the papers presented to the President's Commission on Foreign Language and Area Studies that this country needs people and research familiar with different world areas and those people and that research depends upon access to comprehensive and timely information from and about the areas.

As Dr. Senese has discussed the role of Title II-C, we would only emphasize the importance of the two grants which we have received under that Title to increase the availability of our Collection nationally.

We focus instead on Title VI, which is specifically intended to strengthen international and area awareness. In the history section, we indicated that support for libraries under Title VI was significant as a proportion of the grants which represented a permanent investment in the research resources of the nation (21.7% of the grants to Southeast Asia Centers in 1978/79) and for our Collection in particular. Unfortunately, this has not necessarily been the case. Of the eight universities supporting Southeast Asia Collections, three have been designated as National Centers. As a generalization, a Department of Education paper has documented that for all Title VI Centers, library expenditures as a proportion of the federal grants fell from 21.2% in 1973/74 to 15.9% in 1981/82. Combining Southeast Asia and the Pacific Islands, it noted that an average of only 4.5% of the Title VI funds went for library expenditures (least of any of the world areas) but these accounted for an average of 15.2% of library expenditures for the area collection (highest of any world area).[11] A more recent compilation, by Dr. Ann Schneider of the Department of Education, reports that Title VI Southeast Asia Centers spent an average of 16.9% of the grants for library acquisitions (back to highest among the regions) and 10.4% for library staff.[12]

Our purpose is not to criticize centers but to emphasize the lesson learned at Ohio University, when a Federal grant disappears, the one major legacy is the library collection. Moreover, such collections, built with Federal funds, should be truly National Centers, serving researchers spread throughout the nation. To address this

---

[11]Ann I. Schneider, "Libraries of Title VI Centers: Some Impressions and Questions," unpublished paper provided by U.S. Department of Education, April 13, 1982.

[12]Ann I. Schneider, "Center Budgets -- Analysis of 1983-84 Data," Memo to Directors of Title VI Centers and Fellowships Programs, U. S. Department of Education, Center for International Education, June 24, 1985.

Bill Frederick, a member of the Ohio University faculty, two years ago suggested a rethinking of the "Center Concept" as it applies to Southeast Asia. He emphasized that with only eight centers and programs concentrating on Southeast Asia that "all centers should be treated as national repositories and receive basic support for, in particular, library and other materials.[13] At the same conference, Shiro Saito called for "the formation of a consortium of Southeast Asia collections" to engage in "a nationally coordinated collection plan to acquire systematically Southeast Asian research materials."[14] While we find the suggested levels of funding ($3,000-$5,000) and matching ($800-$1,500) impossibly low, the concept has merit and would be a natural continuation of current discussions within the Collection Development Sub-Committee of the Committee on Research Materials on Southeast Asia (CORMOSEA).

Finally, considering Federal programs, the role of the Library of Congress and its Jakarta Field Office cannot be neglected. Cutbacks in the funding for the Jakarta office, just as a new director has come on board, would be a severe blow to CAP participants for Southeast Asia. The program is significant for both acquisitions and cataloging. If anything greater attention should be given to opportunities afforded by microcomputers to increase productivity and for Jakarta to provide machine readable records to LC which can be added to national online databases such as RLIN and OCLC.

6. **Access.** Previous mention has been made of the importance of access to materials. In citing access as a challenge, we are concerned that researchers can identify materials, can afford to borrow or otherwise use them, and have as full access as possible internationally as well as nationally. In identifying materials, the problem is both the backlogs in cataloging and processing and the problems for institutions in RLIN or OCLC to share records with those in the other utility. For users outside the eight academic Southeast Asia Centers, the problem is even greater. We would hope that the Linked Systems Project might eventually bridge this chasm on a national (and possibly international) basis, but at present print sources seem the only solution.[15] Beyond identifying materials, users need to be able to obtain them. This

---

[13]William H. Frederick, "Adapting the Area Study Center Concept to New Needs," in Ronald A. Morse, ed., *Southeast Asian Studies: Options for the Future* (Papers presented at a conference held at the Woodrow Wilson International Center for Scholars, March 26, 1984; Lanham, Md.: University Press of America, 1984), p. 92. Emphasis in original.

[14]Shiro Saito, "Progress and Needs for Research Tools and Resources in Southeast Asia Studies," in ibid., p. 154. Emphasis in original.

[15]Examples of printed materials which assist in identifying and obtaining materials include the Library of Congress, *Accessions List, Southeast Asia* (Jakarta: Library of Congress Office) and *The John M. Echols Collection on Southeast Asia Accessions List* (Ithaca: Southeast Program, Cornell University). Similar information but with

is particularly critical for graduate students, the next generation of researchers, who are severely pressed to meet the interlibrary lending charges imposed by institutions housing some of the Southeast Asia Collections. There is no easy solution in sight, particularly as the collections at some of the larger institutions, apparently are following an institutional policy in which they have a small voice. In our own institution, we strive to maintain the principle of free access to information by not charging other than for photocopy charges or in reciprocity to those institutions that impose a charge on our institution.

The question of international cooperation remains wide open. Various approaches have been made from the U.S., Australia, and Southeast Asia, but little concrete has been accomplished to date. New initiatives are obviously needed.

7.   New and Special Collecting Problems.   Time and technology are also bringing new challenges to Southeast Asia Collections. In the history of Southeast Asian studies in this country, we are at a point where many of the pioneering researchers have retired or are nearing retirement. This seems an area deserving special attention if potentially valuable ephemeral materials and field notes are not to be lost to future scholars. Obviously those associated with a particular collection or institution may wish to leave their work with that institution but there are many more across the U.S. whose lifework deserves preservation. We have made small steps in this direction, but it deserves national consideration in conjunction with distributed collection development.

Technology is also providing a proliferation of formats in which materials need to be collected: beyond the traditional audio-visual media are data tapes, recordings of events (cultural and historical), microcomputer software, and a range of video products to name a few. We have begun piecemeal to acquire these but they present an entire range of problems in terms of systems (e.g., VHS or Beta, PAL or other video systems) to actually use them. This takes collections into new areas and is virtually impossible to undertake on a single institution basis. The Malaysian Resource Center represents one approach at Ohio University. Also reflecting the new roles, in 1984 an alumnus presented the Library with a sizeable collection of Southeast Asian artifacts, reflecting the art and artisanship of Southeast Asian peoples.[16] These, together with previous gifts of realia of daily life, are being prepared for exhibit as an adjunct of our Southeast Asian Collection.

---

articles and analytic entries can be found in some country newsletters. We are most conversant with the "Malaysia/Singapore/Brunei Bibliography," begun by the Collection at Yale University but produced in recent years by the Ohio University Southeast Asia Collection, in *Berita: Newsletter of the Malaysia/Singapore/Brunei Studies Group* (Philadelphia: John Lent for the M/S/B Studies Group).

[16]The catalog for that collection is: Lian The-Mulliner, *Southeast Asia Through Ethnic Art: The Russell R. Ross Collection at Ohio University* (Athens: Ohio University Library 1984).

8. New Responses. Two years ago, Bill Frederick called for the establishment of a national institute of advanced studies for Southeast Asia. In the absence of any response, he has now stimulated the formation of one such institute at Ohio University. Sri (or SRI--Southeast Asia Research Institute) is still in its developmental phases. Part of its purpose is to respond to some of the new challenges discussed above which fall outside some of the traditional roles and missions of Southeast Asia Collections. It is too early to provide a detailed description. Our purpose in noting it here is that attempts are being made to respond in new ways to the challenges identified above.

Conclusion

In focusing on Ohio University and especially the library, we have responded to the topic which we were asked to address. We are proud of some of the things that we have accomplished, disappointed in what has not, and cowed by what remains. In focusing on Ohio University, our intention is not to claim particular contributions but to begin what we hope will be an ongoing communications process among the few institutions in the country concerned with Southeast Asia and the many more researchers concerned with the field.

OHIO UNIVERSITY THANKS THE DONORS
TO THE TUN ABDUL RAZAK CHAIR

Corporate Contributors

Leadership Gifts

Goodyear Malaysia Berhad
Esso Companies in Malaysia
American International Group
IBM World Trade Corporation
NCR Malaysia Sdn. Bhd.
RCA Sendirian Berhad
R.J. Reynolds Tobacco Co. Sdn. Bhd.
3M Malaysia Sdn. Bhd.
Johnson & Johnson Sdn. Bhd.

Major Gifts

General Instrument Sdn. Bhd.
Colgate-Palmolive (Malaysia) Sdn. Bhd.
Warner-Lambert (Mfg) Sdn. Bhd.
Caltex Oil Malaysia Ltd.
The Chase Manhattan Bank, N.A.
Citibank, N.A.
Ford Motor Company of Malaysia Sdn. Bhd.

Special Gifts

Monsanto Fund
CPC (Malaysia) Sdn. Bhd.
Gillette Companies in Malaysia
Mobil Oil Malaysia Sdn. Bhd.
Uniroyal Malaysian Plantations Sdn. Bhd.
Union Carbide Malaysia Sdn. Bhd.
Ogilvy & Mather (M) Sdn. Bhd.
Burson-Marsteller (Malaysia) Sdn. Bhd.
Bristol-Myers (Malaysia) Sdn. Bhd.

APPENDIX B

About the Tun Abdul Razak Chair

In March of 1980, the Malaysian Ministry of Education announced in Kuala Lumpur and Washington D.C. the establishment of the Tun Abdul Razak Chair in Southeast Asian studies at Ohio University. Jointly endowed by a US$350,000 grant from the Government of Malaysia and by matching funds generously contributed by public-spirited American firms with operations in Malaysia, this Chair represents an extraordinary nation-to-nation commitment in higher education.

Under the agreement with Ohio University, Malaysia annually nominates prominent visiting scholars from a wide variety of academic fields to go to Ohio University to teach, to conduct research, and to travel to academic and other meetings around the nation. As intellectual envoys to the United States from Southeast Asia, these scholars will leave a lasting legacy in America: a new appreciation of our similarities, a new respect for our differences.

The first holder of the Tun Razak Chair, the world-renowned Islamic scholar, Professor Syed Mohd. Naquib al-Attas, served with distinction during the academic year of 1981-1982. He measurably advanced the purposes of the Chair's founders which are to expand American knowledge of the cultural, economic, social, and political life and history of Malaysia and Southeast Asia.

Professor al-Attas made substantial progress on a book of commentary on the great Islamic thinker, Al-Raniri, which will give new insight into the history of Southeast Asia and the impact of Islam in the Malay world. He taught courses, lectured in other parts of the nation, advised Ohio University librarians in their quest to strengthen further an already first-rate Southeast Asian collection, and served as an advisor/consultant to Malaysian and American students and scholars. The second distinguished Tun Razak Professor, soon to be announced, will build upon the foundation of excellence laid by Professor Naquib al-Attas.

The concept of the Razak Chair grew out of the vision and cooperation of many individuals and organizations. Without the inspiration and support of Tun Dr. Hussein Onn, Datuk Seri Dr. Mahathir, Datuk Musa Hitam and other Malaysian leaders, the project could not have been realized. The generous support of the civic-minded American companies being honored here tonight is an essential link in this unique partnership in international education. The leaders of these U.S. firms, here and at home, see this liaison as a natural corollary to their economic partnership with the people and government of Malaysia.

By every measure, the Tun Abdul Razak Chair is a remarkable success. Ohio University is proud to be part of this innovative program in Malaysian-American relations and understanding.

Section II

Bibliographic Control

Scholarly Publications: Considerations on Bibliographic
Control and Dissemination (1975); Co-author:
Stephen W. Massil 49

International Standard Numbering for Books and Serials and
the Standardization of Bibliographic Descriptions (in Chinese)
(1975); Co-author: Jane C. Yang 55

Cooperative Regional Bibliographic Projects in South-East
Asia (1977) 63

SCHOLARLY PUBLICATIONS: CONSIDERATIONS ON BIBLIOGRAPHIC CONTROL AND DISSEMINATION

Co-Author: Stephen W. Massil

This paper discusses certain factors affecting the publishers' responsibilities in catering to the academic community. These factors and responsibilities relate to the process of information transfer, and in following the suggested procedures publishers will find that benefits are opened to themselves as well as to their clientele. Addressed to publishers of scholarly material, it is hoped that this paper can encourage greater cooperation among all publishers, their distributors, and their customers. It may be that publishers, in universities especially, are already aware of the factors under discussion, and have effective procedures of their own. They should be further encouraged, therefore, to take a lead in their countries to ensure wider implementation of the procedures presented here.

Scholarly publications are expensive and have a limited if assured appeal; as contributions to knowledge they have nonetheless a world-wide appeal. It is therefore important for their publishers to make contact with their potential audience as quickly and as efficiently as possible. Publishers in the scholarly field have a duty, in terms of the spread of knowledge and of the educational, intellectual, and research aspects of national development, to contribute to the efficient transfer of information. It is library and documentation services that are of major concern in this process, but the procedures to be implemented will bring publishers closer to the research function of libraries and their users.

Through UNESCO, many basic recommendations regarding national libraries, deposit, and Universal Bibliographic Control (UBC) have recently seen widespread implementation, followed now by the review of bibliographic standards. The implications for publishers need to be adumbrated too.

International Standard Book Numbers (ISBN)

The ISBN scheme grew out of the need to standardize the various systems of numbering that publishers had been utilizing over many years to control and simplify the files identifying their books. It was first put into practice in Britain in 1967. In 1969 the International Standards Organization, with the approval of 23 countries, ratified the scheme, and ISO Standard No. 2108-1972(E) was drawn up to coordinate and standardize the use of book numbers. Different countries (such as Britain and Australia[1]) have their own national ISBN agencies. The International ISBN Agency was set up in the Library of State of the Prussian Cultural Foundation in 1972. Its task is to co-ordinate the work of the national ISBN agencies, and to extend the scheme to non-participating countries, where co-operation amongst publishers, publishers' associations, and national bibliographic services should be instrumental in establishing eventual participation.

The ISBN itself is a ten-digit number divided into four parts (the letters ISBN should precede):

  (a) group identifier
  (b) publisher prefix
  (c) title number
  (d) check digit (for computer manipulation)

A number is unique to a title in a particular edition, and is unchangeable. The number appears on the back of the title page and perhaps on the book-jacket and elsewhere. It is used in all publicity and listings. The advantages for publishers, suppliers, and libraries are great, since they provide an efficient and economical method of communication amongst them.

International Standard Serial Numbers (ISSN)

Similar in concept and purpose to the ISBN for books, the ISSN for periodical and serials publications in the widest sense has arisen in direct response to the needs of UBC, and the system has been integrated with UNISIST activities (UNESCO's World Science Information Programme) in its International Serials Data Systems (ISDS) network. Again, centres for registering titles are being set up either nationally or regionally, and the resulting files are being coordinated by an International Centre in Paris.[2] In countries where centres are operating, publishers should seek their ISSNs from these. Otherwise they should notify the International Centre for the numbers to be assigned. Publishers may already have been notified by R.R. Bowker of ISSNs allocated. These appear in *Ulrich's International*

---

[1]The Australian Standard Book Numbering Agency has issued the following pamphlet: *International Standard Book Numbering in Australia*. 3rd ed. Canberra: Australian Standard Book Numbering Agency, National Library of Australia, 1973. ISBN 0 642 99004 2.

[2]ISDS International Centre, 20 Rue Bauchaumont, 75002 Paris, France. It publishes: *Bulletin de l'ISDS / ISDS Bulletin*, v. 1, no. 1 (1974). ISSN 0300-3000.

Periodicals Directory[3] and *Ulrich's Irregular Serials and Annuals,*[4] and the numbers have been included in the ISDS base file.

The ISSN is an eight-digit divided into two parts separated by a hyphen (and preceded by the letters ISSN); the eighth digit is a check-digit. The number is not publisher-oriented and relates to a particular title uniquely. (In Ulrich's, country or group identifiers precede the ISSN as printed, and do not form part of the ISSN). The number should appear on the cover or title-page of every issue, and in all publicity and listings. Monographs that are published in series need to show their respective ISBN and the ISSN of the series.

Bibliographic Control

Once the framework for the numbering systems has been set up in each country, the onus on publishers in complying with the requirements will be slight. There will be advantages in continuity of identification and ordering, and in other respects, if publishers can reserve numbers at the pre-publication stage; it is especially important to have the ISSN on the first issue as well as on subsequent ones. Adherence to the systems and standards[5] will achieve a great step forward in respect of bibliographic control. This has nothing to do with censorship and regulation of the press (in the countries where publishers are obliged to obtain licenses, a virtue could be made of the arrangement to ensure allocation of the standard numbers by this means). Its purpose is to achieve awareness of what materials have been published, and to disseminate as much information concerning them as possible and as rapidly as possible.

The prime authority for bibliographic control should be vested in national bibliographic services, which in many countries are now operated within the national library. The main means at the disposal of the national bibliography for achieving this control is in most countries some sort of copyright deposit legisla-

---

[3]15th ed. New York, 1974.

[4]2nd ed. New York, 1973.

[5]Following the ISBN and ISSN standards, there are the *International Standard Bibliographic Description for Monographs and for Serials, ISBD(M) and ISBD(S)* (London: IFLA Committee on Cataloging, 1974), which are being discussed by the national libraries of the world. These do not affect publishers directly, but they should be sufficiently aware of them in the interest of clear presentations of their title-pages and publicity materials.

tion[6] whereby publishers are liable to deposit at least one copy of every publication (issued for sale) with the national library (in Britain, the obligation is for six copies, one each to a group of institutions). In its turn the national bibliography is deputed to publish a listing of items received in this way; the work of the national library is severely hampered when the legislation is not strict, and where publishers are lax.

The importance of the measures for bibliographic awareness and control should be compounded by the attempts made by the Library of Congress in its shared cataloguing programme of the last fifteen years, and by the presence of its acquisitions agents - one for south-east Asia, for instance, based in Jakarta - in different parts of the world. The National Library of Australia also has an acquisitions office in Jakarta. Their acquisitions go to build up "area" collections in their respective libraries, and the listings published[7] are relied upon by other libraries for selection and other purposes. Local national bibliographies[8] are used in other parts of the world for the same purposes.

There should be a clear duty for publishers of scholarly material, which may have relevance for world knowledge as well as "area" study, to comply with deposit laws in terms of the needs of national development; the benefit of publicity via the national bibliography, and dissemination of this and other listings abroad, should also be an incentive.

Cataloguing In Publication (CIP)

A further development to consolidate bibliographic control, undergoing development in Britain, the U.S.A., and most actively in Australia in particular, is the procedure whereby publishers notify the national bibliography as early as possible of the publications they are planning, not merely so that the ISBN can be assigned and registered well in advance but so that preliminary cataloguing data can be prepared and printed in the book itself. This, of course, is an experiment geared to library needs, with the supremacy of centralized cataloguing as a goal, but the CIP information also ensures advance appearance in the National Bibliography itself.

---

[6]E.g., Singapore. *Laws, statutes. Chapter 224. Printers and Publishers Act.* Revised ed. 1970.

[7]E.g. *Accessions List: Indonesia, Malaysia, Singapore and Brunei.* Library of Congress. National Program for Acquisitions and Cataloguing (Jakarta: Library of Congress Office). ISSN 0041-7742.

[8]E.g. *Singapore National Bibliography, 1971.* Singapore: National Library, 1974.

Publishers of scholarly works are probably in the best position to co-operate with national bibliographic services in this part of the world, and to undertake such an experiment here. Some such development may seem worth initiating.

Serials

The remarks on bibliographic control apply equally to books and serials. Certain desiderata more specific to serials publishing, especially as they are more likely in the scholarly context to be published by societies and institutions than by commercial publishers, need to be treated separately.

It should be standard practice for each article in a journal to be preceded by a brief abstract or summary. Contents pages should be clear. There should be a title page (or its substitute - a cover or masthead) conveying both the title, the details of the issuing body and editorial board, numbering statement, and frequency. If an ISSN has been assigned, this should appear in the requisite place, and the ISDS key title statement associated with this number may also appear with lesser prominence. Style of presentation is optional, but references and abbreviations in articles and citations should follow recognized standards. A regular index should also be supplied with each completed volume or group of volumes. These details may be obvious, but there is a need to mention them. Standards of editing of scientific journals in South-East Asia have recently been the subject of a series of UNESCO courses. One of the special emphases of these courses was bibliographic control. Copies of the draft lecture notes[9] are available from the UNESCO Field Science Office for Southeast Asia.

Regarding the use of English, the titles of serials and of articles should be given in English in parallel with the vernacular, and those in non-Roman scripts should be transliterated as well. There should be a separate contents page in English, and abstracts of articles should also be given in English.

Regarding the titles of serials, it is library experience that these change often and sometimes quite arbitrarily. Under the ISDS scheme, each change of title requires a new ISSN, and it is quite understood that interested content changes require title changes, that variations, splits, and mergers occur under publishing conditions which need to be reflected in bibliographic systems. Nevertheless, it is recommended that publishers resist as sternly as possible the impulse to change the titles of their serial publications.[10]

---

[9]H. Grunewald, *A Short Course on Scientific Editing; Lecture Notes*. Jakarta: UNESCO Field Science Office for Southeast Asia, 1974.

[10]A group calling themselves Librarians United to Fight Costly, Silly, Unnecessary Serial Title Changes (LUTFCSUSTC) at Michigan State University Library,

Conclusion

Scholarly publishing is the most important wave of the information explosion. The measures for achieving bibliographic control described here are practical, and simple to put into effect. Publishers of scholarly material should take the lead, together with the national libraries, in coordinating the necessary procedures amongst themselves and in the publishing community at large. The benefits to publishers from their participation in this effort will be seen to be quite as great as any accruing to other components of the information process, and in particular the so-called "information gap" will be marginally narrowed.

East Lansing, Mich., is the subject of a letter from D.C. Yaylor, in *Library Association Record*, v. 76 no. 1, (1974).

國際圖書刊物統一編號及著錄的標準化

李華偉* 楊黃晴

一、前　言

　　近幾年來，世界各國的圖書舘界，因鑒於圖書刊物統一編號及著錄標準化的重要，在國際圖書舘協會聯盟(International Federation of Library Associations 以下簡稱「圖協聯盟」)，國際文獻聯盟 (International Federation of Documentation)，國際標準組織 (International Standards Organization)，及聯合國教育、科學與文化組織 (United Nations Educational, Scientific and Cultural Organization 以下簡稱「聯敎組織」)等機構的倡導與實際推動下，陸續地訂定了下列四項國際標準，由美、英、法、德、加、澳洲等國家率先領導，付諸實施：

1. 國際標準圖書編號——ISBN (International Standard Book Number)。[1]
2. 國際標準刊物編號——ISSN (International Standard Serial Number)。[2]
3. 國際圖書著錄標準——ISBD (M) (International Standard Bibliographic Description for Monographs)。[3]
4. 國際刊物著錄標準——ISBD (S) (International Standard Bibliographic Description for Serials)。[4]

　　根據最近的資料，這四種標準已受到世界各國圖書舘界及出版界廣泛地重視，很多國家且已正式採用這些標準。我國亦曾爲圖協聯盟會員之一，對於國際合

* 李華偉博士，現任泰國曼谷亞洲理工學院 (Asian Institute of Technology)圖書舘舘長。
　楊黃晴女士，美國新漢普夏大學助理教授，現服務於該校圖書舘編目部。

作向極重視，應卽採取步驟，將這些標準譯成中文，向國內廣為介紹；並由國立中央圖書舘及中國圖書舘學會，會同有關機構擬訂實施辦法，及早付諸實施。本文因受篇幅限制，祇能將此四種標準的來龍去脈做一個簡要的報導。

二、國際標準圖書編號 "ISBN"

　　圖書編號的作用大致有二：從出版界的觀點來看，圖書編號可以簡化圖書發行，宣傳、推銷、記錄，及管理等手續，為此之故，很多出版商或書商為了業務上的需要，早已採行了各自設計的編號。從圖書舘的觀點來看，圖書編號可以簡化圖書採訪、登錄、出納，及管理等工作，尤其是近年來，因電腦的應用已日漸增廣，圖書編號逐成為簡化電腦作業，資料儲檢及流通的重要方式之一。為使圖書編號全世界一致化，以增進其最大的效能，美國早在一九六〇年卽有此建議，但最先付諸實行者還是英國。現行的國際標準圖書編號是經英國福斯特（F. G. Foster）教授設計，由英國出版者協會（The Publishers' Association）在一九六七年底開始採用。此後，美、加、澳洲等國家相繼起而仿行。經過了廿三個國家的批准，國際標準組織乃於一九七二年，正式將該編號制度訂為國際標準——ISO Standard No. 2108—1972（E）。為了執行及推廣此一標準，一個永久性的國際 ISBN 機構（International ISBN Agency）在一九七二年設立，附設於柏林的普魯士文化協會（Stiftung Preussischer Kulturbesitz）圖書舘內，以綜理協調世界各國有關標準圖書編號的事宜。至於實際分配號碼給出版商的工作，則分由各國的 ISBN 中心負責。

　　國際標準圖書編號是一種十位數的號碼，每一個號碼包括下列四個部份：
1. 地區或國家識別號碼（Group identifier），
2. 出版商號碼（Publisher prefix），
3. 書名號碼（Title number），及
4. 核對數字（Check digit）。

　　前三部份的號碼皆為阿拉伯數字，每一部份的數字長短不一，可以相對的增減，使總數位經常保持九位。第四部份是一個單位數，逢「十」時則以英文字母的「×」代替，每一部份間有一空隔以資區別。

　　地區或國家識別號碼並非因國家而異，有些國家因語言相同，有時可共同使用一個號碼：如「0」卽同時代表英、美、加、澳洲、紐西蘭，及南非等國家。根據手頭的資料，「2」代表法國，「3」代表德國，「82」代表挪威，「90」則代表荷蘭。這些號碼是由國際 ISBN 機構統一分配的。

核對數字則是從每一編號的九個數字中，根據特別公式推算而來，用以查核該號碼是否被誤記。此種核對的方式，以電腦行之，十分方便有效。

因為前三部份的號碼皆可以相對的增減，變化無窮，因此每一部份皆有足夠的號碼可資分配及使用，例如：

ISBN 　 0 　 471 　 　 　 84831 　 X
　 　 美國 　 Becker & Hayes 　 書名 　 核對數字

ISBN 　 0 　 903043 　 02 　 　 5
　 　 英國 　 圖協聯盟 　 書名 　 核對數字

我國在實施此一標準時，最好能參考澳洲的情形，在國立中央圖書館內附設一ISBN機構，以掌管出版商號碼的分配及其他有關事宜。凡本國圖書無統一編號者，國立中央圖書館應在列入全國圖書目錄時，代為編號。

三、國際標準刊物編號 "ISSN"

刊物編號的目的和用途與圖書編號大致相同，在執行的方法上亦無大差異。最初提議設此編號者也是美國。在一九六八年，美國標準局（American Standards Institution 現已改名為 American National Standards Institute）的圖書館工作，文獻與出版業組（Committee Z 39 on Library Work, Documentation, and Related Publishing Practices）特別設立了一個專案小組來研究刊物編號的統一標準。為了使得此一標準能夠國際化，美國標準局特將此一標準的草案送交國際標準組織的第四十六技術小組（ISO/TC/46）審議，於獲得通過後，正式定為國際標準刊物編號。

當此標準正在草擬之時，聯教組織與國際科學團體聯合會（International Council of Scientific Unions）花了四年的時間，在一九七一年共同提出了「建立一個世界科學資料系統可行性的研究報告」。[5] 此一報告與其附帶建議在同年為聯教組織大會所通過，並被列為聯教組織主要任務之一。為簡稱計，此一「世界科學資料系統」乃被定名為——UNISIST。

在此同時，聯教組織與國際科學團體聯合會的一個著錄工作小組（ Joint UNISIST/ICSU—AB Working Group on Bibliographic Description）亦提出建立一個「國際刊物資料系統（ International Serials Data System ）可行性的報告」[6]，獲得 UNISIST 中央委員會通過，成為 UNISIST 的主要活動

之一。在法國政府經費的補助下，一個刊物登錄的國際中心 （International Center for the Registration of Serial Publications）已於一九七二年底在巴黎成立，總管刊物登錄及編號的事宜。根據該中心的指南——Guidelines for ISDS，世界各國或各地區應分別設立各該國家或地區的 ISDS 中心，實際負責刊物登錄及編號的工作。

國際標準刊物編號是一種八位數的號碼，分成兩個四位數，中間由一「連字符號」（Hyphen）連接。其第八位數字是核對數字。每一號碼除代表一個刊物的名稱之外，別無其他意義，例如：

ISSN 0024—2527 為 Library Resources & Technical Services 的標準號碼。

ISSN 0301—4150 為 AGE Current Awareness Service 的標準號碼。

各國家或地區的 ISDS 中心，在設置之初應先向巴黎的國際中心報備，取得一份各該國或地區已編過號的刊物名單，並由該國際中心配給一批未用的號碼做為編號之用。各國家或地區的中心應按照規定，按時將刊物登記及編號的資料，向國際中心呈報，使國際中心能有一套完整的記錄。在沒有設立 ISDS 中心的地區，刊物的出版者可直接向國際中心申請編號。為便捷計，美國的保克公司（R.R. Bowker Co.）便曾事先獲得國際中心的同意，將七萬多登錄在該公司出版的兩種國際刊物名錄上（*Ulrichs' International Periodicals Directory* 及 *Irregular Serials and Annuals*）的刊物予以編號。各國新設的中心，對此批號碼應特別留意，以免重複。

目前我國雖已退出聯敎組織，對 ISDS 的活動仍應參加，最好能在中央圖書舘內附設一 ISDS 的中心來負責全國刊物登記及編號的有關事項。

四、國際圖書著錄標準 "ISBD(M)"

國際圖書著錄標準的起源，可以追溯到一九六一年圖協聯盟在巴黎召開的「國際編目原則會議」（International Conference on Cataloging Principles）。基於國際合作的精神，該會議通過了一項極為重要的「原則說明」（Statement of Principles）。希望能依此原則而達到各國編目的一致化。此原則已經譯成中文，刊載於第十四期「中國圖書館學會會報」上。[7]

由於巴黎會議能在編目原則上獲得各國同意，大會在結束前成立一個統一編目規則（Uniform Cataloging Rules）的委員會，來繼續推廣編目一致化的工作。該委員會後來蛻變爲圖協聯盟的編目委員會（IFLA Committee on Cataloging），並於一九六九年在哥本海根召開了一個「國際編目專家的會議」（International Meeting of Cataloging Experts）。參加此會議的專家們，大家均有四點同感：

1. 每一國家應設立一個國家目錄或編目的機構，以負責該國所出版圖書的編目工作。此國家目錄不僅供國內圖書舘之用，同時亦供給國外圖書舘之用。

2. 在著錄上，所有的國家應採用劃一的格式。

3. 每一國家的編目機構應設法將外國圖書的編目資料供給國內的圖書舘。

4. 有鑒於編目資料的交換終將會使用電腦，各國圖書編目應考慮採用某些統一的標點符號，使電腦能自動識別著錄的項目，以減省資料輸入的費用。

基於這些共同概念，此會議特設一國際著錄標準之工作小組，以兩年的時間擬定了國際圖書著錄標準。此標準在一九七一年公佈後，不到兩年的時間，已獲得英、德、澳洲、南非、法、保加利亞、加、美、南斯拉夫、蘇俄等國家的支持與採用。經過若干澄清與修正，此標準的「標準本」於一九七四年，正式由圖協聯盟出版。

有關此標準的大概，于鏡宇先生在第廿五期「中國圖書舘學會會報」上曾附帶提及。[8] 于先生亦建議我國圖書舘界速將此一標準的全文及因其而修改的「英美編目規則」（Anglo-American Cataloging Rules）第六章等譯成中文，以做爲訂定我編目規則的參考。國際圖書著錄標準的要點有下列三點：

1. 規定著錄所應包括的項目。

2. 規定這些項目的順序。

3. 規定區分這些項目所特用的標點符號及間隔。

茲將著錄的全部項目，順序及標點符號列示於后：

正題書名＝並題書名：別題／第一作者記載；第二或其他作者記載.—版本記載／第一版本作者記載；第二或其他版本作者記載.—第一出版地；第二或其他出版地：出版者，出版時（印刷地；第二或其他印刷地：印刷者）.—頁數或册數：插圖記載；大小和附件.—（叢書記載；次叢書記載；叢書或次叢書編號 ISSN）

註解

國際標準圖書編號　裝訂：價格

在上列例子中，有些項目在實際使用時可以省略；但有些項目亦可因需要而

59

重複一次或多次。例如有些書的並題書名不止一個。此外，國際圖書著錄標準是以書名開始，與我國現行的編目格式相似，頗合我們的採用。

五、國際刊物著錄標準 "ISBD(S)"

國際刊物著錄標準是由圖協聯盟的一個聯合工作小組所擬定。此一小組係由圖協聯盟屬下的編目委員會及刊物委員會在一九七一年共同設立。舉凡此一標準的目的，內容，與要點等皆與國際圖書著錄標準力求相似。此標準草案在一九七二年六月經擬定後卽印發世界各國有關人士供批評及建議。根據各方的反應及多次的修正，此標準在一九七三年底經聯合小組通過，建議各國採用。

有關國際刊物著錄標準的全部項目，順序及標點符號，請參看下列示例：

特殊標題＝並行標題：副標題／作者記載．—第一出版地；第二或其他出版地：出版者，出版日期及編號（印刷地；第二或其他印刷地：印刷者）．—插圖記載；大小和附件．—（叢書記載；叢書編號：次叢書記載：次叢書編號）

註解

國際標準刊物編號：價格

其中應注意的是特殊標題的選取，所謂特殊標題乃指刊物的主要標題，於登錄時須特別留意。採用國際刊物著錄標準最好能由國立中央圖書館率先領導，並將此工作與我國的 ISDS 中心的工作合併在一起，以避免重複。

六、結　論

以上四種國際標準，雖然都是在最近才公佈，但已普遍為世界各國所接受及採用；對促進國際合作及知識流通發生極大的影響。以目前的趨勢，圖書刊物著錄編號的統一化，是勢在必行。由於電腦的應用，國與國間目錄的交換與編目合作等會更趨密切。為了配合這種趨勢，對於已公佈的國際標準，我國的圖書館界及出版界應及早採取步驟，付諸實施。

參 考 資 料:

1. *International standard book numbering in Australia* / Australian Standard Book Numbering Agency. -3d ed. -Canberra: National Library of Australia, 1973. -10p. -ISBN 0-642-99004-2. Paperback: gratis.

2. *Guidelines for ISDS: UNISIST International serials data system (ISDS)* / International Centre for the Registration of Serial Publications-Paris: Unesco, 1973. -58p. -(SC/WS/538) Paperback: gratis.

3. *ISBD(M)-International standard bibliographic description for monographic publications* / International Federation of Library Associations. - 1st standard ed. - London: IFLA Committee on Cataloging, 1974. -X, 36p -ISBN 0-903043-02-5 Paperback: £2.00.

4. *ISBD(S) -International standard bibliographic description for serials* / Recommended by the Joint Working Group on the International Standard Bibliographic Description for Serials, set up by the IFLA Committee on Cataloging and the IFLA Committee on Serial Publications-London: IFLA Committee on Cataloging, 1974, — X, 36p. — ISBN 0-903043-03-3 Paperback: £2.00.

5. *Study report on the feasibility of a world science information system* / by the United Nation Educational, Scientific and Cultural Organization and the International Council of Scientific Unions-Paris: Unesco, 1971. -XII, 161p. -(Unesco/ UNISIST/4) Paperback: gratis.

6. *Report on the feasibility of an international serials data system* / M. D. Martin & C. I. Barnes; prepared for UNISIST/ICSU-AB Working Group on Bibliographic Description-London: INSPEC, 1970. (DM/CB/284) Paperback.

7. "國際圖書編目原則會議。" 中國圖書館學會會報，第14期。民51年12月。p. 51—54, 40。

8. 于鏡宇，"分類編目之改進計劃。" 中國圖書館學會會報，第25期。民62年12 月。p. 8—9,16。

COOPERATIVE REGIONAL BIBLIOGRAPHIC PROJECTS IN SOUTH-EAST ASIA

Introduction

Regional cooperation on joint bibliographic projects has been a recent development in South-East Asia. Despite the seemingly late start, nearly all such projects are carefully planned and have received enthusiastic support from the participating countries. This trend toward regional cooperation stems from the recognition of its importance by library leaders in South-East Asian countries and is fostered by encouragement and financial assistance provided by foundations and several regional and international organizations.

This article intends to trace the development of seven cooperative regional bibliographic projects now in existence in South-East Asia. A detailed description of the current status and major activities of these projects is given, based on the latest information available.

The term 'South-East Asia' is here meant to include that part of the Asian continent lying south of China and east of India, together with the Indonesian and Philippine archipelagos. Owing to political and military conflicts, many projects discussed in this paper are largely confined to the five ASEAN countries, namely Thailand, Malaysia, Singapore, the Philippines, and Indonesia.

Of the joint bibliographic projects to be discussed in this article, some are strictly South-East Asian, others are projects initiated in South-East Asia but covering the whole of Asia. Those strictly for South-East Asia are: (a) the Regional Microfilm Clearing-house; (b) the compilation of a master-list of South-East Asian microforms; (c) the ISDS Regional Centre for Southeast Asia.

Those covering the whole of Asia are: (a) the Asian Mass Communication Research and Information Centre (AMIC); (b) the Asian Information Centre for Geotechnical Engineering; (c) the Agricultural Information Bank for Asia;[1] (d) the Clearing-house for Social Development in Asia.

---

[1]Because the Agriculatural Information Bank for Asia (AIBA) was discussed in another article in the issue in which this was published [see Remedios V. Viloria, "The Agriculatural Information Bank for Asia: Its Development and Activities," *Unesco Bulletin for Libraries*, Vol. 31, No. 6 (Nov.-Dec. 1977), pp. 331-339], the portion of the orginal manuscript relating to AIBA was omitted from the published article.

The Regional Microfilm Clearing-house[2]

The increasing activities in microfilming historical records, archival materials and other publications of importance to South-East Asia as a means of preserving national heritages and facilitating research prompted the establishment of the Regional Microfilm Clearing-house at the Institute of South-East Asian Studies (ISEAS), Singapore, in 1972.

Campaigning most actively for the establishment of the clearing-house, among others, was Mrs. P. Lim Pui Huen, Librarian of ISEAS, who presented a paper on Regional Cooperation in Microfilming Activities at the first General Conference of the South-East Asian Branch, International Council on Archives (SARBICA) held in Manila from 24 to 28 May 1971.[3] Based on her paper and the general awareness of the need, the resolution, '...that a joint SARBICA-CONSAL clearing-house of information pertaining to microform matters be established...', along with a set of guidelines for its implementation, was adopted by the SARBICA conference.

As a result of the resolution, Mrs. Lim was appointed Regional Microfilm Coordinator, and the library of ISEAS was asked to act as the clearing-house responsible for the gathering, publication and dissemination of relevant information on all matters relating to the planning, co-ordination, production, distribution, bibliographic control and use of South-East Asian microforms. In doing so, the clearing-house should 'serve as liaison between interested parties within and without the region and promote efforts for cooperative programs and the sharing of experience and expertise'.[4]

Since its inception, the clearing-house has undertaken the following important work:

1.   The compilation of the *Directory of Microfilm Facilities in Southeast Asia*. As the first order of business, the clearing-house conducted a survey of the existing microfilming facilities in South-East Asia. The results of the survey were published in 1972 as ISEAS's *Library Bulletin*, No. 3. A second edition with much updating was published in 1973 as ISEAS's *Library Bulletin*, No. 7. The

---

[2]The latest account of the clearing-house is in the paper written by Tan Sok Joo, "Regional Microfilm Clearing-house, 1972-75: a report to SARBICA and CONSAL," *Proceedings of the Third Conference of Southeast Asian Librarians, held in Jakarta from 1 to 5 December 1975*, (Jakarta: Pusat Dokumentasi Ilmiah Nasional for Ikatan Pustakawan Indonesia, 1977), pp. 34-51.

[3]The paper was later published in the *Southeast Asia Microfilms Newsletter*, No. 1, December 1972.

[4]Tan Sok Joo, *op. cit.*, p. 1.

directory lists the equipment of each institution, its microfilming programs, and guides to its collection.

2. The publication of the *Southeast Asia Microfilms Newsletter*. Under the editorship of Mrs. Lim six issues of the newsletter were published between 1972 and 1974. Since June 1975, the newsletter is managed by an editorial board, comprising Mrs. Lim and three other members. Under the new arrangement, the newsletter is published twice a year by ISEAS for SARBICA and CONSAL, and printed and distributed by the SARBICA secretariat in Kuala Lumpur.

Thus far the newsletter has disseminated information on serial and other titles filmed or acquired, sets collated for filming, purchases and evaluations of new equipment, microfilm consortia formed, regional cooperative projects, publications available about micrographics and microform applications, etc.

3. Searching out holdings of important or rare research materials for filming. The latest and most significant example of this is the attempt to microfilm national official gazettes of South-East Asian countries. This project is a cooperative effort undertaken at the request of the Library of Congress and the New York Public Library in making national official gazettes of the world available in microform.

As a first step in this attempt, the clearing-house began compiling a checklist of all national and state or other local gazettes, if any, of the region. A preliminary checklist was issued in December 1975 which contains holding information, both hard copies and microforms, of 84 gazettes published in Brunei, Burma, Democratic Kampuchea, Indonesia, Lao People's Republic, Malaysia, Papua New Guinea, the Philippines, Singapore, Thailand, Timor and the socialist Republic of Viet Nam.

The Master-list of South-East Asian Microforms[5]

Although, to some extent, this regional project is closely related to the Regional Microfilm Clearing-house project, it is a separate project which reports to SARBICA and CONSAL. Since SARBICA has a permanent secretariat and was the one that

---

[5]The recent development of this project is described in the report by Winarti Partaningrat, "Progress Report on a Joint SARBICA-CONSAL Project: the Compilation of a (Regional) Masterlist of Southeast Asian Microforms," *Proceedings of the Third Conference of Southeast Asian Librarians, held in Jakarta from 1 to 5 December 1975,* (Jakarta: Pusat Dokumentasi Ilmiah Nasional for Ikatan Pustakawan Indonesia, 1977), pp. 52-66.

negotiated with the International Development Research Centre (IDRC)[6] Canada for the funding of the master-list project, it is therefore responsible for the administration of the project.

The idea of compiling a regional master-list of microforms was first proposed by SARBICA in 1972. At almost the same time, a similar recommendation was made by the Permanent Committee on Socio-cultural Activities of the Association of South-East Asian Nations (ASEAN) calling for the compilation of a catalogue of microfilmed materials to facilitate the exchange of such materials among ASEAN countries. In 1973, the proposal of SARBICA was endorsed by CONSAL at its second conference.

With the cooperation of CONSAL, a proposal for financial support of the project was drafted in 1974 by Mrs. Hedwig Anuar, the SARBICA chairperson, and was submitted to IDRC for funding.[7] In 1975, a grant was awarded by IDRC which enabled the project to commence in May 1975. Miss Winarti Partaningrat, the former director of the Indonesian National Scientific Documentation Center, was appointed Editor, while Mrs. Lim of ISEAS serves as the Project Director. The main objective of the master-list project is to 'collect information regarding South-East Asian documents and publication already reproduced on microform in the region...'.[8]

It is planned that within the two-year funding period, a 3-in. by 5-in. index card file containing complete bibliographic information on all South-East Asian microforms will be set up in the Project Office. This file will then be published. After this, the National Library of Singapore will assume responsibility for continuing the project so that supplementary volumes of the master-list can be brought out at regular intervals.

---

[6]IDRC is a public corporation created by an Act of the Canadian Parliament in 1970. Although most of its funds come from Parliament it is an autonomous body with a twenty-one member Board of Governors drawn from several countries. The aim of IDRC is 'to help developing regions build up their own research capabilities and the innovative skills needed to solve their problems'. Information sciences is one of the five programme divisions of IDRC and it has had a significant impact on the development of information systems for the benefit of developing countries.

[7]Hedwig Anuar, *Proposal for the Compilation and Publication of a Masterlist of Southeast Asian Microforms*, Singapore: SARBICA, 1974, 4 p.

[8]*Guidelines for the Compilation of a Masterlist of Southeast Asian Microforms*, Singapore: The Project Office, 1975, 4 p.

The ISDS Regional Centre for South-East Asia[9]

The latest regional bibliographic project, which was initiated in 1973 by Thailand and has had strong support from Unesco and other South-East Asian countries, was formally established in March 1976 in Bangkok.

ISDS (International Serials Data System) is an important component of Unesco's UNISIST program.[10] The major aims of ISDS are 'to provide a reliable registry of world serial publications covering the full range of recorded knowledge' and to assign 'to each serial published under a given title, a unique and unambiguous numeric code identifier, the International Standard Serial Number (ISSN)'.[11]

In order to attain these aims and to carry out its intended activities, a two-tier organizational structure consisting of an international centre and a network of national and regional centres has been adopted. Through an agreement between Unesco and the French Government, the International Centre for the Registration of Serial Publications was established in Paris in 1973. Since then, pursuant to resolution 2.141(c) adopted by the sixteenth session of the Unesco General Conference, a number of national centres and one regional centre have been established, mostly in developed countries.[12]

Many countries in South-East Asia felt that for reasons of economy, manpower, technology and regional cooperation, a regional centre instead of separately founded national centres would be more desirable and advantageous. Because of this, at the request of Mrs. Maenmas Chavalit, Director of the National Library of Thailand, a consultant was provided in November 1975 by Unesco to undertake a one-month

---

[9]Information concerning the background of the regional centre is contained in the Unesco mission report and recommendations prepared by Hwa-Wei Lee, *The Possibility of Establishing a Regional Centre for the International Serials Data System in Thailand*, Paris: Unesco, 1975, 42 p.(SC-76/WS/7.)

[10]UNISIST is a Unesco programme concerned with international co-operation in the field of information, particularly with a view to promoting systems interconnection and facilitating access to the world information resources.

[11]*ISDS Bulletin*, Vol. 1, No. 1 (1974).

[12]Thus far, fifteen countries have announced the establishment of their national centres: United States, United Kingdom, Australia, Canada, Federal Republic of Germany, France, Argentina, Japan, Finland, Yugoslavia, Nigeria, Tunisia, Netherlands, Sweden and Brazil. Not all of these national centres are operational. The first regional centre was established in Moscow; it consists of the U.S.S.R., Bulgaria, Czechoslovakia, the German Democratic Republic, Hungary, Mongolia, Poland and Cuba.

exploratory mission in South-East Asia to examine the feasibility of establishing such a regional centre. After meeting with library officials in Thailand, Malaysia, Singapore, Indonesia and the Philippines, a positive recommendation was made and, based on the recommendation, a special fund was provided by Unesco to convene an organizing meeting[13] in Bangkok in March 1976. The organizing meeting was attended by representatives from the five above-mentioned countries and by M. Rosenbaum, Director of the international centre.

To participate in the ISDS regional centre, each member country has designated a national centre which is responsible for reporting all serials published in the country in accordance with the Guidelines for ISDS.[14] Upon receiving such reports on standard forms the ISDS Regional Centre for Southeast Asia, which was established in Bangkok under the auspices of the National Library of Thailand, will assume the following responsibilities:

1. Check for the completeness of the bibliographic information required.
2. Assign an ISSN for each serial publication reported.
3. Help national centres to promote the use of ISSN in their countries.
4. Create and maintain a computerized regional serials data bank.
5. Report newly registered serials to the international centre.
6. Publish a regional list of serial publications and separate national lists of new serial titles.
7. Answer inquiries concerning serial publications.
8. Provide training opportunities to serials librarians and documentalists in the region.

The cost for operating the regional centre is to be shared by the cooperating countries, but, for an initial period of five years, financial support from outside sources is also needed. A request for such support has been submitted to IDRC for consideration.

Asian Mass Communication Research and Information Centre(AMIC)[15]

To serve as a regional clearing-house for mass communication in Asia, AMIC was established in 1971 in Singapore under the joint sponsorship of the Friedrich Ebert

---

[13]The final report is available from the National Library of Thailand.

[14]International Centre for the Registration of Serial Publications, *Guidelines for ISDS*, Paris: Unesco, 1973, SC/WS/538).

[15]Lena U Wen Lim, "Asian Mass Communication Research and Information Centre," *Information*, December 1974, p.318-19.

Stiftung, a German foundation,[16] and the Singapore Government. In addition to its clearing-house functions, AMIC also aims at the promotion of teaching, training, and research in mass communication in Asia. At the international level, AMIC is one of six regional mass communication centres whose work is encouraged and co-ordinated by Unesco.

The activities of AMIC may be grouped under three broad headings: research and training program, publication program and documentation program. It is the documentation program that is the focus of this article.

To facilitate the dissemination of information on mass communication in Asia, five major bibliographic projects have been undertaken by AMIC. Each of these is described briefly below:

AMIC Documentation List. This annotated list comprised of selected recent acquisitions by AMIC is published as a regular feature in AMIC's quarterly journal, *Media Asia* (No. 1, 1972). In its columns 'Cues' and 'Findings', *Media Asia* also carries popularized 'rewrites' of important research reports and findings of interest to its readers.

AMIC Communication Bibliographies Series. This annotated subject bibliography series is issued from time to time in support of other activities organized by AMIC. The first one, issued in 1973, was on broadcasting in Asia.

Asian Mass Communication Bibliography. The activities leading to the publication of various country sections of this bibliography are a cooperative project, sponsored, co-ordinated and initiated by AMIC in 1973. This project, which involves the compilation of separate country bibliographies, each by a national team, to be published separately but under a unified title, includes Hong Kong, India, Indonesia, Republic of Korea, Malaysia, Nepal, Pakistan, the Philippines, Singapore and Sri Lanka.

List of Theses, 1971. Studies in Mass Communication in Asia. These annual lists are to include bibliographic information on all theses dealing with various aspects of mass communication in Asia completed either in Asian universities or elsewhere in the world.

---

[16]The Friedrich Ebert Stiftung (FES) is an independent German foundation established in 1925 as the cultural legacy of Friedrich Ebert (1871-1925), the first President of the Weimar Republic. FES receives grants from both governmental sources and private donations. In the sphere of international co-operation, FES devotes itself to adult education, assistance to trade union training and co-operatives, aiding improvements in social structure, and use of mass media in education and training.

In addition to its bibliographic publications, AMIC provides a document delivery service whereby it supplies upon request photocopies, microfilms, microfiches or translations of any material in its collections.

Asian Information Center for Geotechnical Engineering (AGE)[17]

The Asian Information Center for Geotechnical Engineering (Asian Geotechnical Engineering for short, abbreviated AGE) was founded in January 1973 at the Asian Institute of Technology in Bangkok under the joint sponsorship of the institute's Division of Geotechnical Engineering and the Library and Information Center.

The idea of establishing AGE was conceived at a meeting held in Bangkok in July 1971 of the representatives of the national societies of soil mechanics and foundation engineering in Asia. Arising from a generally felt need for a relevant, timely and responsive information service on geotechnical engineering especially tailored to the needs of Asian engineers, the meeting passed a resolution requesting the Asian Institute of Technology to establish and operate AGE for the purpose of selecting, acquiring, analyzing, storing, retrieving, publicizing and disseminating useful information on Asian geotechnical engineering for the benefit of all those who are concerned. Recognizing the significance of geotechnical engineering work in relation to social and economic development in Asia as well as the importance of providing an information service on a regional basis to serve the needs of geotechnical engineers and specialists, a grant was made by the International Development Research Centre to support the operation of AGE for a three-year period.

Some major activities of AGE are as follows:

1.   To seek, select, and acquire both published and unpublished literature on geotechnical engineering which is relevant to Asia, with particular emphasis on literature published in Asia, preferably in English, but materials of importance in other languages are also included.

2.   To establish both a card-index file and a machine-readable database for the relevant literature completely indexed and abstracted for easy retrieval. Both the International Geotechnical Classification System (IGC) and the Soil Mechanics Thesaurus are used.

---

[17]This part of the article is based on an earlier paper by the present author, "The Experience of a Specialized Information Service in Asia--AGE," presented at the Round-table Conference on Documentation Problems in Developing Countries held in Khartoum, Sudan, on 10-11 April 1975. The conference was organized by FID/DC and the FID National Member in Sudan.

3.   To prepare periodic directories of geotechnical engineers, specialists and organizations in Asia as well as reports in their ongoing projects.

4.   To disseminate information on available literature and survey results through the following publications:

> *AGE Current Awareness Service*--a quarterly publication informing readers of recent geotechnical engineering publications and contents of selected geotechnical engineering journals received at AGE.

> *Asian Geotechnical Engineering Abstracts*--a quarterly publication consisting of abstracts of available publications and reports in geotechnical engineering in or about Asia.

> *AGE Conference Proceedings List*--an annual list of conference proceedings on various subjects of geotechnical engineering in AGE's collection.

> *AGE Journal Holdings List*--an annually revised list of geotechnical engineering journals held at AGE.

> *Asian Geotechnical Engineering in Progress*--an annual publication which will provide information on current design, construction and research projects in geotechnical engineering being undertaken in Asia.

5.   To provide the three 'R' services (Reference, Reprography, and Referral) to members and other users. It is planned that at some future date, the centre will also publish state-of-the-art reviews and bibliographies on subjects of interest to geotechnical engineers.

6.   To cooperate with ot⁷ information and documentation services on, or related to, geotechnical engineering both in and outside Asia to enhance information resources and service on geotechnical engineering on a global basis through reciprocal arrangement and systems interconnection.

The operation of AGE has been guided by two committees: the Policy Advisory Committee and the Technical Committee. An effective link between AGE and its users has been established through appointed liaison officers in many of the Asian countries.

In order to find the pattern of information usage by geotechnical engineers in Asia, a questionnaire survey was conducted among AGE users in March 1974. Findings concerning the general characteristics of AGE users, their information channels, the library facilities available to them, the types of technical information they often require, their appraisals of the AGE publications and services were reported in the paper "User and Use Analysis: A Case Study of the Information Utility by Geotechnical Engineers in Asian Countries."[18]

To evaluate the role of AGE now and in the future, a Workshop on Geotechnical Information Systems was held at AGE from 5 to 9 April 1976. The workshop was co-sponsored by IDRC and AGE and had forty-two participants including members of the Policy Advisory Committee and the Technical Committee, liaison officers and representatives of other geotechnical information services from Australia, France, Federal Republic of Germany, Norway, Sweden, and the United States.

Clearing-house for Social Development in Asia[19]

The recent establishment of the Clearing-house for Social Development in Asia which is located in Bangkok is due largely to the Friedrich Ebert Stiftung in cooperation with the National Research Council of Thailand.

Recognizing the need for relevant information on social development in Asia by planners, policy-makers, government officials, researchers and others who are interested in the social development in various countries or regions of Asia, a feasibility study for the establishment of a regional clearing-house for such information was conducted in 1972-73 by Erwin Kristofferson, then the regional representative for Asia of FES. During the course of this study, it was found that the idea of establishing a Clearing-house for Social Development in Asia was highly favoured by many Asian countries.

Subsequent to the study, Preparatory Meeting of Experts was held in Bangkok in April 1973 and an information specialist, Dr Gottfried Voelker, was sent by FES to take charge of the preparatory work. Through his efforts, an organizing meeting was held in Bangkok in February 1975 which resulted in the formation of an interim Governing Council and a Standing and Advisory Council. Since then the following activities have been undertaken by the clearing-house either through its own staff or local consultants contracted by the clearing-house:

1.   A regional survey on the demand for and supply of information in Asia has been carried out in Singapore, the Philippines, Thailand, Malaysia and

---

[18]This paper by the author was presented at the thirty-seventh Annual Meeting of the American Society for Information Science, Atlanta, Georgia, 13-17 October 1974, and was published in *Information Utilities: Proceedings of the 37th Annual Conference of the American Society for Information Science*, p. 133-6, Washington, D.C.: ASIS, 1974.

[19]Clearing-house for Social Development, *Annual Report, February 15, 1975-April 30, 1975*, Bangkok, 1976, 8 p.

Indonesia. Findings of the survey have been published in the *Clearing House Journal*.

2. A regional bibliographical study on social development data in the five ASEAN countries has also been conducted. All relevant materials which are available in these countries were collected, abstracted and indexed using the OECD Macrothesaurus. Results of the study have also been published in the *Clearing House Journal*.

3. The clearing-house is working on a number of selected topics which are important to the region: 'Women Participating in Family Income,' 'Formal Associations and Development,' and 'Migration and the Impact on Social and Economic Development.'

4. The preparation of a regional card catalogue on social development, comprising both published and unpublished materials, is in progress. All materials, including reports of ongoing research, are classified according to the OECD Macrothesaurus system and given four entries: author, title, subject and country. Relevant summaries are entered back of each card.

5. The *Clearing House Journal* reports on the findings of both the regional survey and the bibliographic study, along with any other relevant information. There are two issues to each volume. Each issue is devoted to a special country or topic; for example, Vol. II, No. 1 (February 1976) was devoted to 'Social Development in the Philippines'.

In addition to the above activities, the clearing-house also plans to conduct seminars and to publish occasional papers on subjects of significance to social development. Translation of selected literature from Asian languages into English is also contemplated.

According to the planning documents, the clearing-house will eventually become an independent, self-supporting regional institution. For the initial five years, it will be completely funded by FES. After that, the support from FES will be phased out gradually and the cost of operating the clearing-house will be shared by member countries.

Conclusions

This article has described in some detail six of the seven ongoing regional bibliographic projects in South-East Asia: three strictly South-East Asian in scope and coverage and four others covering some other Asian countries as well.

It is of interest to note that six out of the seven projects have been funded by two foundations: (a) the International Development Research Centre funds the master-list of South-East Asian microforms, the Asian Information Center for Geotechnical Engineering, the Agricultural Information Bank for Asia, and partly the ISDS Regional Centre for Southeast Asia; (b) the Friedrich Ebert Stiftung funds the Asian Mass Communication Research and Information Centre and the Clearing-house for Social Development in Asia.

The generous financial support provided by IDRC and FES has made it possible to develop cooperative regional bibliographic projects in South-East Asia. This support has encouraged countries to work together in joint bibliographic projects.

Two regional professional organizations--CONSAL and SARBICA--although they have met infrequently in the past, have, nevertheless, provided a forum for librarians, documentalists and archivists in South-East Asia to discuss problems of mutual concern and to work out cooperative projects.

Unesco's UNISIST program--with its emphasis on the needs of developing countries--has been instrumental in the establishment of the ISDS Regional Centre for Southeast Asia. The Organization, through both its UNISIST and NATIS programs, has also greatly assisted countries in South-East Asia in the setting up or strengthening of their national library and information infrastructures, as well as in the training of librarians, documentalists and archivists, and in the promotion of closer regional cooperation.

Recent developments in several of the international information systems such as the International Nuclear Information System (INIS), the International Information System for the Agricultural Sciences and Technology (AGRIS), and the Development Sciences Information System (DEVSIS) have encouraged many of the count⁻ ⁻ in South-East Asia to participate in these international information systems by pro, ⁻g bibliographic information relating to their countries, in standard format, to tne⁻ international databases. Such participation is very important both in terms of helping the countries in South-East Asia to improve their bibliographic apparatus and in making their bibliographic information more readily available world-wide. It is only through cooperation in bibliographic projects that there can be true sharing of information among all nations.

Section III

International Cooperation

An Approach to Regional Cooperation in Scientific
and Technical Information Services for Southeast
Asia (1972) 77

Regional Cooperation for ISDS (1977) 91

Educating for International Interdependence: The Role
of the Academic Library -- Ohio University and
Malaysia (1985); Co-author: K. Mulliner 101

AN APPROACH TO REGIONAL COOPERATION IN SCIENTIFIC AND TECHNICAL INFORMATION SERVICES FOR SOUTHEAST ASIA[1]

Introduction

The developing countries in Southeast Asia, especially Malaysia, Singapore, Indonesia, the Philippines, and Thailand, are in a stage of rapid economic, socio-political, and industrial development. In order to expedite the development process, seeking to close the technological gap between the "developing" countries and the "developed" countries instead of widening it, as it has been the case in the past, an expanded, more responsive scientific and technical information service is urgently needed.

The relationship between "development" and "information" can be seen as mutually dependent. This is especially so in the development of science and technology. There is a positive correlation existing between the degree of industrial and technological development and the level of information requirement. The higher the degree of development, the greater the need for information services, and vice versa. It is also predictable that more development in science and technology will generate more need for information and more readily available information will stimulate and accelerate further scientific and technical development.

Aware of the full impact of scientific and technical information in national development, in recent years, many countries in Southeast Asia have taken effective measures toward setting up national documentation centers or strengthening their national libraries for the purpose of improving the scientific and technical information services in their respective countries. These attempts were made either under the assistance and encouragement of Unesco or under their own initiative. It seems to be the time to promote the idea of regional cooperation as a necessary step for the developing countries in Southeast Asia to join forces for better information services throughout the entire region. Effective regional cooperation will serve to complement the national efforts and plans rather than to be a substitute for them. The cross fertilization of this parallel approach both at the national level and at the regional and international level will be mutually beneficial.

---

[1]This article is based on a paper delivered by the author at the Conference on Scientific and Technical Information Needs for Malaysia and Singapore held in Kuala Lumpur on 24-26 September, 1971 under the joint sponsorship of the Library Associations of Malaysia and Singapore.

The Necessity for Regional Cooperation

The needs for regional and international cooperation in meeting the scientific and technical information requirement is no longer a questionable supposition. Many international organizations, both inter-governmental and non-governmental, have been in fact eagerly pursuing and promoting this objective. Among them are Unesco, the International Council of Scientific Unions (ICSU), the International Federation for Documentation (FID), the International Standards Organization (ISO), and the International Federation for Information Processing (IFIP), to name just a few.[2]

Recently, there have been a few regional organizations taking concrete moves toward regional cooperation in scientific and technical information policies and cooperative activities. The most notable and successful one is NORDFORSK (the Scandinavian Council for Applied Research) founded jointly by the four Scandinavian countries: Denmark, Finland, Norway and Sweden, and also Iceland. Since 1952, NORDFORSK has had a special committee on technical information, Scandinavian Committee for Technical Information Services (NORDinfo), which has tried to act as a policy-formulating body in the technological information field, and it has initiated several cooperative projects.[3]

The Organization for Economic Co-operation and Development (OECD) has also set up an office within its Science Directorate to help in developing and coordinating the science information policies among its member-countries. In 1969, the eight member-countries of the Council for Mutual Economic Assistance (CMEA) also established an International Centre of Scientific and Technical Information in Moscow for the purpose of coordinating the science information policies of member countries.[4]

Several factors and recent developments have provided a favorable environment for regional cooperations. They are: 1) The universality of scientific and technical knowledge and the desire for information transfer across national boundaries; 2) the

---

[2]F. A. Sviridov, "International Trends in Documentation and Information Services", *Library Trends*, V. 17 No.3 (January 1969), pp. 326-338.

[3]Bjorn V. Tell, "Scandinavian Developments in Documentation and Information Services", *Library Trends*, V. 17 No. 3 (January 1969), pp. 289-298.

[4]United Nations Educational, Scientific and Cultural Organization/International Council of Scientific Unions, *UNISIST: Synopsis of the Feasibility Study on a World Science Information System* (Paris: Unesco, 1971), p. 26. The eight countries are Bulgaria, Czechoslovakia, German Democratic Republic, Hungary, Mongolia, Poland, Rumania and USSR.

recent technological advancement in computer technology, reprography, and telecommunications; and 3) the development of "UNISIST".

1.   The Universality of Knowledge and the Desire for Information Transfer.

It has been said that knowledge has no national boundary. Knowledge is built on knowledge.[5] Therefore it is an international asset and resource. This is very true in science and technology. Scientific and technical knowledge flourishes only when it is freely exchanged and readily available among the researchers and technologists in the world. The transfer of scientific and technological information from developed countries to the developing countries is of particular importance and is viewed as one of the prerequisites by which a developing nation can narrow the gap between the "have" and the "have-not" nations of the world.

2.   The Advancement of Communication Technologies and Information Transfer.

Information transfer is as old as civilization. Several major innovations in the past have accelerated the pace of such transfer. The creation of written languages, the invention of paper and printing, the growth of presses and publications, the development of modern transportation and communication systems, etc. have all contributed to the transfer of information and have accelerated the growth of the world's knowledge. The most recent and significant developments which serve to revolutionize information handling and service are 1) the development of computer technology and its potential application in information processing, 2) the improvement in the reprographic techniques, and 3) the advancement in telecommunications. These new technological developments have both directly and indirectly affected the process of information collecting, analyzing, indexing, handling, retrieving and disseminating. They have brought about drastic change both in the concept and in the practice of library and information services.

The computers, which have the power and versatility to process data with high speed and precision, are increasingly being used in libraries and information centers as an effective means to cope with the proliferation of today's information. Although the computers are without doubt a powerful tool which can be employed by the librarians, documentalists, and information specialists to cope with the problem of the "information explosion", it is expensive in terms of hardware acquisitions and software developments. For the developing countries in Southeast Asia, an elaborate information system operated by computers with an extensive storage of bibliographical data prepared both externally and internally can only be achieved by a joint force of as many countries in the region as possible.

---

[5]Ibid., pp. v-vi.

The improvement in reprographic techniques such as microfilming and various methods of copying and duplicating have enabled the wide dissemination of information some of which may not be available or accessible otherwise. It has made it possible for the libraries and information centers in many countries to interchange reproduced information on request.

The spectacular advancement in telecommunications, particularly satellite communications, is another reason for regional and international cooperation. The satellite communications can overcome the geographical barriers which formerly prohibited the free flow of information. The capability of communication satellites to transmit voice, teletype and facsimile signals to a distant place without recourse to telephone lines has a distinct advantage over other communication media. A combination of telephone, teletype, radio, and satellite communications can provide an effective network of national, regional, and world information systems which will greatly facilitate interlibrary communications and cooperation and bridge the distance gap.

3.   The Development of UNISIST.[6]

Another important recent development having significant meaning for regional and international cooperation is the joint feasibility study on a world science information system undertaken by Unesco and ICSU. The report of the study which has just been published reaffirms the belief that a world-wide information system is both desirable and feasible. The broad principles embodied in the study are quoted below:[7]

--   the unimpeded exchange of published or publishable scientific information and data among scientists of all countries;

--   hospitality to the diversity of disciplines and fields of science and technology as well as to the diversity of languages used for the international exchange of scientific information;

--   promotion of the interchange of published or publishable information and data among the systems, whether manual or machine, which process and provide information for the use of scientists;

---

[6]UNISIST is an acronym which stands for the feasibility study and for the recommended future program to implement its recommendations. Ibid., p. v.

[7]Ibid., pp. vi-vii.

-- the cooperative development and maintenance of technical standards in order to facilitate the interchange of scientific information and data among systems;

-- promotion of compatibility between and among information processing systems developed in different countries and in different areas of the sciences;

-- promotion of cooperative agreements between and among systems in different countries and in different areas of the sciences for the purpose of sharing workloads and of providing needed services and products;

-- assistance to countries, both developing and developed, wishing access to contemporary and future information services in the sciences;

-- the development of human and information resources in all countries as necessary foundations for the utilization of machine systems;

-- the increased participation of scientists in the development and use of information systems, with particular attention to the involvement of scientists in the evaluation, compaction, and synthesis of scientific information and data;

-- the involvement of the coming generation of scientists in the planning of scientific information systems of the future;

-- the reduction of administrative and legal barriers to the flow of scientific information between and among countries.

While the UNISIST feasibility study was in progress, a conference focusing on the application of science and technology to the development of Asia convened in New Delhi in August 1968. The conference considered the development of information and documentation facilities and the organization and promotion of international and regional cooperation as two of the priority areas where action is needed. Among other recommendations, the conference recommended to participating governments for priority action in Asia "the development of information and documentation facilities through strengthening existing centres; establishing new centres and links between national centres; rationalizing existing systems and making maximum use of modern techniques of reproduction, abstracting and data processing; considering the establishment of one or more regional information clearing-houses."[8]

---

[8]Conference on the Application of Science and Technology to the Development of Asia, New Delhi. August 1968, *Science and Technology in Asian Development* (Paris: Unesco, 1970), p. 215

Besides the foregoing factors and developments which have provided the necessary impetus for regional and international cooperation, there are also many specific reasons calling for effective and immediate regional cooperation in Southeast Asia. The two most important reasons are:

First, the countries in Southeast Asia generally suffer from a scarcity of library and information resources and services, inadequate funds necessary for their support, and a shortage of trained librarians, documentalists, and information specialists. In order that the limited resources may be best utilized to meet the developing needs, a pooling of the available resources in the region through voluntary cooperation and a carefully worked out system of coordination is needed.

Second, the close approximation of social and economic conditions prevailing in the countries of Southeast Asia and the intimate relationship and geographical distance among them provide.a favorable environment for regional cooperation. It is now time to undertake some concrete actions.

Possibilities and Important Considerations in Regional Cooperation

There are a score of possibilities for cooperation on a regional basis all of which are fundamental in the realization of a region-wide information system and, when implemented, would yield good results.

1. Establishment of subject oriented or discipline oriented bibliographical data centers in a few selected libraries and documentation centers or in a single location where both strong library facilities and computer capability exist. Externally generated databases in machine-readable form are to be acquired and the subject coverage of each database should as far as possible not be overlapped or duplicated. These centers should be considered as regional information centers in the particular subjects or disciplines in which each of them specializes.

2. Establishment of communication linkage between the bibliographical data centers and other national libraries, documentation centers, and selected academic and research libraries in the region. Satellite communications should be employed as soon as possible to provide an effective linkage not just among the national centers in each of the participating countries within the region but also with other major libraries and documentation centers in countries outside the region. Other media of communication such as telephone, teletype, and facsimile transmission should be developed to interconnect each of the national centers with the libraries and documentation centers in their respective countries.

3. Each of the bibliographical data centers should also maintain a region-wide union list of serials, reference works, etc. in the subject or discipline in which each of them specializes. The frequently updated computer printout of such lists should be deposited in other bibliographical centers, national libraries, and documentation centers.

4. Each of the bibliographical data centers should also collect, analyze, index, abstract, and store the scientific and technical publications and reports, both published and unpublished, by the participating countries in the region. Agreement may be worked out so that at least one copy of such publications and reports can be deposited in the bibliographical center which specializes on the subject or the discipline.

5. Each of the bibliographical data centers should serve as a clearinghouse for announcement, reproduction, and dissemination of the scientific and technical publications and reports collected or deposited in the center.

6. Each of the bibliographical data centers should maintain effective contact and close cooperation with other national, regional, and international centers throughout the world.

7. A regional coordinating council for scientific and technical information needs to be established to plan and coordinate regional cooperation and other activities. The council should seek to identify the needs, and establish priorities and guidelines in regional cooperative programs and activities. The functions of the council should also include the following:

    a) To encourage the publication of national bibliographies, union list of serials, union catalogs, etc.;

    b) to formulate policies which will facilitate exchange of publications, interlibrary loans, photoduplications, and reference and referral services among participating countries;

    c) to hold regional conferences for the communication and exchange of ideas among the librarians, documentalists, and information specialists;

    d) to conduct short courses and in-service training programs at the advanced level for training or upgrading the professional staff in library and information services;

    e) to establish standards and uniform formats for bibliographic records and other library and information services;

    f) to provide consultation services to national libraries, documentation centers and other libraries in the development of scientific and technical information resources and services. There is a special need for consultation service in the planning and design of computerized library and information systems; and

g)   to consider the financial matters of joint activities.

The possibilities elaborated above are all basic and necessary for the region. The establishment of a region-wide subject or discipline oriented bibliographical data center or centers is not impractical if each of them evolves from an existing center or library within the region. The utilizing or reprocessing of bibliographical tapes produced by the existing abstracting and indexing services in the developed countries is an economic necessity for the developing countries. For example, at present no one country in Southeast Asia can afford to produce the Chemical Abstracts itself with the limited financial, technical. and human resources at its disposal. The regional centers can, however, supplement the acquired databases by adding to them the locally indexed and abstracted inputs produced from local scientific and technical publications and reports.

To successfully carry out the possible activities already mentioned, there are a few basic considerations which must be kept in mind.

1.   Regional cooperation should be based on the voluntary participation of national libraries, documentation centers, and major academic and research libraries within the region. The network of regional information systems should be flexible in structure as suggested in the UNISIST report.[9]

2.   The establishment of regional information centers should be in the spirit of cooperation instead of competition. Unnecessary duplication of efforts should be avoided.

3.   Regional cooperation should be planned according to the specific conditions and requirements of the region. It should be tailor-made rather than transplanted.

4.   It is recommended that the make up of the "region" should not be strictly defined. Although initially the cooperation may be confined to Malaysia, Singapore, Indonesia, the Philippines, and Thailand, other countries in the region are welcome to join if they so desire.

AIT's Role in Regional Cooperation

---

[9]United Nations Educational, Scientific and Cultural Organization/International Council of Scientific Unions. op. cit., p. 19.

In considering the scientific and technical information needs of the region and the cooperative efforts to provide for it, it is desirable to examine the unique role the Asian Institute of Technology (AIT) plays in the region and its plan to build up strong library and information resources which, when fully developed, will suffice to serve as a regional information center.

The Asian Institute of Technology located centrally in Bangkok, is a regional graduate school of engineering. It has an international faculty and its students come from 18 countries in Asia to study in the Diploma, Master's and Doctoral programs and to do research. Its graduates stay in Asia to apply their newly gained knowledge to the development of this vast region -- only 4 per cent have left Asia to work in the West. The AIT is uniquely chartered as a private non-profit regional institution and is recognized as an "international organization" in every respect.

Since its inception in 1959 AIT has grown steadily and its sphere of activities in Asia has widened greatly -- both geographically and in services and programs offered.[10] Its objectives are to provide:

1.   Educational opportunities at the master's and doctorate levels.

2.   Through post-graduate diploma courses and short-term institutes, opportunities for practicing engineers in the region to keep abreast of technological developments and their application to the needs of the region.

3.   Stimuli for the development of research oriented specifically to the needs of the region by the establishment of a major research center within AIT.

4.   Opportunities for faculty members from other educational institutions to study and conduct research at AIT.

5.   A focus for the development of engineering education to meet the unique needs of the region.

6.   Mechanisms for the introduction into the region of the latest developments in technology and for the development of their application to its needs.

7.   A center for the development of equipment for research and instructional laboratories.

8.   An outstanding library to serve the needs of both AIT and the region.

---

[10]Before 1967, AIT was known as the SEATO Graduate School of Engineering. It is now totally independent from SEATO.

9.   A major computing center, designed and operated to serve AIT and other institutions in the region.

10. A regional focal point and catalyst for the development of professional activities, including conferences and seminars, and a center for the publication of technical information for the region.

The fields of study presently offered at AIT encompass the following divisions:

Environmental Engineering
Geotechnical Engineering
Structural Engineering and Mechanics
Systems Engineering and Management
Transportation Engineering
Water Science and Engineering

Additional fields will be added according to the needs of the region:

Agricultural Engineering (to commence in January 1972)
Electrical Engineering -- Power Systems (to commence in August 1972)
Computer Science
Economic Geology
Chemical Engineering
Food Technology
Mechanical Engineering

It is anticipated that by 1980 AIT will become a complete institute of technology with a total enrollment of 1,000 graduate students.

In order that AIT can achieve its long-range goals and broad objectives, a new campus on a site of 400 acres 42 kilometers north of Bangkok is being constructed. The total capital investment for the new campus will be in the amount of 20 million U.S. dollars. The first phase of construction costing 6.2 million U.S. dollars will be completed in August 1972. A 1.6-million U.S. dollar Library and Computer Center Complex which will occupy 100,000 sq. ft. of space is being planned for 1974.

Pursuant to the objectives, particularly number 8, the Institute has, ever since its conception, devoted a large portion of its resources to the development of a well stocked library. According to the long-range projection of the library, its collection of books will be expanded from 30,000 volumes at present to 300,000 volumes in the 1980s. During the same period, its journal titles will be increased from 1,000 to 5,000.

The long-range development plan of the AIT Library also includes the following which are significant to regional cooperation:

1.   To establish a computer-based bibliographical data bank.

Because of the critically high cost in cataloging, indexing, and abstracting of books, documents, technical publications and reports, journal articles, and papers of conference proceedings, the library seeks to utilize the existing cataloging, indexing, and abstracting services available in machine-readable form as the major input of its data bank and to supplement them with its own selected bibliographical data cataloged and indexed from its own collections.

Based on the recently published survey of scientific and technical tape services,[11] there are 55 known bibliographical data sources now available on magnetic tapes which can be obtained either by subscription or by special arrangement.[12] A few of the widely known tape services are listed below:

Chemical Abstracts -- Condensates.
Engineering Index -- Compendex.
Institute of Electrical and Electronics Engineers -- IEEE REFLECS (Retrieval from the Literature on Electronics and Computer Sciences).
Institution of Electrical Engineers -- INSPEC Tape Service.
International Atomic Energy Agency -- INIS Output Tape.
U.S. Government Research and Development Reports (USGRDR).
U.S. Library of Congress -- MARC Distribution Service.

Initially AIT will seek to acquire bibliographical data in engineering and related subject areas such as CA Condensates, EI Compendex, INSPEC, USGRDR, HRIS, and CAIN, and to add others later as may be needed. Close coordination will be undertaken with other libraries and documentation centers in the region that may also plan to establish such bibliographical data banks in other subject areas so that unnecessary duplication of efforts and subject coverage can be avoided.

Besides the above databases, the AIT Library also plans to make use of the MARC (Machine Readable Cataloging) tapes of both the U.S. and U.K. to aid in book selection, acquisition, cataloging, processing, SDI (selective dissemina-

---

[11]Kenneth D. Carroll, *Survey of Scientific-Technical Tape Services* (New York: American Institute of Physics, 1970), 64 p. (PB 196 154)

[12]Although the survey by Carroll does not include those tapes made by government sources not available to the general public (e.g., NASA and DDC - U.S. Defense Documentation Center), it also omits a number of other tape services known to exist (e.g., MIT INTREX--Information Transfer Experiment--tape, Highways Research Information Service--HRIS, MEDLARS--Medical Literature Analysis and Retrieval System of the U.S. National Library of Medicine, and CAIN--Cataloging and Indexing--tape of the U.S. National Agricultural Library).

tion of information) service, and current and retrospective bibliographical search, etc. Once they are in operation, most of these services will undoubtedly be made available to other libraries and documentation center as well as to industries, government agencies, and individual researchers and engineers on a cost-sharing basis in order to bring down the unit cost. This experiment will begin as soon as there is access to a large computer system capable of processing the magnetic tapes and the required financial support which is being sought by the Institute becomes available.

2. To experiment with satellite communication for immediate interconnection with major libraries and national documentation centers in and outside the region.

There is now a very promising experiment underway at the University of Hawaii called "PanPacific Education and Communication Experiments by Satellite" (PEACESAT). The essence of this experiment is to use the ATS (Applications Technology Satellite) geostationary satellite owned by the U.S. National Aeronautics and Space Administration (NASA) as a relay to interconnect institutions of higher education in the Pacific basin for purpose of two-way voice, teletype, and facsimile communications. The University of Hawaii has developed a very effective low-cost ground station capable of transmitting and receiving the three types of information. We are now making contact with both the University of Hawaii and NASA for participation in the experiment and in the use of ATS satellites. Once the arrangements are made, we plan to set up a ground station in Bangkok with communication linkage with the Library of the University of Hawaii and other major libraries in California, U.S.A., in Australia, and in New Zealand where such ground stations will he installed. This communication network when established will greatly facilitate the flow of scientific and technical information into the region. Furthermore, if the cost of such equipment is low enough, a regional network of ground stations can be strategically located with interconnections of at least one library or documentation center in each country.

3. To plan and design a computerized library system providing the necessary support for the two major undertakings mentioned. Currently, two such sub-systems employing an IBM 1130 computer system are already in operation -- one in journal listing and control and one in acquisitions and accounting.[13] Restricted by the limited capacity of the present computer, further computer applications will have to wait until a large computer system is installed on the campus.

---

[13]Detailed description of these two operations are reported in the author's article "Library Mechanization at the Asian Institute of Technology", *International Library Review*, V. 3 No. 3 (June 1971), pp. 257-270.

Planning and Implementation Strategy

In view of the future plans of the AIT Library and the two projected major undertakings which will have a region-wide implication and significance, it is necessary that a regional coordinating council be founded to coordinate the program and development of the AIT Library in relationship with the national libraries, documentation centers, and major academic and research libraries in the region and to plan for other cooperative activities among the libraries and documentation centers.

It is suggested that the council members should consist of national representatives as well as representatives from Unesco, FID/CAO (Commission for Asia and Oceania of the International Federation for Documentation). ASPAC (The Asian and Pacific Council), ASAIHL (The Association of Southeast Asian Institutions of Higher Learning), SEAMEO (South East Asian Ministers of Education Organization), and AIT who are interested in and concerned about regional cooperation. It is further suggested that a planning committee for the establishment of the proposed "Regional Coordinating Council" be founded as soon as can be arranged under the sponsorship of Unesco and AIT. The planning committee should consist of one representative from each of the participating countries such as Malaysia. Singapore, Indonesia, the Philippines, and Thailand plus one each from Unesco and AIT.

The time has come for concrete action in regional cooperation. The developing countries in Southeast Asia will be greatly benefitted by the joint force of their national libraries, documentation centers, and academic and research libraries in searching for effective ways and means to share their information resources and services in science and technology for the betterment of life and the well-being of their people. This spirit of cooperation is imperative if the scientific and technical information needs of the region are to be fulfilled.

REGIONAL COOPERATION FOR ISDS

Introduction

Perhaps the most significant development in the library and documentation field, world-wide, during the 1970s is the major surge of international cooperation in information transfer and sharing through the standardization of bibliographic description and improved tools for systems interconnection. The role played by UNESCO to spearhead this movement has won great acclaim the world over, but the success of this development is also the result of the cooperation and support of many other international organizations such as the International Council of Scientific Unions (ICSU) which, in collaboration with Unesco, jointly sponsored the inquiry into the feasibility of a World Science Information System (UNISIST)[1].

The International Federation of Library Associations (IFLA), long active in international cooperation, contributed to the standardization of bibliographic description which culminated in the publication of ISBD(M)[2] and ISBD(S)[3] and in the establishment of an Bibliographic Control (UBC)[4] among all nations.

To establish the foundation necessary for effective Universal Bibliographic Control and information transfer, in September 1974, Unesco together with IFLA, FID (International Federation of Documentation), and ICA (International Council of Archives), convened an Intergovernmental Conference on the Planning of National

---

[1]*Study Report on the Feasibility of a World Science Information System by the United Nations Educational, Scientific and Cultural Organization and the International Council of Scientific Unions* (Paris: Unesco, 1971). (Unesco/UNISIST/4)

[2]International Federation of Library Associations. *ISBD(M) - International Standard Bibliographic Description for Monographic Publications.* 1st standard ed. (London: IFLA Committee on Cataloguing, 1974). ISBN 0-903043-02-5

[3]*ISBD(S) - International Standard Bibliographic Description for Serials, Recommended by the Joint Working Group on the International Standard Bibliographic Description for Serials set up by the IFLA Committee on Cataloguing and the IFLA Committee on Serial Publications* (London: IFLA Committee on Cataloguing, 1974). ISBN 0-903043-03-3

[4]Dorothy Anderson, *Universal Bibliographic Control*, Intergovernmental Conference on the Planning of National Documentation, Library and Archives Infrastructures, Paris, 23-27 September 1974. (Paris: Unesco, 1974). (COM-74/NATIS/Ref.3)

Documentation, Library and Archives Infrastructures in Paris.[5] At this conference which was attended by delegates from 86 countries, a new program called "National Information System" (NATIS) was launched. This string of developments beginning with the UNISIST program has turned the pages of library history to an exciting new chapter.

The UNISIST program which was formally established by Unesco in 1972 at its 17th Session of the General Conference grew out from the feasibility study undertaken jointly by Unesco and ICSU from 1967 to 1971 and the recommendations made at the Intergovernmental Conference that convened in October 1971 specifically to consider the program proposal put forth in the study report.

While the long-range goal of the UNISIST program is to develop international networks of information services in the various sectors of sciences, it also establishes five intermediate objectives on which many program recommendations are based. These objectives are:

1.   To undertake activities for improvement of the tools of systems interconnection.

2.   To provide assistance for strengthening the functions and improving the performance of the institutional components of the information transfer chain.

3.   To help in the development of the specialized manpower essential for the planning and operation of information networks, especially in the developing countries.

4.   To encourage the development of scientific information policies and national networks.

5.   To assist Member States, especially the developing countries, in the creation and development of their infrastructure in the field of scientific and technical information.

Under these five broad objectives, a variety of programs have been planned or are being carried out by the Division of Scientific and Technological Information and Documentation of Unesco which acts as the executive office for the UNISIST program.

---

[5]*Final Report, Intergovernmental Conference on the Planning of National Documentation, Library, and Archives Infrastructures, Paris, 23-27 September 1974* (Paris: Unesco, 1975). (COM/MD/30)

What is ISDS?

The International Serials Data System (ISDS), an important component of the UNISIST program, was established in 1972 after its original proposal which was contained in the "Report on the Feasibility of an International Serials Data System, and Preliminary System Design"[6] was approved by the UNISIST Central Committee, and recommended to Unesco for implementation. The system as outlined in the report envisions a two-tier organizational structure consisting of an International Centre (IC) and a network of national and regional centres (NC and RC) jointly responsible for the creation and maintenance of computer-based data banks, which hold essential information for the identification of serials.

According to the first issue of the *ISDS Bulletin* published in 1974, "The aim of ISDS is to provide a reliable registry of world serial publications covering the full range of recorded knowledge. It is responsible for assigning to each serial published under a given title, a unique and unambiguous numeric code identifier, the International Standard Serial Number (ISSN)."

Through an agreement between Unesco and the French Government, the International Centre for the Registration of Serial Publications was established in Paris with funds provided by the two founding bodies.

The operation policy of the ISDS network is based on a set of common rules and standards which cover the ISSN, rules for ISSN assignment, the content of ISDS data files on international, national and regional levels, the use of standard data element specifications, tagging schemes, character sets and magnetic tape formats for interchange and integration purposes. Detailed descriptions of the structure, policies, procedures and specifications of ISDS are given in the Guidelines for ISDS which is available in English, French, Japanese, Russian and Spanish.[7]

Since the success of the ISDS network depends to a large extent on the establishment of national or regional centres in every part of the world and the effective coordination of their activities, the Unesco Member States and associate members were invited in November 1972 by the Director General of Unesco to establish such centres. To date, 19 national centres and one regional centre have been declared. The 19 national centres are: U.S.A., U.K., Australia, Canada, Federal Republic of Germany, France, Argentina, Japan, Finland, Yugoslavia, Nigeria,

---

[6]In M. D. Martin and C. I. Barnes. *Report on the Feasibility of an International Serials Data System*, prepared for UNISIST/ICSU-AB Working Group on Bibliographic Description. (London: INSPEC, 1970). (DM/CB/284)

[7]*Guidelines for ISDS: UNISIST, International Serials Data System (ISDS)*. International Centre for the Registration of Serial Publications. (Paris: Unesco, 1973). (SC/WS/538)

Thailand, Tunisia, Holland, Sweden, Brazil, Indonesia, and the Philippines. The one Regional Centre in Moscow consists of the U.S.S.R., Bulgaria, Czechoslovakia, the German Democratic Republic, Hungary, Mongolia, Poland and Cuba. More than half of the national centres have already begun operation.

Why a Regional Centre?

Although three national centres in the Southeast Asian Region have been declared, none is in operation as yet. While planning is still in progress for some, it is felt that, perhaps, the concept of having a regional centre in Southeast Asia should be explored and their advantages be examined. Some of the advantages are:

1. From the economical point of view, because the number of current serial publications in most of the Southeast Asian countries is relatively small, it will not pay for each country to develop and maintain a computer-based serial data bank separately. The regional centre is economically feasible when, particularly, if the use of a computer is considered.

2. In terms of funding, the regional centre will have far more leverage than a national centre in seeking financial supports.

3. The regional centre also provides an answer to the scarcity of trained manpower in the Region. In addition, the proposed regional centre can provide training opportunities for serial librarians in the Southeast Asian countries.

4. The establishment of a regional centre will help those countries that may otherwise not be able to participate in ISDS for some time to come.

5. With a computer-based serial data bank, a variety of services can be provided as a by-product to the participating countries, e.g., the printing of new serial titles, both regional and national at desired intervals.

6. The computer-based serial data bank can be easily duplicated to provide each participating country a ready-made serial record in machine-readable form whenever needed.

7. The regional centre could serve as a catalyst for further cooperation in the Region.

How to Proceed?

With the many advantages given in the preceding section of this paper, it seems clear that the establishment of a regional centre in Southeast Asia is highly desirable. But the question immediately coming to mind is "How is this to be done?" To answer this, Unesco, at the request of the Royal Thai Government, has engaged the author, the former Director of the Library and Information Center, Asian Institute of Technology, to return to Southeast Asia for a three week mission to prepare a program proposal for the potential pilot project.

In order to carry out his mission, the author plans to visit Thailand, Malaysia, Singapore, Indonesia, and the Philippines between November 21 and December 14, 1975. The visit would have the following six objectives:

1.   To assess the present situation of serial publications in these countries.

2.   To evaluate the current status of bibliographical control for serial publications in these countries.

3.   To identify the national body and, possibly, the individual person(s) responsible for the bibliographical control of serial publications in each of these countries.

4.   To negotiate with appropriate authorities in each of these countries for their participation in the proposed regional centre.

5.   To solicit inputs from various sources for the establishment of the centre.

6.   To hold an open discussion on the preliminary plan of the Centre at the Third Conference of Southeast Asian Librarians to be held in Jakarta from December 1 to 5, 1975.

It is hoped that at the conclusion of the visit, a detailed program proposal can be prepared based on the data gathered and the feedbacks received during the discussions.

To facilitate such discussions, it is felt that a written outline of the preliminary plan as conceived by the author should be made available as a base for discussion. A sketch of this preliminary plan which covers such considerations as objectives, organization, operation, and financing is presented below:

The Preliminary Plan

1.   Objectives:

    A.   To establish a computer-based regional serials data bank for serials published in each of the participating countries using the ISDS format and ISSN.

    B.   To serve as a regional node of the ISDS International Centre by putting the local data into the data bank of the International Centre and by acting as a liaison between the International Centre and the representatives of participating countries in the Region.

C.   to improve the bibliographical control of serial publications in each participating country.

D.   To facilitate the information transfer on serial publications both within and beyond the Region.

E.   To foster a spirit of cooperation among participating countries.

2.   Organization:

A.   It is proposed that the Regional Centre be established in Thailand under the auspices of its National Library. The Director of the National Library also serves as the Director of the Regional Centre.

B.   The countries interested in participating in the Regional Centre may do so on a voluntary basis.

C.   Each participating country should designate a national agency to act as the national representative for the Regional Centre. The national agency should be the one which has a general responsibility in the handling of serial publications of the country, such as the national library.

D.   There should be an advisory committee consisting of 5 to 10 members with one representative nominated by each national agency and 1 to 3 technical experts appointed by the Director. The committee should meet once a year to consider policy, procedure and budget of the Centre.

E.   A full-time executive secretary should be appointed by the Director to take charge of day-to-day operations.

F.   The Centre should have an adequate number of staff to handle the flow of work.

3.   Operations:

A.   The national representative in each participating country should supply information on serial publications of its country at least once a month, on the standard worksheet adopted by the International Centre and in accordance with the rules set out in the Guidelines for ISDS and its supplements. A photocopy of the cover and the title page of each serial publication should accompany the worksheet.

B. The Regional Centre will check the correctness of each worksheet and will assign an ISSN to each serial publication. The national representative will be notified of the ISSN assigned and should in turn inform the publisher concerned and persuade him to use the ISSN in all issues of the serial publication.

C. The national representatives should prepare promotional materials and conduct workshops for serial publishers in their respective countries to acquaint them with the purpose and intend of ISSN.

D. The Regional Centre will be responsible for the development of a computerized system to handle the input, merge and update of all serial records and to generate magnetic tapes for submission to the International Centre.

E. The Regional Centre will provide the national agency of each participating country with a periodic printout of the complete regional record together with a separate national list of new serial titles.

F. The Regional Centre will act as a regional clearinghouse on information concerning serial publications. It should maintain a complete list of serial records of the International Centre and the necessary reference and bibliographic tools on serials.

G. An annual workshop for the national representatives will be conducted in Bangkok in conjunction with the annual meeting of the advisory committee to familiarize them with the operations and latest development of both the International Centre and the Regional Centre.

H. In cooperation with library schools and other educational institutions the Regional Centre may conduct in-service training programs, short courses, seminars, etc. on bibliographic control of serial publications and other related subjects.

4. Financing:

A. Because the Regional Centre is conceived as a regional pilot project of Unesco, it is proposed that for the initial period of five years the financial support for the Regional Centre is to be sought from UNDP or from other funding sources.

B. Budget requests of the Regional Centre for the first two years of operation should include such line items as:

Salaries and fringe benefits for the Executive Secretary and other staff members.

97

- - Meeting expenses of the advisory committee.
- - Expenses of the annual workshop for national representatives.
- - Travel expenses for the Director and the Executive Secretary to attend regional and international meetings on ISDS.
- - Cost of developing a computerized system and computer time.
- - Equipment and supplies.
- - Postage, telegraph, TWX, etc.
- - Miscellaneous.

C. Long-range financial requirement of the Centre should be reviewed by the advisory committee which is responsible for the establishment of fiscal policies and the approval of future budgets.

Conclusions and Recommendations

This paper has reviewed the recent major developments in international cooperation with particular reference to the UNISIST program and ISDS. A proposal is made to establish a Regional Centre for ISDS in Southeast Asia as a pilot project of Unesco. To facilitate discussions in connection with the Unesco sponsored mission, the author has drafted a preliminary plan for the establishment of the Regional Centre to be used during his three-week visit to Thailand, Malaysia, Singapore, Indonesia, and the Philippines. Communications to the author on any aspects of the preliminary plan are most welcome.

In order that the Regional Centre can be established at the earliest date possible it is recommended that:

1. All countries interested in participating in the regional project are urged to designate a national agency which will then appoint one of its staff as national representative,

2. the National Library of Thailand is requested to take immediate action to convene a planning meeting for the Regional Centre and to establish an ad hoc committee for the organization of the Regional Centre. All national representatives should be invited,

3. Unesco is requested to act swiftly on the program proposal and to provide funds for the planning meeting to be held in Bangkok early in 1976,

4. the final program proposal should be submitted to funding sources as soon as possible, and

5. besides the five countries already identified, other Southeast Asian countries that are interested in participating in the Regional Centre are requested to inform the ad hoc organization committee about their intents.

It is hoped that the participants of the Third Conference of the Southeast Asian Librarians would give their endorsement and support to this regional project which shares the same aspiration as the conference: to further library development through regional cooperation.

EDUCATING FOR INTERNATIONAL INTERDEPENDENCE: THE ROLE OF THE ACADEMIC LIBRARY -- OHIO UNIVERSITY AND MALAYSIA*

Co-Author: K. Mulliner

We are pleased to address you today both because of the fond memories that we have of visiting Malaysia and working with many fine librarians from Malaysia in regional programs and because of the special relationship which exists between our Library and Malaysia. We do not have to remind many of you that this conference coincides with the inauguration of the Malaysian Resource Center in the Southeast Asia Collection of Ohio University Libraries. We will return to that subject later.

Before beginning our remarks, we should commend the Minister and his predecessors. The academic libraries, library collections, and the librarians of Malaysia set a standard which other nations in the region struggle to approach. This is particularly noteworthy when one recalls that, with one exception, the development of universities in Malaysia, and previously in Malaya, has been accomplished during the past twenty-five years. We trust, that in discussing the role and contributions that the Ohio University Library has made and can make, that we do not convey the idea that academic libraries within Malaysia have done less than an outstanding job, and certainly the strong support of the government and the respective universities over the past quarter century have made this possible.

We do believe that there is a role, and even a responsibility, for academic libraries in the United States in cooperating with students, scholars, colleagues, institutions, and governments in Third World nations. In reviewing the possible themes that we would like to discuss today, we have decided to focus on two.[1]

We have chosen these complementary themes because we believe that they are of considerable importance but also because they reflect particular strengths and contributions of Ohio University Library, and thus we are able to discuss practice

---

*Paper presented to First Tun Abdul Razak Conference on Southeast Asia Studies, "Higher Education and Economic Development in Malaysia -- Thinking Ahead," at Ohio University, May 10, 1985.

[1]A wider range of activities was described in K. Mulliner, Hwa-Wei Lee, and Lian The-Mulliner, "International Information Exchange and Southeast Asia Collections -- A View from the U.S.," *Journal of Educational Media Science*, Vol. 18, No. 2 (Winter 1980), pp. 3-18; reprinted in this volume.

rather than theory. In brief, the themes are:

1. affording opportunities for continuing education and growth among professional librarians in Malaysia (exemplified in the international internship program pioneered by Ohio University Library and its Southeast Asia Collection in 1979) and

2. the two-fold task of providing appropriate resources for students from abroad in the U.S. and for increasing awareness among Americans of other nations and cultures with which they share the planet (of which the new Malaysian Resource Center marks a new direction).

International Library Internships

We have described our international library internships in some detail elsewhere[2] and today will confine our remarks to a few highlights and a brief consideration of the relevance of this program for today's theme, "Higher Education and Economic Development in Malaysia -- Thinking Ahead," and for libraries in Malaysia, particularly libraries serving institutions of higher education.

In Asia, and in Malaysia in particular, librarianship has generally been recognized as an important professional activity. An active undergraduate library science curriculum is offered at the MARA Institute of Technology. Recognition of the importance of qualified professionals has led to programs to send those who will occupy professional positions in the libraries for schooling in the U.K., U.S., Australia, and elsewhere. The result is a well-trained cadre of librarians.

It is perhaps this success that creates the challenge which we address through the international library internship program. As in other high-technology fields (yes, today librarianship is certainly a high-technology endeavor), change is the one constant with which we live in library and information science. As a result, the professional education which librarians received a decade ago now is dated, and education from earlier, no matter how germane at the time, seems almost quaint. Of course, professional activities help compensate for this -- the Congress of Southeast Asian Librarians (CONSAL), of which we have been fortunate to attend meetings, is

---

[2]Hwa-Wei Lee, "International Library Internships: An Effective Approach to Co-operation," *International Library Review*, Vol. 17 (1985), pp. 17-25; reprinted in this volume. Also, K. Mulliner and Hwa-Wei Lee, "International Exchange of Librarians and the Ohio University Internship Program," *College & Research Libraries News*, Vol 43, No. 10 (November 1982), pp. 345-348; reprinted in this volume.

a particularly valuable interchange within the region[3] -- and it would be possible to send the librarians back to school.

As neither is completely satisfactory (conferences are too brief for real hands-on experience and schooling is too lengthy, costly, and also lacking in practical experience), the international library internship program addresses a real need in providing opportunities to work with the latest in library and information technology in a library setting. Briefly, professional librarians at the middle-management level spend three to six months undertaking a personally tailored program of practical experience. Usually, interns will divide their time roughly in half between working in their particular areas of responsibility (i.e., cataloging, acquisitions, or reference) and half their time spending brief periods in all of the other library departments. This permits the development of the specific skills and knowledge needed for an individual's immediate responsibilities and also a greater understanding and appreciation of the activities of the other departments in the library and how these mesh to support the library's mission -- providing perspectives which will prepare them for greater management responsibilities in their home institutions.

For librarians and library science faculty from Southeast Asia, our internationally recognized Southeast Asia Collection, headed by Ms. Lian The-Mulliner, affords additional opportunities to work with many of the same materials and languages which they will encounter in their home institutions.

In addition to our outstanding Southeast Asia Collection, Ohio University Library can offer ample opportunity to become familiar with the latest in library and information technology, to investigate how such technology impacts on library organization and management, and to discuss with librarians familiar with the region how such technology might fit into the Southeast Asian context. Of course, it is up to each intern to draw on her or his own special knowledge of the context in which s/he works to interpret the information given. The goal is not to provide pat answers and uncritical adoption of Western answers to an Asian environment but rather to provide stimulating experiences and professional guidance to assist the interns in determining such answers for themselves.

Beyond our valuable staff who bring human qualities as well as an awareness of Asia and Southeast Asia, Ohio University Library has other advantages which make it an ideal site for such a program. We would be remiss if we did not mention the support and assistance which the Library receives from our University President, our

---

[3]The published proceedings of the recent meetings are informative. D. E. K. Wijasuriya, Yip Seong Chun, and Syed Salim Agha (eds.), *Access to Information: Proceedings of the Fifth Congress of Southeast Asian Librarians, Kuala Lumpur, 25-29 May 1981* (Kuala Lumpur: CONSAL V, 1982), and *The Library in the Information Revolution: Proceedings of the Sixth Congress of Southeast Asian Librarians, Singapore, 30 May-3 June 1983* (Singapore: CONSAL VI, 1983).

Provost and other senior administrators, our outstanding Center for International Studies under Dr. Felix Gagliano and the International Student and Faculty Services Office as well as the faculty, staff and students of the University in general.

In assisting the interns to explore the applications of technology to library services, we have a relatively long history in such applications. In the 1960s, we were a founding member of OCLC (now the Online Computer Library Center but then the Ohio College Library Center), a national and international library network with 6,000 member libraries and which, within its database, contains almost 12 million library records and is adding over 1 million more each year. In 1971, Ohio University Library was the first member institution to input a record online into that system. Today, with OCLC, we are able to share the demanding tasks of cataloging with all other member institutions, to identify which other member institutions may have a copy of a book or article which our library users may need, and online to ask that, or several, institutions to lend it to us. Conversely, all of the other member institutions are able to identify the materials which we have and to request to borrow them from us -- a valuable plus for the Malaysian Resource Center and one of which I hope all of the Malaysian and American visitors from other institutions in this country are aware. The networking through OCLC is a striking example of cooperation to share scarce resources and to maximize the effectiveness of skilled personnel.

In serving our local users, we have an automated library system based on the Virginia Tech Library System (VTLS), known locally as ALICE, which provides an automated circulation system, an online public access catalog for users, and all of this is based on our computerized cataloging through OCLC. Other enhancements to automate serials control and acquisitions are expected in the next year.[4] This system also permits users of terminals from anywhere on campus or microcomputers in their homes to access the public catalog to identify materials. As this is not a library meeting, we will not amplify on our pride and joy with the system.

Augmenting the system to identify the latest information available, we offer computerized searching of most indexes using microcomputers to download the information identified. Beyond these, microcomputers are used for a large and growing number of administrative and routine tasks. The import, for the intern, is that there is ample opportunity to encounter and work with virtually the gamut of computer applications to library service.

---

[4]The system and our experiences are described in Hwa-Wei Lee, K. Mulliner, E. Hoffmann-Pinther, and Hannah McCauley, "Alice at One: Candid Reflections on the Adoption, Installation, and Use of the Virginia Tech Library System (VTLS) at Ohio University," paper presented at the Integrated Online Library Systems Second National Conference, September 13-14, 1984, Atlanta, Georgia. Published in the *Proceedings* (Canfield, Ohio: Genaway and Associates, 1984), pp. 228-242; reprinted in this volume.

We will mention only one additional strength of the internship program, that of location. The Columbus, Ohio, area is a major center of information technology today. OCLC is headquartered just outside in Dublin, Ohio, and Chemical Abstracts, which is in the forefront in providing online information services, is in Columbus as are Battelle and a range of other information services and companies. Major library and information science academic programs are available at Indiana University, Kent State University, the University of Kentucky and the University of Pittsburgh. In describing the information-rich environs, we cannot neglect Athens and the Ohio University campus. Here the intern encounters a cosmopolitan university with a large international student enrollment and a university and community committed to international understanding, all of this in a beautiful and relatively safe environment, some distance from the distractions of urban centers.

Lest we wax poetic, let us conclude the discussion of the international internship program with some realities. In the past six years, internship training has been provided to more than 20 professional librarians from all of the ASEAN countries (except Brunei and Singapore), from the Republic of China on Taiwan, the People's Republic of China, Papua New Guinea, and Saudi Arabia. Support for the program has been provided by UNESCO, the Asia Foundation, the U.S. Agency for International Development, the U.S. Department of Education, and from the interns' home governments and institutions. We would add that while we have direct costs which must be met, the costs are only a fraction of what it would cost for a formal educational program abroad and the results, based on the evaluations which we have received from the interns and their home institutions, have been impressive. To date, we have only had one participant from Malaysia, but we would hope that such an opportunity might be extended to others in the future.

Malaysian Resource Center

Earlier this morning, we had the pleasure of attending, with our distinguished guests from Malaysia, the opening of the Malaysian Resource Center within the Library's Southeast Asia Collection. All of you have received a brochure describing the Center and its projected activities. Without repeating that information, we will make two points.

The first is that today's ceremony was an impressive step, but only one of many which have gone before and many that will follow. Since its creation in 1967, the Southeast Asia Collection has, in less than two decades, grown into a major national and international resource for research on Southeast Asia (in this, it is not unlike the nation of Malaysia which traces its prominence to *Merdeka* [independence] only a decade earlier than the Collection). Some years ago, the Southeast Asia Collection undertook a serious assessment of its national and international role. It was recognized that publications from and about Southeast Asia were ballooning to an extent that no academic library in the U.S. could hope or afford to collect everything from and about every country in the region. The wisdom of this analysis was attested to at a meeting this past March in conjunction with the national Association for Asian Studies Annual Conference in Philadelphia, in which representatives from the eight academic research libraries with Southeast Asian Collections and the Library of Congress discussed ways in which responsibilities might be shared.

In its decision to concentrate its collection development efforts, the Southeast Asia Collection considered its historical, local, and national roles. Historically, when the Collection was created concurrently with the Southeast Asia Studies Program (under the direction of Professors Norman Parmer and Paul van der Veur), the Program and the Collection focused on Malaysia and Indonesia. Locally, the University has developed significant ties with Malaysia (personified today in holder of the Tun Abdul Razak Chair in Southeast Asian Studies, Datin Professor Fatimah Hamid Don) while the Southeast Asia Studies Program (now Center) has built on those beginnings to also develop strengths on the Philippines. Nationally, the Collection observed that, while Cornell had unapproachable strengths for Indonesia and most other countries in the region were receiving major attention from one or more of the other collection, no Collection had identified Malaysia and its neighboring states of Brunei and Singapore as foci. As a result, in the past decade, the Southeast Asia Collection has concentrated on these nations with secondary emphasis on the Association for Southeast Asian Nations (ASEAN) and its other member nations.

For Malaysia, as the occasion of our discussion, this means that Ohio University receives as much and usually more materials from Malaysia than any other academic institution in the U.S. We believe that it is safe to say, despite the outstanding growth and development of libraries in Malaysia, only the National Library and libraries serving some of the major universities in Malaysia, have larger collections on Malaysia than Ohio University.

With this background and with Ohio University Library's commitment to resource sharing, the Malaysian Resource Center is a logical step. In part it recognizes the reality that the Southeast Asian Collection should be a primary source for anyone seeking research materials on Malaysia. It also represents a long standing commitment to service beyond the immediate users at Ohio University. Companies and U.S. government officials are increasingly aware that we may be the only institution with particular Malaysian materials. We would add that the service which they receive is also an important attraction.

Beyond those who need materials for research, academic, policy, or financial interests, there are millions of Americans who know little about Malaysia and whose lives are the poorer for that ignorance. Within the Center for International Studies, there have been, and continue to be, active programs to increase international awareness in the schools of Southeastern Ohio and to engage in citizenship awareness to make the wider population more cognizant of the cultural richness of the world. While the Malaysian Resource Center will not, with the simple cutting of a ribbon, banish the ignorance in this country of Malaysia and things Malaysian, it is a further step on the road. It will support the outreach program of the Center for International

106

Studies and similar programs elsewhere in the U.S. It is lighting a candle rather than cursing the darkness.

We are particularly pleased that the Malaysian Resource Center will offer films, tapes, and other materials beyond those usually thought of as information. It is consonant with the role of the library as a repository of the human record, not just the written record. Such materials offer the opportunity of reaching citizenry with a wide range of interests, who may be little interested in a scholarly tome but will find relaxation and common threads of human experience in a *noblat* record or a Shahnon Ahmad novel. We are sure that scholars, with the increasing attention given to popular history, will also find a rich repository in the future.

The second quality of the Malaysian Resource Center directly addresses the theme of this gathering. The more than 15,000 Malaysians studying in institutions of higher education in North America represent a serious challenge and responsibility for the academic community. Some of us who are older may recall schooling during a colonial era. The curriculum frequently focused on the colonial center with more information provided about the towns and provinces in the West than about neighboring *kampong*s and states. Not that such learning is necessarily bad, only that when it displaces students' awareness of their home history, heritage, and neighbors, something has been lost. This is not unlike what Malaysian students encounter when enrolled in academic institutions in North America. Few will find many courses on Asia, not to mention Southeast Asia. We are more fortunate at Ohio University, with its strong Southeast Asia Studies Center and numerous faculty who have taught and done research in Malaysia, but students should not expect that all of their American teachers will be familiar with the Malaysian and Southeast Asian situations.

If this is the case in general, it is much more true for students enrolled at other North American universities in specialized fields of knowledge such as science, engineering, education, and business, as so many Malaysians do--recognizing the economic development needs of Malaysia. Even if few Malaysian courses are offered, there is an alternative. As a student climbs the educational ladder, there are increasing opportunities for individual research and exploration, for testing the theories and lessons presented in class in contexts of the student's choosing.

The Malaysian Resource Center and the strength of the Southeast Asia Collection provide the substance for such testing, using Malaysian data and contexts. It is important to recognize that the mission of the Malaysian Resource Center is national. It serves not only the students and faculty at Ohio University or the citizenry of Southeastern Ohio. It is available to students and faculty across North America (the OCLC systems helps make this possible) attending or affiliated with American institutions. As an anonymous example, there is a Malaysian studying taxation at a major institution in a neighboring state. The student contacted our Collection to ask about property taxes in Malaysia, based on what the student is learning in courses in that institution. Based on the subsequent materials borrowed, it is evident that the student has discovered that Malaysia has a very different

107

approach than that in the U.S. Multiply this example by hundreds and thousands and the potential value of the Malaysian Resource Center for Malaysia becomes clearer.

Certainly, not every student from Malaysia will want or need to use Malaysian materials. But it is important for the student, and for Malaysia in the longer run, that such materials be available and that Malaysian students be encouraged to take advantage of them. We would only add that we are already very pleased to help make our resources available to numerous Malaysians from other institutions who come here to do research during academic vacations. We would welcome more.

We are very pleased with the support and the materials of the Malaysian Embassy. We look forward to a continuing mutually beneficial association. We hope that the Minister and other government officials in Malaysia can help to identify Ohio University as a repository, if not a depository, for Malaysian materials. We also encourage the Embassy and the Malaysian Students Department to assist us in making Malaysian students in the U.S. more aware of the Malaysian Resource Center, of the materials in our Southeast Asia Collection, of our willingness to help and to share these materials, and of the advantages to the students and to Malaysia resulting from this effort.

As we closed the initial section with a discussion of realities, perhaps that is a fitting theme for the conclusion of the paper as well. While we have dealt at length on the strengths of the Malaysian Resource Center (current and potential) and of the Ohio University Library's Southeast Asia Collection, we hardly need remind everyone that such strengths do not come cheap. In the past two decades, the Collection has achieved its present stature as a result of substantial support from Ohio University, from the Library, and from the U.S. Government. Since the establishment of the Tun Razak Chair, some funding is also provided to assist us in strengthening our holdings of Malaysian materials and to address the research needs of the Tun Razak Professor. At the same time, publishing costs and the quantities of materials available in Malaysia and from other countries on Malaysia are rising.

We have emphasized the positive points in the growth of the Southeast Asia Collection. There have been other times, in the mid-1970s, when Ohio University faced severe financial crises. Those are painful to remember and, we hope, behind us. Still, it was instructive. As a result of that experience, we are aware that public budgets are subject to many factors. To prevent such pain in the future, the Library is pleased to announce that, with the support of the President and the University administration and the Development Office, we have launched a campaign to provide an endowment for the Southeast Asia Collection of $1 million. We have already received initial gifts of more than $100,000 toward that goal. We believe that, with this endowment, we can assure that the next two decades of the Southeast Asia Collection and of the Malaysian Resource Center will be as fruitful as the past.

Section IV

International Exchanges and Internships

International Exchange of Librarians and the Ohio
University Internship Program (1982); Co-author:
K. Mulliner 111

International Library Internships: An Effective Approach
to Cooperation (1985) 117

INTERNATIONAL EXCHANGE OF LIBRARIANS AND THE OHIO UNIVERSITY INTERNSHIP PROGRAM[1]

Co-Author: K. Mulliner

Introduction

"International exchange of librarians" is often interpreted as those bilateral arrangements between institutions to exchange librarians on a short-term basis. The details of such arrangements vary from agreement to agreement and, as a rule, are expected to work out to the mutual advantage of both institutions and of the individuals. But, practically speaking, not all exchanges are bilateral nor on a one-to-one basis. Some may begin as unilateral and later become bilateral as a result of the relationships established while others may lead to multilateral or other asymmetrical relationships. No matter the form, it is likely that exchanges will require considerable negotiation, patience, and time to finalize a multitude of details. This paper will illustrate the above points by discussing some of the exchange opportunities available for American librarians and then by focusing on the library internship programs offered by the Ohio University Libraries.

Opportunities for American Librarians

Many of the exchange arrangements among American librarians and their foreign counterparts result from personal contacts. While this means that those individuals with international connections are most likely to develop further contacts, those wishing to join the international library community are not excluded. One of the media for initial contacts which has been little utilized is the advertisement section of professional journals.[2] This year, in response to an ad in *College & Research Libraries News*, April 1981, p. 108, placed by a French librarian, a colleague is arranging to switch jobs with his French counterpart. The realization of such exchanges requires not only the willingness of both individuals to agree to mutually satisfactory arrangement but also the strong yet flexible support of their respective library and institutional administrations. This latter is

---

[1]This paper was originally presented to the American Library Association International Relations Round Table at the Annual Conference in Philadelphia, Pa., on July 12, 1982.

[2]Also potentially valuable are the exchange notices sometimes carried in the *IFLA Journal*.

individual; therefore, special administrative actions may be required to make an exchange possible.

In addition to personal contacts, a variety of other approaches may also prove fruitful.

The Fulbright Exchange Program and the Peace Corps, for examples, are two of the best known programs administered by the U.S. government. The Fulbright Program offers opportunities for teaching or research in professional fields, including library science, in many parts of the world - both developed and less developed. The Peace Corps, which lists library science as a programming emphasis is suitable for both young and experienced librarians interested in library service in less developed countries. Opportunities for Peace Corps Volunteers with library background or expertise include teaching, consulting, and service. Although monetarily the Peace Corps may not be the most attractive, the experience itself can be both challenging and rewarding. Two of my colleagues on a field trip to Southeast Asia last year reported encountering Peace Corps Volunteers working in libraries and teaching in library science programs. For such positions the Peace Corps offers a standard of living comparable to locally employed peers within libraries and other institutions. And, while it is not stressed by the Peace Corps, Volunteers receive a "readjustment allowance" of $175 for each month that they serve at the end of their assignments, reflecting a level of savings that many of us in the U.S. wish we could maintain.

Funded by U.S. government agencies and private foundations, the Committee on Scholarly Communication with the People's Republic of China (a joint standing committee of the American Council of Learned Societies, the National Academy of Sciences, and the Social Science Research Council) maintains a number of exchange programs with the People's Republic of China. The Committee has a program for American graduate students and postdoctoral scholars to carry out long-term study or research in affiliation with Chinese universities and research institutes; a short-term reciprocal exchange of senior-level Chinese and American scholars; a bilateral conference program; and an exchange of joint working groups in selected fields. Although American librarians have not actively participated in these programs, a visit by a group of Chinese librarians to this country was among the first exchange visits under the auspices of the Committee.

For experienced librarians and library educators, opportunities for short-term consulting or teaching assignments are frequently available through the U.S. Agency for International Development, the U.S. International Communication Agency [Ed.: since reverted to the more familiar U. S. Information Agency), the United Nations, Unesco, the World Health Organization, and others. Some comparable opportunities may also be available through foundations and foreign governments and institutions. With the financial support of the Asian Development Bank and other international agencies, many universities in the developing nations of Asia are embarking on long-term development projects which will require the services of library consultants.

With rising standards of living in many developing countries, some can now offer salaries and employment attractive to librarians from the U.S. In Asia many American librarians are known to be (or to have been) employed in Hong Kong, Malaysia, Singapore, Taiwan, and Thailand, all of which have a strong demand for experienced librarians as they modernize their library services. There is a shortage of trained librarians in many of these countries.

Internships for Asian Librarians

To provide experience in modern library practices and concepts for middle and upper-level professionals in some Asian nations, Ohio University inaugurated a library internship program in 1979, initially at the request of Chulalongkorn University in Bangkok, Thailand. Since its inception, the program has been designed to serve two distinct groups of librarians from East and Southeast Asia. The first is comprised of middle or upper management personnel who have been working for several years and are now in need of upgrading their knowledge and skills, particularly with regard to the applications of technology to the information field. This group has since been broadened to include library science faculty, to provide them with practical experience to enhance their teaching capabilities. The second group includes recent graduates from professional degree programs in the U.S. and has aimed at providing hands-on experience with automated systems prior to returning to their home institutions to assume responsible positions.

The geographical preference indicated in this program arises from the strong ties of the Ohio University's Southeast Asia Collection with libraries and librarians from East and Southeast Asian countries. Thus far, three librarians from Thailand, one from Indonesia, and five from Taiwan have completed internships ranging from two to six months (although three months has been the preferred minimum). Among the interns, three are library science faculty and six hold responsible library positions at the middle management level or higher. Three of these also teach part-time in the library science programs of their institutions.

The success of these programs has attracted Unesco funding for two of the library school faculty last year and two more this fall, each for three months. Another program, which is being carried out in cooperation with the Graduate School of Library and Information Science of Simmons College with partial funding from Unesco, provides graduate library education at Simmons and practical training at Ohio University for a staff member from the Institute of Scientific and Technical Information of China (ISTIC). This program is especially tailored to combine education and training to meet a special need.

The internship programs at Ohio University Libraries[3] have, among others, the following special features:

1. As much as possible, the training program for each intern is planned to suit the individual needs of the intern and his/her institution. It takes into consideration the intern's educational background, previous training and experience, and career goals.

2. The length of an internship, normally three to six months, proves to be mutually beneficial for the interns and for the Ohio University Libraries. It provides sufficient time for the interns to be trained in their chosen areas of specialization plus it affords an overview and some experience in library management and departmental operations. During the internship period, the Library in return receives the services of the interns. Their area and language expertise are welcome additions to the Southeast Asia Collection and the Cataloging Department. The internships also include attendance at selected library workshops and conferences as well as visits to major libraries in the eastern United States. For instance, within easy driving distance is Columbus, the home of OCLC, Chemical Abstracts Service, and Ohio State University. Several library schools (including Kent State, Case Western Reserve, Pittsburgh, and Indiana) are also conveniently accessible.

3. Although the internships stress modern library concepts and the practice includes computerization and networking such as OCLC online cataloging and interlibrary loan systems, database searches, etc., special attention is given to the applicability of the technologies to the interns' home countries. The Library's Southeast Asia Collection, one of the best in the U.S., provides an ideal learning environment for the interns to relate their training to familiar materials and situations.

4. Complementing the Southeast Asia Collection, Ohio University Libraries also has a number of staff members familiar with library development in Asian countries. These professionals are able to guide and advise the interns with regard to their individual needs. Additionally, Ohio University has strong ties with a number of educational institutions in Asia, particularly Malaysia. This is evidenced in the recent joint gift by the Malaysian government and U.S. corporations to establish the endowed Tun Abdul Razak Chair for Malaysian Studies at Ohio University. These associations which span diverse faculty and

---

[3]The article by Ron Coplen and Muriel Regan, "Internship Programs in Special Libraries: A Mutually Beneficial Experience for Librarian and Student," *Special Libraries* 72 (January 1981):31-38, capably highlights many of the general characteristics of internships and thus the discussion here focuses on characteristics special to international exchanges.

administrators contribute to a cordial and supportive working and learning environment for the interns.

Adequate financing is of course essential to implementation of the intern program. Essentially, there are three types of direct costs involved:

1. **Travel Expenses**. These include the international travel to Ohio and return, local transportation for visits, and the costs of participating in conferences and workshops. Depending on the distance to the home country, the number of visits to be made, there can be considerable variation in cost, but $3,000 should be considered an absolute minimum for interns from Asia (based on mid-1982 air fares).

2. **Living Expenses**. These include room and board, insurance, and personal and incidental expenses. For a rural locale such as Athens, Ohio, $600 per month is adequate for subsistence. Obviously, this figure depends on local costs and must be adjusted for inflation.

3. **Administrative Expenses**. These include the travel expenses (but not salaries) of library staff who will accompany the intern(s) for visits and conferences as well as the cost of telephone and telex usage, postage, photo-copying, and database searching. To this should be added receptions and official entertainment. The minimum estimate for these expenses is about $1,000.

Applying these figures to a three-month internship, the direct costs would be about $5,800. The estimated indirect cost to the University for staff time spent programming, coordinating, supervising, training, and counseling plus overhead will amount to about $1,500 each month for each intern. These indirect cost can be partially and justifiably returned by assigning the intern to work approximately one-half time in a library department. This benefits the intern by deepening his/her understanding of how the library really works and how things are accomplished but at the same time contributes to the library's productivity. An important mutual benefit which cannot be monetized is the exchange of ideas between the interns and the library staff through daily contacts.[4] Funding for the internship programs with the Ohio University Libraries has come from a number of sources. These have included full support from Unesco for four library school faculty from Southeast Asia, shared Unesco and home-institution support for a technical librarian from China, support for travel and living expenses for five librarians from Taiwan by their universities and information agencies with Ohio University underwriting the administrative costs, and other combinations. U.S. Federal funding under Title VI (Foreign Language and Area Studies) also partially supported two interns from

---

[4]The benefits to the institution hosting an intern, described in the Coplen and Regan article, ibid., p. 32, are all applicable to the international context and often heightened as a result of the cross-cultural dimension of the interaction.

Thailand and, beginning in October 1982, intern support was included in our Title II-C (Strengthening Research library Resources) project for cataloging Southeast Asian materials. In this project, the intern from Southeast Asia will profit from the opportunity to work in a modern automated library and the Library will profit from having a professional librarian with linguistic and cataloging skills not available in the U.S.

Despite the importance of outside funding, the success of the programs relies on the strong commitment by Ohio University, and particularly its top administration, to international cooperation. And, as is evident above, the support from Unesco, both financially and through encouragement, has also been vital in the program's growth.

In summarizing the internship programs, we consider them to have special merit. They are relatively inexpensive in comparison with formal library science education programs and have far more substance than study tours. The programs are particularly advantageous for professional librarians from Third World nations as they are afforded concentrated training and experiences which provide both depth and breadth within a relatively short period. As these individuals occupy or will be occupying responsible positions within the library profession in their own countries, the opportunity to use and understand contemporary technological applications and management processes can impact on the advancement of entire nations.

Conclusions

International exchanges have many benefits. In the long run, they not only benefit the individuals but also foster inter-institutional cooperation, information sharing, networking, and standardization on a global basis. Library internship, such as those at Ohio University, fulfill an important need. This is evidenced by the growing number of requests received and the availability of external funding. The fact that many institutions are willing to send their librarians to Ohio University Libraries for internship training at their own expense manifests the value of such short-term training. It is hoped that more libraries in the U.S. will open their doors to foreign librarians either on exchange or on internships. Standing in the forefront of modern library developments, the U.S. has much to offer in librarianship. Yet, at the same time, there is much that U.S. librarians and libraries can learn from others through such interchanges.

INTERNATIONAL LIBRARY INTERNSHIPS: AN EFFECTIVE APPROACH TO COOPERATION[1]

Introduction

Cooperation for library development in the Asian and Pacific Region takes many forms. Such diversity is necessary to address the varying needs and levels of development among and within the countries in the Region. One important area for cooperation is the education and training of library and information professionals. Adequate manpower resources are crucial for library development at a time when the importance of information for national development is widely acknowledged. I have found, in my years of professional involvement in the Region, that the pace of library development in a given country is often dictated by the quality and quantity of its library professionals. Without these, little happens.

Given this need, the development of professional manpower in library and information science is a fertile area for cooperation between the developed countries and the developing nations. As pioneers and leaders in library education, American and Canadian library schools have led in educating large numbers of information professionals from the Asian and Pacific Region. In the past two decades, Great Britain and other European countries also have been educating increasing numbers of library and information professionals. More recently, Australia and a regional program in the Philippines have made significant contributions as well. Most of the graduates who have returned to their homes hold responsible positions in libraries and information centers. Many are contributing to national library development in their respective countries. Yet, despite these educational opportunities, the number of trained professionals is still far short of actual needs.

In addition to formal library education, which requires the greatest investment in time and money, there is an urgent need for a diversity of training programs and professional opportunities, ranging from short courses, seminars, workshops and conferences to exchanges of personnel, professional visits, and internships. All of these provide training and retraining for library and information workers not only in the "basics" needed in their jobs but also in the new concepts, skills, and technologies in this rapidly changing profession of librarianship. Nothing can compare with a formal library education -- the value of which is beyond doubt -- yet there is a definite need to supplement or complement it with a variety of training programs especially

---

[1]Revised version of a paper originally presented to the Joint Annual Program of the Asian/Pacific American Librarians Association and the Chinese-American Librarians Association, June 28 - 29, 1983, in conjunction with the American Library Association Annual Conference, Los Angeles, California.

designed and tailored to the needs of the individuals involved. Unlike formal library education which often is bound by a fixed program of study and course sequences, training programs can be far more flexible and responsive to individual needs.

Recognizing this, since 1979 the Ohio University Library has been offering internship programs to library and information professionals from the Asian and Pacific Region.

Origin of the Internship Program

The internship program at Ohio University was begun in response to a number of requests from libraries and information centers in Indonesia, Taiwan, and Thailand. A number of factors made this possible, including:

--   the support of the Ohio University administration and its strong commitment to international education and cooperation,

--   the University's long standing association with educational programs in Malaysia and the University's Center for Southeast Asian Studies which originally stimulated the development of the Library's internationally recognized Southeast Asia Collection,

--   the interest and enthusiasm of the library staff especially those in the Southeast Asia Collection which provides an excellent home base for many of the interns, and

--   the financial support of the Division of General Information Programme of Unesco for several of the interns and the support of other funding sources including the interns' own institutions.

One additional factor of importance was my own working and teaching experience in Southeast Asia between 1968 and 1975 when I was seconded by the U. S. Agency for International Development to work as the Director of Library and Information Center at the Asian Institute of Technology (AIT) in Bangkok, Thailand. My close involvement in library development during those seven years led me to recognize the importance of internship programs. In fact, back in 1970, I started an internship program at AIT for several librarians from Indonesia and other libraries in Thailand. The current internship program at Ohio University could properly be seen as a continuation of this earlier program.

Purpose of Internships

Since its inception, the prime purpose of our internship program has been to provide practical experience in a major American library for selected library and

118

information professionals from the Asian and Pacific Region on modern concepts and developments in library and information services. Given our strong Southeast Asia link, (although one of our most recent programs was the training of two Saudi Arabian professionals in the management of a micrographic department for the National Center for Financial and Economic Information) our special focus has been Southeast Asia.

Three main groups of library and information professionals have benefitted from the training. The first group consists of middle- and upper-level professionals who received formal library education or training several years ago and now need to update their knowledge and skills for our rapidly changing profession. The second group consists of mostly younger faculty members of Southeast Asian library schools who wish to refresh their library skills with the hope of integrating theory and practice through the internship. The third group consists of new graduates of American library schools from the Asian and Pacific region who, before returning to their home countries, would like an opportunity to apply what they have learned in the context of a major American library. Of the 15 interns who have participated in the program, the majority divided almost equally between the first two groups. Some of the first group have dual responsibilities, i.e., in addition to working in the library, they also teach part-time in library schools at their home institutions. Thus far seven countries have been represented in the program. They are Thailand, Taiwan (Republic of China), Indonesia, Malaysia, the Philippines, People's Republic of China, and Saudi Arabia.

Structure of Internships

As was mentioned earlier, nearly all training is individually designed so that each intern has a tailor-made program to suit his or her special background and needs. In order to provide the utmost care in the training of each intern, we prefer no more than two interns at any one time. In fact, our experience has been that it is desirable to work with a single intern, although there are definite advantages in terms of mutual support in having a peer intern to whom to turn. Also, there needs to be a sufficient lapse of time between programs to give the participating staff a break. This is necessitated by the considerable time participating staff must give in the training and supervising of the interns.

While finalized only after his/her arrival and after a face-to-face meeting, much of the preparation for the program takes place several months in advance through correspondence. Once the specific background and needs of an intern have been identified, an appropriate library staff member is assigned as the training coordinator to oversee the entire training of the intern from arrival to departure. This staff member will be assisted by others as required. Our experience further suggests that three to six months are desirable to permit sufficient hands-on experience. A longer time period also permits the intern to make a greater contributions to the primary mission of the library. Six months is recommended for those interns whose English language proficiency requires a longer adjustment period. To give each intern greater awareness of various library practices, visits to other libraries in the vicinity are arranged. Depending on funding, visits to OCLC and Chemical Abstracts, which are located in Columbus, Ohio, and attendance at relevant library conferences, workshops, seminars, etc. are often a part of the program as well. For library school faculty members, a visit to the nearby library schools such as Kent State, Case Western Reserve, Pittsburgh, Kentucky, and Indiana may be added if so desired.

Scheduling of the training normally takes two forms. One is a stationary assignment in which an intern is assigned to one or two library areas (or departments) for half of each day during the entire internship period. This assignment is made according to each intern's needs for in-depth training in a given library or information service. The other form is a rotating assignment in which, during the other half of each day, the intern is assigned to a different library area for a period ranging from one to ten days each. This is designed to give the intern overall experience in a wide range of library operations. Some of the interns who have specific training objectives may be asked to carry out a project under the supervision or guidance of experienced staff members, in addition to the two forms of assignments.

It is of interest to note that among the areas most interns have wished to learn are:

1. Modern organization and management of a library or information center including particularly the many aspects of human resources management;

2. Applications of modern technologies to library and information services including computerized online cataloging and interlibrary loan, such as the systems provided by OCLC, and online searching of remote databases through Dialog, SDC, BRS, MEDLINE, etc. [our local online public access catalog and circulation system became available only this summer];

3. Networking of library and information services; and

4. The applicability of the above for the intern's home institution.

The last is of utmost importance in our view since unless most of the practical experience gained by the interns can be applied in their own environment, there is little value in the internship program. At the same time, the interns must be expected to interpret what they learn rather than expecting to be able to directly transplant each technological application.

Costs of Internships

To insure the success of the internship program, adequate funding for the following three types of direct costs[2] must be secured:

1. Travel Expenses. These include international travel to Ohio and return, local transportation for visits, and the costs of participating in conferences and workshops. Depending on the distance to the home country, the number of visits to be made, and the number of conferences to be attended, there can be considerable variation in cost, but $3,500 should be considered a minimum for interns from Asia (based on 1983 air fares).

2. Living Expenses. These include room and board, insurance, and personal and incidental expenses. For a rural locale such as Athens, Ohio $600 per month is adequate for subsistence. Obviously, this figure depends on local costs and must be adjusted for inflation. Expenses for interns accompanied by family members would be higher.

3. Administrative Expenses. These include the travel expenses (but not salaries) of library staff who will accompany the intern(s) for visits and conferences as well as the cost of telephones, textbooks and reading materials, telex, postage, photocopying, and database searching. To this should be added receptions and official entertainment. The minimum estimate for these expenses is about $1,000 for a three-month training with an increment of $150 per additional month -- depending on activities.

Applying these figures to a three-month internship, the direct costs would be about $6,300 (or $8,650 for six months).

The estimated indirect cost to the University for staff time spent programming, coordinating, supervising, training, travelling, and counseling plus overhead will amount to about $1,500 each month for each intern. Although part of this indirect cost may be recovered from the work performed by the interns during their internship, that part not recovered can be considered as a contribution made by the Ohio University Library to international cooperation. It is our hope that more libraries in North America, particularly those with area resources and expertise, will consider offering internship training to library and information professionals from the Asian and Pacific Region. Currently, because of the success of our internship program, we receive more requests than we can possible handle.

---

[2]Adapted from Hwa-Wei Lee and K. Mulliner, "International Exchange of Librarians and the Ohio University Internship Program," *College & Research Libraries News*, Vol. XLIII. No. 10, November 1982, pp. 345-348; reprinted as the preceeding article in this volume.

Funding Sources

Financial support for the direct costs of the internship programs has come from a number of sources. Most important of these has been from the General Information Programme of the United Nations Educational, Scientific and Cultural Organization (Unesco). The two Saudi Arabian interns were supported by their Government through the U. S.-Saudi Arabian Joint Commission on Economic Cooperation. Others were financed by funds made available through U. S. federal grants, that the Library was awarded under Titles II-C and VI of the Higher Education Act or by the interns' home institution.

It is necessary for the interns' home institutions to convince their government of the importance of a library internship and to seek financial support for it as well. Beyond this, Third World institutions should recognize their unique ability to inaugurate programs. Many international and bi-lateral agencies are more responsive to requests from recipient institutions than to proposals from the West. In this regard also, recognition by Third World governments of the importance of libraries and information centers for development efforts will affect the willingness of aid-granting and technical assistance agencies to support internships.

Program Review and Evaluation

To assure continuing flexibility in the programming and scheduling for an intern, I conduct a monthly review with the intern and his/her program coordinator. The review often leads to program modifications and improvements. In addition to periodic program reviews, two separate evaluations are carried out at the end of each internship: one by the intern using a standard evaluation form and one by the training coordinator. Although we have received highly satisfactory and complimentary evaluations from most of the interns, we actively seek their suggestions for the refinement of the program. Many of the suggestions have been adopted in subsequent programming and training. Some of the more important suggestions include: improved housing arrangements, assigning a staff member for each intern throughout the internship, preferred timing of internships during the year, and the value of some of the visits and the lack of value of others. Another form of evaluation which we hope to conduct is to ask for an evaluation by the intern's home institution of the effects of the training on an intern's performance after return. The findings could provide useful information and insights from a different perspective.

Summary and Recommendations

This paper thus far has described in some detail the internship program of Ohio University which has proven both popular and successful. Among the special features of the program are its flexibility and adaptability. Each intern receives an individually designed program based on his/her background and needs. In describing the program I have briefly traced its origin, purpose, format, costs, sources of funding, program review and evaluation, etc. Based on our experience, I would like to offer a few recommendations for the continuation of the program and for those others who may want to do the same.

First, I hope to see more libraries offering this program. There is an urgent need to upgrade and improve the knowledge and skills of a large number of library and information professionals in the Asian and Pacific Region in view of rapid social, economic and technological changes. The need for improved library and information services is increasingly recognized. It is an opportune time for library and information professionals to take part in the development and to gain recognition for their services.

Second, although there may be no monetary advantage for libraries to offer internship training, the experience itself can be richly rewarding. From my own experience, shared by my Ohio University colleagues, I have learned a great deal from each intern and have made lasting friendships with many of them. In fact, among other contributions, each intern has brought to our library a rich cultural experience and an opportunity to view our operations and procedures from different perspectives. Not unimportantly, they also pave the way for further inter-institutional cooperation and meaningful information exchanges for our Southeast Asia Collection.

Third, in order that more internships can be made available to the large number of library and information professionals who need them, expanded sources of funding are needed. In addition to increasing current financial support from international organizations and foundations, there is a need for greater awareness by governments of the value of internship programs as an important component for development. Such awareness, of course, must be followed by financial commitments. This applies to nations in the Region and to nations providing development assistance. Sending library and information professionals abroad for internship training should be strongly supported by the home institutions as well.

Fourth, in the selection of interns, particularly from non-English speaking countries, a moderate level of English proficiency should be required as this will facilitate the learning process and assure maximum benefit from the short-term training.

Fifth, another factor affecting the results of internships is the desire and determination to learn by the interns. It is very important that each intern be made aware early in his/her training that the responsibility to learn rests on the intern. The staff members assigned to coordinate the internship training should also be carefully selected and matched. They should have the professional ability, cultural sensitivity and commitment to do justice to the program. A successful internship program is often the result of good planning and team work. It requires the support

123

and participation of a major segment of the library staff who will not only help the interns in their training but also will go out of their way to make the interns feel welcome and at home.

Sixth, the commitment from the intern's home institution must extend beyond financial support. Unless the institution is prepared to capitalize on what the intern has gained, our time and effort might be more usefully directed to other areas. Important to this process is not only providing opportunities for the returned intern to apply what she/he has gained but also to share the lessons with others. Even with major expansion in internship opportunities, adequate addressing of the regional needs for professional development demands that those individuals selected serve not only as practitioners but as teachers for their colleagues after returning. Teaching in this instance refers to professional development programs rather than necessarily to a classroom role.

In conclusion, the internship program at Ohio University has offered a new approach to cooperation. Both the interns and we have learned from and about each other and ourselves. The experiences have been mutually rewarding.

Section V

Library and Information Services

User and Use Analysis: A Case Study of the
Information Utility by Geotechnical Engineers
in Asian Countries (1974) 127

The Application of Information Technology to
Close the Information Gap (1974) 137

The Experience of a Specialized Information Service
in Asia -- AGE (1975) 149

Approaches to Development of Water Resources
Scientific Information Systems (1978); Co-author:
Marjorie H. Rhoades 157

Challenges for the Library and Information Profession (1983) 171

USER AND USE ANALYSIS: A CASE STUDY OF THE INFORMATION UTILITY BY GEOTECHNICAL ENGINEERS IN ASIAN COUNTRIES

Introduction

The need for engineering and technical information in Asia is increasingly felt as the pace for economic and industrial development is accelerated. Engineers and technical experts in Asia are often frustrated by the inaccessibility of relevant information at the time of need. Although to some degree this situation is also true in the developed world, it more seriously affects progress in the developing countries where both expertise and financial resources are in critically short supply.

As a regional institution for advanced engineering education and research, the Asian Institute of Technology (AIT) is deeply involved in the technical development of the Asian region and it is this involvement which has led AIT to an awareness of the urgent needs of Asian engineers for relevant information. To this need, AIT has, since its inception, given top priority to the development of a first class library and information center within the Institute. Steps have been taken to expand this facility into a regional information center for engineering and related fields, embracing the collection, organization and dissemination of useful technical information.

To experiment with the setting up of a regional information service, a very important but highly specialized field -- Geotechnical Engineering, has been chosen for the pilot project. The idea of establishing a regional information center for geotechnical engineering was conceived at the meeting held in Bangkok in July 1971, of representatives of national societies of soil mechanics and foundation engineering in Asia. One of the resolutions of the meeting requested AIT to establish and operate the specialized information center for the benefit of all those who are concerned with geotechnical engineering in Asia. The importance of this undertaking was recognized through a grant awarded by the International Development Research Centre of Canada to partially support the operations of the Center for the initial three-year period. As a result, The Asian Information Center for Geotechnical Engineering (Asian Geotechnical Engineering for short, abbreviated AGE) was founded in January 1973 within the AIT Library and Information Center in collaboration with AIT's Division of Geotechnical Engineering. The operation of AGE is guided by a Policy Advisory Committee whose members are either leading subject specialists or information experts and a Technical Committee whose members are largely from AIT. At least one liaison officer from each Asian country has been appointed to provide close linkage between AGE and its users.

Major Functions of AGE

Serving as a clearing house in Asia for information on all aspects of geotechnical engineering such as soil mechanics, foundation engineering, engineering geology, rock mechanics, earthquake engineering and other related fields, the Center undertakes the responsibility to collect all relevant information and data useful to the region, to design a computer-based information storage and retrieval system, to disseminate such information through its publications and reproduction services, and to provide the three-R service (reference, referral and reproduction).

The three present publications of AGE are:

AGE Current Awareness Service. A quarterly publication informing readers of recent geotechnical engineering publications and contents of selected geotechnical engineering journals received at AGE.

Asian Geotechnical Engineering Abstracts. A quarterly publication consisting of abstracts of available publications and reports on geotechnical engineering relevant to Asia.

AGE Journal Holdings List. A list of geotechnical engineering journals held at AGE.

Other publications soon to be published are:

AGE Conference Proceedings List. A list of conference proceedings on various subjects of geotechnical engineering in AGE's collections.

Asian Geotechnical Engineering Directory. A bi-annual publication to consist of information on various organizations and individuals who are doing geotechnical engineering work in Asia or work relevant to Asia.

Asian Geotechnical Engineering In Progress. A semi-annual publication to consist of information on current design, construction and research projects in geotechnical engineering being undertaken in Asia.

Users of AGE

Basically, AGE's services are available at a subsidized cost to all who are concerned with any aspect of geotechnical engineering work in Asia. Regular users of AGE are encouraged to join AGE either as an individual member or as an institutional member in order to receive the wide range of information services at a very low annual fee.

As of April 15, 1974, 33 individuals and 41 institutions, mostly in Asia, had joined AGE as fee-paying members. In addition, there were 50 complimentary members consisting of those who serve either on the Policy Advisory Committee and the Technical Committee or as liaison officers. Table 1 gives the breakdown of the membership.

User and Use Analysis

In a continuing effort to make AGE more responsive to the information needs of its members, this study was conducted in March 1974. A total of 88 questionnaires was sent to all individual and institutional members in Asia as well as to all liaison officers. Before the middle of April, 36 questionnaires were returned constituting 40.9% of the total number of questionnaires sent. Results and findings derived from the returns in conjunction with other membership data previously gather by AGE are presented in the remaining part of this paper.

User Analysis

There are a few general characteristics of AGE's membership that can be summarized below. These include all individual members and one representative from each institutional member.

1. A majority are middle-aged, 46.15% between 31 and 40 and 23.08% between 41 and 50. All are college graduates with 46.43% having a Master's degree and 17.85% having a doctoral degree.

2. A very high percentage of them (79.4%) are either chief engineers or are holding senior executive and teaching positions.

3. As shown in Table II, a high percentage of both individual and institutional members are from engineering and consulting firms.

4. One phenomenon among individual members is the large number of engineers working in foreign countries. Of the 33 individual members, 11 are working in countries other than their own. For example, one Thai works in China, two Chinese work in Indonesia, one Australian works in Nepal, three Americans, one Dutch and one Indian work in Singapore, one Japanese works in Thailand, and one Indian works in the U.S.

TABLE I: AGE MEMBERSHIP

Country	Indiv. Member	Instn. Member	Complimentary Policy	Complimentary Technical	Liaison	Total
Bangladesh	0	0	0	0	1	1
Burma	0	0	0	0	1	1
China, ROC	3	15	1	0	2	21
Guam	0	1	0	0	0	1
Hong Kong	1	5	0	0	1	7
India	1	3	2	0	3	9
Indonesia	4	1	1	0	1	7
Iran	0	0	0	0	1	1
Israel	0	0	1	0	1	2
Japan	3	2	2	0	2	9
Korea, South	2	0	0	0	1	3
Malaysia	3	1	1	0	1	6
Nepal	1	0	0	0	0	1
Pakistan	0	1	0	0	1	2
Philippines	2	0	0	0	1	3
Singapore	5	0	1	0	1	7
Sri Lanka	0	1	0	0	1	2
Thailand	6	8	4	11	0	29
Asia Totals	31	38	13	11	19	112
Outside Asia						
Australia	0	2	2	0	0	4
Belgium	0	0	1	0	0	1
Brazil	0	0	1	0	0	1
Denmark	0	1	0	0	0	1
Un. Kingdom	0	0	1	0	0	1
United States	2	0	2	0	0	4
Non-Asia Totals	2	3	7	0	0	12

TABLE II: SOURCES OF FEE-PAYING MEMBERS

Sources	Individual No.	%	Institutional No.	%
Engineering & Consulting Firms	21	63.64	19	46.34
Universities & Research Organizations	9	27.27	7	17.07
Government Agencies	2	6.06	15	36.59
Unknown	1	3.03	0	.00
Total	33	100.00	41	100.00

Use Analysis

In regard to information seeking behavior, library facilities, and types of information often required, a rather uniform pattern was found among the population surveyed. No significant deviation can be detected either among the two membership groups and liaison officers or among those with different types of employment. Also differences in countries, nationalities, ages, education, and experience do not seem to affect the general pattern in any significant way.

Channels for Technical Information

The frequently used channels for technical information a shown in Table III are the "reading relevant literature" particularly in books, journais, proc dings, reports and papers, "visits and field trips" and "membership in professional societies".

When asked to indicate the three most important channels, an overwhelming majority (77.8%) indicated "reading of relevant literature" as the most important channel while a clear majority each (27.8% and 33.3% respectively) indicated "contacts with specialists in the same institution" and "attending conferences, seminars, workshops, etc." as the second and third most important channels.

TABLE III: CHANNELS FOR TECHNICAL INFORMATION

Channels	Frequently Used	Casually Used	Not Used	No Answer
Personal contacts and correspond. with outside persons	12	22	2	0
Contacts with specialists in the same institution.	14	16	3	3
Attending conferences, seminars, workshops, etc.	4	30	2	0
Reading relevant literature in:				
Books	30	6	0	0
Journals	26	10	0	0
Proceedings	22	12	2	0
Reports/papers	24	10	2	0
Patents	0	10	16	10
Documents	8	16	6	6
Visits and field trips.	20	16	0	0
Membership in professional societies	20	14	0	2
Enrolling for further studies.	2	4	26	4
Use of current awareness services, indexing and abstracting services, bibliographies, etc.	8	20	8	0
Others.	0	0	2	34

Library Facilities Available

In regard to personal library facilities, 11% rated their personal libraries as "adequate", 38.9% rated theirs as "average" or "inadequate". The highest number of books reported is 4,330 volumes while the lowest is 20 (the average is 490.7 and the median is 100). The highest number of journal titles reported is 114 while the lowest is 2. The number of journals currently received range from 2 to 27 with an average of 3 titles on geotechnical engineering. The geotechnical engineering journals most frequently owned are: *Geotechnical Engineering*, *Geotechnique*, and the *Journal of the Soil Mechanics and Foundations Division, Proceedings of the American Society of Civil Engineers*.

When asked about library facilities of the employer institutions, 11% rated theirs as "adequate", 55.6%, as "average" and 11% as "inadequate". The number of books ranged from a maximum of 200,000 volumes to a minimum of 60 volumes (the average is 32,582 and the medium is 7,000). The number of journal titles ranged from 2,600 down to 20. 38.9% of the libraries have *Engineering Index*, 27.8% own *Geotechnical Abstracts* and the *GEODEX*

Retrieval System for Geotechnical Abstracts, and 22% have their own indexing systems.

For other library and information facilities available, 27.8% rated those they use as "average", 38.9%, as "inadequate" and 27.8% gave no answers.

When asked how much of the information needs of each member has been met from the various library facilities available, the answers for the majority are that the personal libraries satisfy from 25% to 50% of their information needs while very little help was received from other library facilities.

TABLE IV: PERCENTAGE OF INFORMATION NEEDS SATISFIED

Library Facility	0-25%	25-50%	50-75%	75-100%
Personal	4	14	8	4
Employer's	16	4	6	0
Others	22	2	2	0

Types of Technical Information Often Required

Concerning the types of technical information often required by members, a great majority indicated "Practical information" as most often required. This is followed by "Site investigations", "Field performance data" and "Engineering design and construction details".

Table V shows not only those types of technical information which are often required but also those types of technical information which are not often required by the members.

Evaluation of AGE

The effectiveness and usefulness of AGE in meeting the information needs of its members were evaluated in terms of its publications and services.

AGE Publications

The appraisal of two of the published AGE publications were conducted through the questionnaire. The majority of responses were favorable. One

TABLE V: TYPES OF TECHNICAL INFORMATION REQUIRED

Types	Most Often	Average	Not Often	No Answer
Theoretical work.	2	10	14	10
Research findings or reports.	6	12	8	10
State-of-the-art review.	8	8	10	10
Practical information.	26	6	0	4
Field performance data.	20	12	0	4
Site investigations.	24	8	0	4
Engineering design and construction details.	18	8	2	8
Bibliographies, indexes, abstracts, etc.	4	8	16	8
Others.	0	0	4	32

suggestion for the *Asian Geotechnical Engineering Abstracts* was to give more coverage to the practical aspects of geotechnical engineering relating to Asia.

TABLE VI: APPRAISAL OF AGE PUBLICATIONS

AGE Current Awareness Service

	Good	Average	Poor	No Answer
Coverage	18	14	2	2
Arrangement	14	20	0	2
Timeliness	16	16	2	2

	Very Useful	Moderate	Not Useful	No Answer
Overall	14	16	2	4

Asian Geotechnical Engineering Abstracts

	Good	Average	Poor	No Answer
Coverage	16	12	2	6
Arrangement	12	16	2	6
Timeliness	16	12	2	6

	Very Useful	Moderate	Not Useful	No Answer
Overall	6	20	4	6

AGE Services

The finding was that 33.3% of the members have used the reproduction service of AGE at least once, 22.2% have used the reference service, and 5.6%

134

have used the referral service. In all cases, the ratings for the services received by those who used them were considered "satisfactory". For those members who have not used AGE's services, the following reasons were indicated:

1.   There has not been a need for such services yet. (16 indicated)
2.   Because of the distance which prevents direct access to such services. (12 indicated)
3.   Because of the long time required to receive such services, it would not help to solve immediate problems. (6 indicated)
4.   Did not know that such services are available. (2 indicated)
5.   Because of the difficulty in paying for such services. (2 indicated)

Summary and Conclusions

The study on information utility by geotechnical engineers in Asia based on the analysis of data provided by the AGE members points out the following facts which are worthy of attention:

1.   The majority of information users in geotechnical engineering are from engineering and consulting firms or are those who are engaged in such work. They are in the middle age bracket, well trained, and holding senior or executive positions.

2.   There seems to be a rather uniform pattern among them in their information seeking behavior. For example, the frequently used channels for information by the majority of respondents are reading of relevant literature from books, journals, proceedings, reports and papers.

3.   The library facilities available to them are generally "average" or "inadequate" to meet their information needs. Only one third of them have access to the *Engineering Index* and other specialized indexing and abstracting tools. As a consequence, few use these tools regularly for finding information. They are confined to their personal libraries for up to 50% of their information needs.

4.   The types of technical information often required are practical in nature. Theoretical work, bibliographical publications, research reports, and state-of-the-art review are less often required.

5.   The responses to two of the AGE publications are generally favorable with a greater number considering *AGE Current Awareness Service* as more useful than *Asian Geotechnical Engineering Abstracts.*

6.   Although the reasons given for the low level of use of AGE services by members are mainly the lack of needs and the factors of time and distance, some marketing efforts are necessary to convince the members and other potential users of AGE's ability to supply needed information as quickly and as economically as possible.

7.   The user and use analysis contained in this study has been confined mainly to the members of AGE. Further study is needed to include the uses made by non-members.

AGE has been in existence slightly more than one year. The two publications mentioned in this study have just completed their first annual volumes. Many of its services are beginning to become known among potential users in Asia. The continued growth of its membership and services used should be closely monitored to provide additional information on the pattern of information needs and uses of engineers in the developing countries of Asia.

THE APPLICATION OF INFORMATION TECHNOLOGY TO CLOSE THE INFORMATION GAP[1]

Introduction

One of the most pressing problems facing the developing nations in Asia today is the inability of their libraries and information centers to respond effectively and expediently to the wide range of information needs which are required for national development.

It has been observed that there exist two types of "information gap" in Asia. One is the lack of immediate access to the ever widening frontier of new knowledge resulting from the rapid advancement of science and technology in the developed world. Another is the lack of an effective mechanism to uncover useful indigenous information available within one's country or in the region.

A great deal of human and financial resources have been wasted in Asia as a direct result of these two types of "information gap." The perpetuation of this situation has rendered the works of Asian scientists, research workers, and technical specialists both inefficient and ineffective.

Recognizing such a serious problem, most of the Southeast Asian nations already have taken steps to correct it. This is shown in the findings of a 1972 Unesco report[2] which states:

> In each country visited there is active interest in the development of scientific and technical information, and plans for improvement of the present system. In Indonesia, a Ford Foundation mission recently advised on the establishment of a national network of science information centres to be co-ordinated by the National Scientific Documentation Centre, and the Government has requested UNDP (United Nations Development Programme) consultant services to assist in the actual planning. In Malaysia a mission was carried out in late 1971 under

---

[1]Based on an earlier paper presented by the author at the Regional Seminar on Information Storage, Retrieval and Dissemination organized by Asian Mass Communication Research and Information Centre in cooperation with National Research Council of Thailand, Bangkok, March 26-30, 1973. It was brought up to date as of June 1974.

[2]*Report of UNESCO Fact-Finding Mission on the Regional Information Network for Science and Technology in Southeast Asia.* 1972. 20 p. (SCP/425/2-25)

British Council sponsorship to advise on "Scientific and Technical Library and Information Services in Malaysia" In Singapore there has been no direct follow-up on the 1969 Unesco sponsored "Proposals for the setting-up of a Scientific and Technical Information Centre", but there is active interest in revising this study to bring it in line with the changing situation in Singapore. In the Philippines the NSDB (National Science Development Board) is setting up a new National Science Information Centre which will serve as the national co-ordinating body and as the linkage to regional and international networks or systems. The Government has requested UNDP advisory services in planning the Centre. In Hong Kong the Committee for Scientific Co-ordination has set up a Sub-Committee on Scientific and Technical Information to consider the establishment of a "Centralized Technical Information Service." In Thailand the Thai National Documentation Centre (TNDC) which is already well established is planning further services, and the Asian Institute of Technology has advanced plans for development of a complete information service on a regional level. In all countries the value of regional linkages was recognized and the concept of a regional information network in science and technology was strongly supported.[3]

In the Republic of China, a Science and Technology Information Center has been founded and is in operation under the National Science Council. A plan to form a nation-wide library and information network was proposed by this author in early 1974.[4] It is hoped that this plan will be considered for adoption.

In the field of social sciences, a study was made by Mr. Erwin Kristoffersen, former regional representative of the Friedrich-Ebert-Stiftung which resulted in a well documented proposal to establish a Clearing House for Social Development in Asia as an effective measure to meet the information needs in the Social Sciences.[5] The study pointed out the serious deficiencies existing in the exchange and dissemination of indigenous information in the social sciences, much of which is vital for developmental planning.

In the light of these two studies and the important groundwork they have laid, I would like to direct attention to the possible tools made available by recent

---

[3]Ibid., p. 4.

[4]Hwa-Wei Lee, "Proposal for the Establishment of a National Library and Information Network," *Central Daily News*, Feb. 26-27, 1974 (In Chinese); reprinted in this volume.

[5]Erwin Kristoffersen, *Clearing House for Social Development in Asia; Project Proposals and Report on the Findings of a Feasibility Study* (Bangkok: Friedrich-Ebert-Stiftung, Bangkok Office, 1972). 35 p.

advancements in information technology which can be applied to improve library-information services in the region.

Information Technology

Information technology is a term referring to those technologies which can be applied to library-information work. There are many such technologies available at present. They generally come under the labels of 1) Reprography, 2) Computers, or 3) Telecommunications.

Each of these three actually represents a variety of applications and different degrees of sophistication. They may work independently or together in either simple or complex library and information systems. Just as with other tools, not all the technologies are suitable for all situations and at all times. It is necessary that we give our attention to those technologies which are considered relevant to each of our particular environments.

Reprography

Despite the fact that "Reprography" is a relatively new term, this technology is already under widespread use by many libraries and information centers in this region. Unlike the newness of the name, reprography consists of many not-too-new techniques such as microfilming and various methods of copying and duplicating.

The techniques of reprography are very important for the developing countries in that:

1)   they enable a wider dissemination of information some of which might not be available or accessible otherwise;

2)   they have made it possible for libraries and information centers to interchange reproduced information;

3)   various microforms are by far the most economic means for information storage and for dissemination to distant places by mail; and

4)   the computer-output-microforms (COM) reduces the problem of storage and dissemination for the large amount of computer generated data including library catalogs and union lists of serials. The process of transferring bibliographical data from the magnetic tape output on to microfilm is relatively simple and economical.

Computers

Although the use of computers in library-information work has found wide acceptance throughout the world, it has just begun in Southeast Asia. The computer is a very promising tool in that it has the power and versatility to process data with high speed and precision. The main obstacles standing in the way of wider application by libraries and information centers in Asia are the factors of high cost, especially in the initial stage, the language barriers and the lack of trained staff. The language barriers are beginning to be overcome as more and more input and output devices for non-Roman languages have been developed and are being put into operation, e.g., Thai and Japanese. The other obstacles can be overcome by methods of sharing and pooling of available resources. One feasible approach is to set up cooperative information processing centers for libraries and information centers that wish to participate in it. This type of center can be established in large libraries or information centers which have easy access to computer facilities.

The essence of this setup is to share the costs of not only the use of a computer system and the developing of the software necessary for its support, but also the pooling together of specially trained personnel. By means of this arrangement, even small libraries and information centers can have the benefit of sharing a computer with large libraries and information centers. The work which can be best handled by such centers would be:

1) Establish and maintain a national (or regional) data bank on indigenous publications. A by-product of this data bank is the publication of national (or regional) bibliographies.

2) Establish and maintain a national (or regional) data bank on major library collections in the country (or region). A by-product of this data bank is the publication of a national (or regional) union catalog and separate book catalogs for each participating library or information center.

3) Establish and maintain a national (or regional) data bank on periodicals and serial publications held by major libraries and information centers in the country (or the region). A by-product of this data bank is the publication of a union list of periodicals and serials and separate lists of holdings for each participating library or information center.

4) Establish and maintain a national (or regional) data bank for scientific and technical literature of relevance to the country (or the region). A by-product of this data bank is the publication at regular intervals of abstracting journals. A score of other services such as SDI service, current awareness service, and retrospective search of the data file can also be initiated.

5)   Establish and maintain a national (or regional) data bank on such vital information as census data, demographic data, land use data, hydrological and meteorological data, inventories of communications and transportation, industrial and housing facilities, geological and natural resources, etc., and relevant economic and sociological data.

6)   Act as a centralized processing center for the acquisitions, cataloging, and processing of books, journals and other materials for the libraries and information centers that want to participate in such labor- and cost-saving operations. There are a wide range of activities that can be channeled through such a central processing service.

7)   Some of these centers may also consider the possibility of acquiring the MARC (MAchine-Readable Cataloging) tapes of both the U.S. Library of Congress and the British National Bibliography for local storage and manipulation. Arrangements may also be made to have either direct or indirect access to some of the major databases in the developed countries by means of modern telecommunications.

8)   The various data banks or processing centers may be integrated within a national (or regional) library and information system or network. Other activities of such a system or network are:

A.   Develop a library of computer programs for various library-information work.

B.   Provide consulting services to libraries or information centers in the application of appropriate information technology.

C.   Provide various computer services to individual or special library-information projects.

D.   Conduct short courses, seminars and workshops for the training and up-grading of librarians and information scientists in the use of computer and other information technology for library-information work.

Telecommunications

Telecommunications is an important part of the new information technology which holds great promise for improving library-information services in Asia.

An effort has been made by the United Nations Economic Commission for Asia and the Far East (ECAFE) to make the countries of Asia into an "Asian Telecommunity." The program intends to develop in every Asian country a telecommunication network and to link the various national networks from Iran to Indonesia by a system of modern communication services provided at the most economical rates. It, when fully realized, will undoubtedly accelerate the interchange of information amongst the libraries and information centers in the region by making possible information transmission and facsimile reproduction at high speed and at low cost. It will also facilitate the development of national library-information systems and regional library-information networks similar to those systems and networks already in operation in many parts of the world. One such example is the ESRO system which was reported by Isotta.[6]

ESRO system is the information system for the Space Documentation Service of the European Space Research Organization located in Darmstadt, Germany. The ESRO system was designed on the concept of a centralized file maintenance and software responsibility, coupled with decentralized searching of the files by remote terminals sited in the member states. The total configuration consists of the central computer facility in Darmstadt, together with its own local terminal; a single leased line to Paris where two terminals are installed; a party-line connection from Paris to St. Mary Cray in Kent where a terminal is installed at the Technology Reports Centre; a party-line connection from Paris to Bretigny, where a terminal is installed at the Centre Nationale D'Etudes Spatiale; a terminal in the ESRO establishment in Noordwijk, Holland; and another terminal in the ESRO establishment in Frascati near Rome.[7]

This type of system can be adopted in Asia if the "Asian Telecommunity" becomes a reality and the cost of telecommunications is substantially reduced.

Another important recent development in telecommunications which has an encouraging implication for Asia is the ability to transmit information among widely dispersed points of the world via satellites. The capability of communication satellites to transmit voice, teletype and facsimile signals to a distant place at the speed of light has a distinct advantage over other communication media for inter-continental communications. An inter-connection of computers, telephones, teletypes and communication satellites can provide a most effective network of national, regional and world information systems.

A highly sophisticated network system which saw the interfacing of all these was demonstrated at the 35th annual meeting of the American Society for Information Science held in Washington, D.C. on October 23-26, 1972. The system demonstrated was called the "International Information Retrieval Network." Through the several on-line terminals located on the conference grounds, participants of the

---

[6]N.E.C. Isotta, "International Information Networks: 1. The ESRO System" *Aslib Proceedings*, V. 24, No. 1 (January 1972) pp. 31-7.

[7]Ibid., p. 33.

annual meeting were able to query not just the many databases on computers located several hundred miles away in different parts of the U.S.A. but also the data files of the ESRO in Darmstadt, Germany via the INTELSAT IV communication satellite. The demonstration featured several recent innovations:

1) International communications via satellite.
2) Remote video and printing terminals.
3) On-line, interactive retrieval systems using both natural-text and index-based techniques.
4) Networking.
5) Access to multiple databases.

The demonstration showed that international networks are technologically feasible, economically conceivable, and usable with minimal instruction.[8]

Another less sophisticated but operating system using only teletype machines and the INTELSAT IV F-2 satellite is the satellite linkage between John Crerar Library (JCL) in Chicago, U.S.A. and Consejo Nacional de Investigaciones Cientificas y Tecnicas (C.N.I.C.T.) in Buenos Aires, Argentina. The basis of the system consists of some fourteen technical libraries in Argentina which are linked by Telex to each other and to C.N.I.C.T. in Buenos Aires. When an institution cannot fill its needs from its own collection, a message is sent to C.N.I.C.T. which then attempts to locate the needed item in one of the other libraries by use of the Union Lists and catalogs. If this is unsuccessful, the request is then transmitted to JCL and the latter provides a microfilm copy by return airmail. The costs of photocopies and the relay messages are borne by the National Academy of Sciences in the U.S.[9]

The JCL/C.N.I.C.T. system is a good example of what the developing countries can do to close the information gap existing within and among countries. Financial assistance of this kind is probably available from many international or foreign aid organizations.

AIT's Plans

As a regional institution for advanced engineering education and research, the Asian Institute of Technology (AIT) is deeply involved in the technical development of the Asian region and it is this involvement which has led AIT to an awareness of the urgent needs of Asian engineers for relevant information. To meet this need AIT

---

[8]From "A World of Information", program of the 35th annual meeting of ASIS. p. 8.

[9]From the letter of William S. Budington, Executive Director and Librarian of the John Crerar Library dated August 30, 1971 and from correspondences with Miss Judith A. Werdel of the National Academy of Science in 1973.

has devoted a large portion of its resources to develop an outstanding library and information center within the Institute. Steps have been taken to expand this facility into a regional library and information center for engineering and related fields, embracing the collection, organization and dissemination of useful technical information. The recently founded Asian Information Center for Geotechnical Engineering, under the joint sponsorship of the AIT Division of Geotechnical Engineering and the Library, is an example of one such endeavor.

To improve library-information service in the region, especially in the application of the latest information technology, AIT is in a very unique position. We are now in the process of undertaking five major steps which, if successful, will undoubtedly have a far reaching effect on the development of a regional library-- information network. These steps are (1) expanding computerized library-information service with a regional outlook, (2) establishing the Asian Information Center for Geotechnical Engineering, (3) leading a project for a computer-based union list of serials in Thailand, (4) collaborating with the National Library of Australia to set up a regional MARC data processing and distribution center, and (5) planning for an information transfer experiment via satellite between AIT and the Knowledge Availability Systems Center (KASC) of the University of Pittsburgh.

1)   Expanding computerized library-information service:

With the installation in January 1974 of a large computer system (CDC 3600) at AIT to replace the currently overloaded IBM 1130, the Library plans to greatly expand its existing computerized systems in acquisitions, accounting, serials listing, etc. while converting them from IBM 1130 to CDC 3600. The existing applications which began in 1969 were reported in the *International Library Review*.[10] As a part of this plan, a library systems analyst from the U.K. has been employed to undertake the designing and implementing of the expanded operations. This specialist, Mr. Stephen W. Massil, from the University of Birmingham joined AIT Library as the Associate Director in September 1973. Mr. Massil has been actively working with the Birmingham Libraries' Cooperative Mechanization Project which utilizes MARC records in three libraries (Aston and Birmingham Universities, and the Birmingham Public Libraries) on a cooperative basis. Work of the Project has been reported regularly in *Program*.[11] It is hoped that with the background of this specialist on library cooperative mechanization, many of our new programs will have a

---

[10]Hwa-Wei Lee, "Library Mechanization at the Asian Institute of Technology," *International Library Review*, V. 3, No. 3 (June 1971), pp. 257-270.

[11]The most recent is: D.G.R. Buckle and others, "The Birmingham Libraries' Co-operative Mechanization Project: Progress Report, January 1972 - July 1973," *Program: News of Computers In Libraries*, V. 7, No. 4 (October 1973), pp. 196-204.

broader perspective and regional outlook and will tie in with the regional library-information network development.

2) Establishing the Asian Information Center for Geotechnical Engineering (AGE):

To experiment with the setting up of a regional library-information service, we have selected a very important but highly specialized field -- Geotechnical Engineering, as our pilot project. The idea of establishing AGE was conceived at the meeting of representatives of national societies of soil mechanics and foundation engineering in the Asian region which convened in Bangkok in July 1971. Through one of the resolutions of the meeting, AIT was requested to undertake the task of establishing and operating AGE for the benefit of engineers in Asia. The importance of this undertaking was recognized through a grant awarded by the International Development Research Centre of Canada to partially support the activities of the Center for the initial three-year period. Because of this support, AGE was formally established in January 1973.

Serving as a clearing house in Asia for information on all phases of Geotech-nical Engineering such as soil mechanics, foundation engineering, engineering geology, rock mechanics, earthquake engineering and other related fields, the Center will undertake the responsibility to collect all relevant information and data useful to the region, to design a computer-based information storage and retrieval system, to disseminate such information through its publications and photocopying and microfilming services, and to provide the three-R services (reference, referral and reproduction).

The detailed information concerning the data files, the publications, and the services of the Center are contained in an introductory brochure published by the Center.[12] Subscriptions to the service have come from 17 countries, mostly from Asia.

3) Leading a project for a computer-based union list of serials in Thailand:

The project for a computer-based union list of serials in which all major libraries in Thailand will participate has been undertaken since February 1974. Data input is in accordance with the UNISIST's Guidelines for ISDS.[13] The input data are being keypunched and will be stored in AIT's CDC 3600 computer for many of the possible uses envisioned by the participating

---

[12]*Introducing Asian Information Center for Geotechnical Engineering* (Bangkok: Asian Institute of Technology, 1973). 9 p.

[13]International Centre for the Registration of Serial Publication, *UNISIST: Guidelines for ISDS* (Paris: Unesco, 1973). 58 p.

libraries. It is further planned that such a machine readable union list of serials will found the base of a national center, or eventually a regional center or network, for the International Serials Data System (ISDS).

4) Collaborating with the National Library of Australia to set up a regional MARC data processing and distribution center.

Considerable progress has been made in the setting up of a regional MARC (**MA**chine **R**eadable **C**ataloging) data processing and distribution center at AIT in collaboration with the National Library of Australia which would provide search service of the MARC files it owns and operates including both the U.S. and the U.K. MARC tapes plus the Australian MARC tapes at request to participating libraries in Southeast Asia channeled through AIT. During the process, AIT will maintain a computerized MARC file of library collections represented by the participating libraries in lieu of a union catalog. Local inputs in MARC format can be entered into the file to form the base for a national MARC database of various Southeast Asian countries. National bibliographies and other desired products can be produced from such database as needed. Detailed explanations of this project is given in two recent papers by Massil.[14]

5) Planning for an information transfer experiment via satellite between AIT and the Knowledge Availability Systems Center of the University of Pittsburgh:

This experiment which is now being planned is patterned after both the ESRO system and the JCL/C.N.I.C.T. system already described. The Knowledge Availability Systems Center (KASC) is one of the six NASA Regional Dissemination Centers in the U.S. Under the directorship of Professor Allen Kent who is also the Chairman of the Department of Information Science at the University of Pittsburgh, KASC has not only the expertise in information/computer/communications areas but also the immediate access to almost every important computerized database in science and engineering. The linkage to KASC via satellite will be a great advantage for both AIT and the region in that we will have remote, immediate access to the many computerized databases which are vital to our information requirement and yet, too expensive for us to own. It is our plan that subsequent arrangements will be made with all parties concerned to supply information drawn from KASC through AIT to other libraries and information centers in the region. This experiment will commence as soon as funds for its support are available.

---

[14]Stephen W. Massil, "The co-operative use of MARC tapes," a paper presented at the Conference on National and Academic Libraries in Malaysia and Singapore, Pulau Pinang, March 1-3, 1974. 8 p.; and Stephen W. Massil, "Local and regional use of MARC in Southeast Asia," a paper submitted to the IFLA Committee on Mechanization, May 1974. 5 p.

These above mentioned recent developments will have an important effect on the overall improvement of library-information service in the region. The advancement of information technology definitely offers excellent possibilities for rapid improvement. It is of prime importance that the libraries and information centers in Asia will take full advantage of this development to close the "information gap" existing between the developed world and the developing world and to become a true partner in national and regional development.

THE EXPERIENCE OF A SPECIALIZED INFORMATION SERVICE IN ASIA -- AGE[1]

Introduction

The many documentation problems in developing countries often stem from similar causes. These problems show a remarkable unity of focus despite the scattered location of developing countries over the various parts of the world. In seeking appropriate solutions to these problems which in some cases may require separate approaches for peculiar circumstances, an identification of these prevailing problems and their causes is the necessary first step. This paper intends to identify some of the documentation problems and difficulties encountered by the Asian Information Center for Geotechnical Engineering (AGE) in its first two years of operation and to suggest necessary actions needed for their remedies.

AGE

The Asian Information Center for Geotechnical Engineering (Asian Geotechnical Engineering for short, abbreviated AGE) was founded in January 1973 at the Asian Institute of Technology, a Bangkok based regional post-graduate school for engineering and related sciences. AGE is jointly sponsored AIT's Division of Geotechnical Engineering and the Library and Information Center. In general, the term "Geotechnical Engineering" comprises five subject areas:

Soil mechanics
Foundation engineering
Rock mechanics
Engineering geology
Earthquake engineering

The idea of establishing AGE was conceived at a meeting held in Bangkok, July 1971, of the representatives of the national societies of soil mechanics and foundation engineering in Asia. Arising from a generally felt need for a relevant, timely and responsive information service on geotechnical engineering especially tailored to the needs of Asian engineers, the meeting passed a resolution requesting the Asian Institute of Technology to establish and operate AGE for the purpose of selecting, acquiring, analyzing, storing, retrieving, publicizing, and disseminating useful information on Asian geotechnical engineering for the benefit of all those who are concerned. Recognizing the significance of geotechnical engineering work in relation

---

[1]This paper was presented at the Round Table Conference on Documentation Problems in Developing Countries held in Khartoum on 10-11 April 1975. The conference was organized by FID/DC and the FID National Member in Sudan.

to social and economic development in Asia as well as the importance of providing information service on a regional basis to serve the needs of geotechnical engineers and specialists, a grant was made by the International Development Research Centre (Canada) to support the operations of AGE for a three-year period.

Among the major activities of AGE are:

1. Searching, selecting, and acquiring both published and unpublished literature on geotechnical engineering which are relevant to Asia. Emphasis is given to literature originating in Asia, preferably in English, but materials of importance even in other languages are also included.

2. Establishing both an index card file and a machine-readable database for the relevant literature completely indexed and abstracted for easy retrieval. Both the International Geotechnical Classification System (IGC) and the Soil Mechanics Thesaurus are used.

3. Disseminating information on available literature through the following secondary publications:

    AGE Current Awareness Service: A quarterly publication informing readers of recent geotechnical engineering publications and contents of selected geotechnical engineering journals received at AGE.

    Asian Geotechnical Engineering Abstracts: A quarterly publication consisting of abstracts of available publications and reports on geotechnical engineering in or about Asia.

    AGE Conference Proceedings List: An annual list of conference proceedings on various subjects of geotechnical engineering in AGE's collections.

    AGE Journal Holdings List: A list revised annually of geotechnical engineering journals held at AGE.

    Besides these four publications, a SDI service by computer is currently being developed and is expected to be ready for service early in 1976.

4. Conducting periodic surveys on geotechnical engineers, specialists, and organizations in Asia as well as their on-going projects and works in progress. Results of these surveys are published in the following two publications:

    Asian Geotechnical Engineering Directory: A biennial publication to consist of information on various organizations and individuals who are doing geotechnical engineering work in Asia or work relevant to Asia.

150

Asian Geotechnical Engineering in Progress: A semi-annual publication to consist of information on current design, construction and research projects in geotechnical engineering being undertaken in Asia.

5. Providing the three "**R**" services (**R**eference, **R**eprography, and **R**eferral) to members and other users. It is planned that at some future date, the Center may also publish state-of-the-art reviews and bibliographies on subjects of interest to geotechnical engineers.

6. Cooperating with other information and documentation services on or related to geotechnical engineering both in and outside Asia to enhance information resources and service on geotechnical engineering on a global basis through reciprocal arrangement and systems interconnection. Discussions on this have been in progress with Geotechnical Abstracts, Inc. (Germany); the Division of Applied Geomechanics, Commonwealth Scientific and Industrial Research Organization (Australia); the Swedish Geotechnical Institute; etc.

Basically, AGE's collections, database, publications, and services are available to its "individual members" and "institutional members". With the financial support generously provided by IDRC, AGE is able to keep the fees for the two kinds of membership at a very low level with a special rate to Asians in order to give them the maximum benefit at a cost the majority of them can afford. As of December 31, 1974, AGE had a total of 149 members; 52 are institutional members and 97 are individual members. They represent 17 Asian countries and 8 non-Asian countries. It is hoped that the number of members will be greatly increased in the years ahead so that AGE could eventually support itself through membership fees and incomes drawn from publication sales and service charges received from non-members.

In order to find the pattern of information usage by geotechnical engineers in Asia, a questionnaire survey was conducted among AGE members in March 1974. Findings concerning the general characteristics of AGE members, their channels for information, the library facilities available to them, the types of technical information they often require as well as their appraisals of the two quarterly AGE publications: The AGE Current Awareness Services and the Asian Geotechnical Engineering Abstracts, and other services provided by AGE were reported in the paper entitled "User and Use Analysis: A Case Study of the Information Utility by Geotechnical Engineers in Asian Countries."[2]

---

[2]Hwa-Wei Lee, "User and use analysis: A case study of the information utility by geotechnical engineers in Asian countries," Paper presented at the 37th Annual Meeting of the American Society for Information Science, Atlanta, Georgia, October 13-17, 1974, preceding paper in this collection.

A follow-up study on the usage of all six AGE publications and the three "R" services by AGE members is being undertaken at present also by means of questionnaire. The second study is designed to seek answers to the following questions:

1. How appropriately have AGE publications and services served the needs of its members?

2. How would they rate the relative importance among the six AGE publications and among the various services?

3. What tangible effects have these publications and services had upon the members?

4. What improvement is needed in the existing publications and services?

5. Are there other publications and services which the members would like AGE to provide?

6. Does AGE meet their general expectation as a regional information center for geotechnical engineering?

7. What are some of the effective ways AGE can get more new members?

8. What are some of the effective ways AGE can obtain more technical literature from the member's country?

The answers to these questions are very important for the planning and future programming of AGE during its next phase of development.

Documentation Problems

The common problems for documentation in developing countries as were experienced by AGE included language differences, bibliographical control, availability, currency, and information consciousness. A brief discussion of each of these problems together with their implications and possible solutions are presented below:

1. The language differences:

   This problem is not unfamiliar to documentalists in that there are many little known languages with which very few documentation services, including AGE, have the capability to deal. Being a regional post-graduate school, the students and faculty members of the Asian Institute of Technology come from 22 Asian countries. This gives AGE the advantage of accessible linguistic assistance whenever needed. But even so, for practical reasons, AGE's collection is predominantly in English with a very small percentage of relevant literature in other languages. This practice is dictated by practicality and user demand rather than by the proportion of the literature available. This act of "discrimination" in the search and selection of relevant literature has restricted the coverage of AGE's collection.

In order to improve this situation, it is felt that the following measures should be taken by authors and editors of technical publications in every country, but particularly in those countries whose languages are less commonly known.

-- For the authors, it will be very useful if they can supply the titles of their papers in a widely used language, preferable in English, in addition to their own. Furthermore, it will be very helpful if they can also prepare an abstract with key words or descriptors in such a language to accompany each of their papers.

-- For the editors of proceedings, serial publications, and journals, they should either require their author to provide title, abstract, and key words in a widely used language in addition to their own or help them in providing these as a standard feature. A bi-lingual title page and table of contents will facilitate literature search and simplify the documentation process.

2. Bibliographical control:

The lack of a comprehensive bibliographical control of publications and literature generated in most of the developing countries in Asia presents another serious problem for documentation work. Although the number of national bibliographies published by developing countries in Asia is increasing, a majority of them are neither complete nor current. This is also true in regard to indexes to journal literature and technical papers prepared by many of the Asian countries. Up until recent years scholars and researchers both in Asia and elsewhere have relied heavily on published library catalogs, international indexes and bibliographies produced by developed countries as the main sources for publications and literature of developing countries. Because of the inadequate coverage of these externally published bibliographical tools, many of the works of Asian origin are not included and therefore are unknown to others. From the AGE's experience, there is a very large amount of relevant literature on geotechnical engineering in most of the Asian countries which has not been listed anywhere.

In terms of the importance of indigenous material for engineers in Asia and the demand for it as shown by 58% of the photocopying requests received by AGE in 1974 which were for materials generated in Asia, a major effort should be made by as many Asian countries as possible to provide full bibliographical coverage of publications and literature originating in each of their countries.

153

The steps to be taken to remedy this problem include the publication of a national bibliography and national indexes by designated agencies such as the national library and the national documentation center or other suitable agencies in each country. The coverage of both should be as complete and current as possible. This must be supported by appropriate depository laws which govern not just trade publications, but also documents, reports, and technical literature by a variety of sources.

The basic principles of Universal Bibliographic Control (UBC) which were proposed by FID and endorsed at the Intergovernmental Conference on the Planning of National Documentation, Library and Archives infrastructures, convened by Unesco on September 23-27, 1974 should be implemented by each country to the fullest extent possible. The tools for standardization such as ISBD(M), ISBD(S), ISDS Guidelines, etc. should be adopted. Efforts should be made to participate in various international information systems such as INIS, AGRIS and DEVSIS so that a worldwide coverage of useful information in fields of importance can be made possible through international cooperation.

3.   Availability:

The problem of availability or to put it more accurately "unavailability" of many indigenous publications and report literature is another headache for documentalists in Asia. Based on AGE's user survey, the most frequently required technical information by geotechnical engineers are field performance data, site investigation information, and engineering design and construction details. But, according to AGE's experience, much of this information is not published for wide distribution and is, therefore, very difficult to obtain.

The original sources for report literature of this kind, either published or unpublished, are government offices responsible for engineering works, academic and research institutions involved in engineering research and projects, and engineering and consulting firms. They have large amounts of report literature, but most of it is not easily available due to government red tape or unnecessary restrictions imposed by some of their issuing bodies. Furthermore, many international or inter-governmental organizations, various foundations, and a score of foreign-aid agencies of the aid-given countries also generate a considerable number of documents and reports. It takes an extraordinary effort, frequently involving personal knowledge and contacts, to acquire some of this information which often proved to be most useful to engineers.

The experience of AGE serves to illustrate a serious need existing in developing countries where a great deal of financial and human resources could be saved or be channeled to better use if much of this report literature, not just that on engineering, could be deposited in national documentation centers of the respective countries and be adequately listed. The operation may be patterned somewhat after the National Technical Information Services (NTIS) of the U.S. to which all publications and reports of government funded or sponsored research and development projects must be deposited. By means of weekly announcements and monthly indexes, and supported by reprographic services, all such publications and reports are made easily available at low cost. It would be more advantageous if the national documentation center or an appropriate agency in every country could expand its coverage to include not just government related publications and reports but others as well, that originate in its country.

4.   The Currency Problem:

A serious obstacle which prevents the inflow of useful information to the developing countries is the lack of convertible currency or foreign exchange in most of the developing countries. Because of this problem, both individuals and institutions in developing countries are unable to purchase needed publications, to subscribe to essential journals, to join professional societies, to obtain reprographic services, or to take advantage of specialized information services available to them from sources outside their countries. The use of Unesco coupons has not functioned well as they, also, are difficult to obtain. There are also regulations on import controls which serve to discourage foreign publications from entering some countries or to step up their prices.

From AGE's experience, the currency problem has made it very difficult if not impossible for some individuals and institutions in Asian countries to join AGE or to use AGE's services despite the nominal rate of charge made possible by an IDRC grant.

To simplify this problem, permission has been granted by AGE to its members and users in those countries where foreign exchange is hard to obtain to pay their membership fees or service charges in local currencies to the appointed AGE liaison officer in their country. The local currency collected is to be used by the liaison officer to purchase local publications for AGE and to pay for packing and mailing costs. But even this provision is considered illegal in some countries. This unfortunate situation is not only responsible, in part, for the slow growth of AGE's membership, but also restricts many Asian users from taking advantage of the services provided by AGE.

Unless the governments can take affirmative action to ease the regulations on foreign exchange, particularly when it is used for the acquisition of publications and technical information, the information users of these countries will continue to be impoverished information-wise.

5.   Information Consciousness:

Documentation services exist for their users. In the developing countries, the needs of information users are sometimes hidden or invisible at first but reveal themselves in an accelerated rate of use once started. Because of this, the temporary absence of visible needs should not be taken to mean that documentation services are not needed or at least not urgent. The main cause for the hidden needs stems from the long absence of adequate library and information services in most of the developing countries. People simply become accustomed to this situation and learn to get along without the benefit of information. This situation has resulted in a vicious circle of slowness in national development as well as in an "inferior" state of documentation service.

In order to improve such a situation, a special effort must be made to break the vicious circle by establishing a few model documentation services in developing countries or by improving their existing documentation services within the national documentation, library and archives infrastructures. These documentation services should serve to stimulate an "information consciousness" among the people they serve and to unearth the hidden needs.

One of the heartening experiences of AGE thus far has been the seeing of the changes taking place in the use pattern of its users. Those AGE users who have used AGE's service once tend to make more and frequent uses thereafter. This proves that once a confidence is established, an increased information use can be expected. The awakening of "information consciousness" is therefore a major task of any documentation services in the developing countries.

Conclusions

This paper has presented a brief description of a regional documentation service-- the Asian Information Center for Geotechnical Engineering--and some of the documentation problems it has encountered. Since the causes of these problems are quite similar among developing countries in different regions of the world, the solutions to these common problems may also be unified. It is hoped that this paper will bring about further discussions on other documentation problems and their possible solutions so that a joint effort could be developed to improve documentation services in the developing countries.

APPROACHES TO DEVELOPMENT
OF WATER RESOURCES
SCIENTIFIC INFORMATION SYSTEMS

Co-Author: Marjorie H. Rhoades

Easy access to the wide range of scientific information on water resources is a basic necessity for policy makers, planners, managers, scientists, engineers, and researchers, as well as for private citizens who are concerned with various aspects of water resources planning, development, and management in their efforts to ensure an adequate supply of clean water for mankind's consumption.

Because of the interdisciplinary nature of water resources information and the needs of a diversity of users, there has been an increasing demand for specialized, mission-oriented information systems at local, state, national, and international levels covering the whole spectrum of water resources activities.

The international model described in the first paper "An International Model for the Transfer of Water Resources Information" is an excellent design for a global information system on community water supplies and sanitation. In order to complement that presentation, this report will concentrate on the discussion of approaches to the development of water resources information systems on the local, state, and national levels, with particular consideration given to the applicability of these approaches in developing countries. Also to be examined is the current trend toward the development of national and international information systems along with the possibility for interconnection of existing information systems into large national and international networks utilizing the latest computer and telecommunication technologies available.

Conceptual Information System and Some Operational Definitions

During the past thirty years there has been a great proliferation of both published and unpublished materials in the form of books, journals, reports, proceedings, documents, patents, specifications, data sheets, charts, etc. Many of these also appeared in a variety of media from paper copies and microtexts to punched cards. The body of information has greatly expanded and the demand for information by users has vastly increased. This has placed undue pressure on various information systems to expand subject, language, and geographical coverage, to deepen content analysis, to share resources with other information systems through cooperation and networking, and to make resources and services readily available and accessible.

Although it has been observed that many scientists and researchers still rely on their personal contacts and direct correspondence as the primary approach to obtain new information, this one-to-one approach in information transfer as shown in Figure I is no longer adequate to meet the information needs of today's world.

Because more information is transmitted through various communication channels in ever increasing speed and frequency, it is becoming difficult for scientists and researchers to keep up. To find the information available in one's field, as well as to obtain it when needed, necessitates the services of well-established information systems and the aid of up-to-date, comprehensive bibliographical apparatus which includes card catalogs, book reviews, indexing and abstracting publications, selective dissemination of information (SDI), and on-line bibliographical databases. A diagram showing the transfer of scientific information through a multitude of communication channels including the various information systems and a wide range of primary and secondary publications is provided in Figure II.[1]

From these diagrams one can derive a simple definition for the term **Information System**, that is:

Information System refers to the methods, materials, media producers, and recipients involved in an organized way to effect information transfer within a specific field, activity, or organization.[2]

INFORMATION here is defined as knowledge, intelligence, facts, or data which can be used, transferred, or communicated. It has four basic qualities: namely, 1) **existence**, 2) **availability**, 3) **language** (or a recognizable representation) and 4) **meaning**. It is the quality of "meaning" that differentiates information from DATA. The distinction between information and KNOWLEDGE is in the degree of permanency. KNOWLEDGE is generally longer in life and more persistent. The term DATA is regarded as raw facts or observations and is often characterized by a tendency toward numerics or quantification. One can also say that quantified DATA intellectually processed become INFORMATION and produce KNOWLEDGE.

The Variety of Information Systems

Information systems exist to effect information transfer in an organized way. In order to maximize the effect for various user groups or organizations which may have different information needs and requirements, a variety of information systems each

---

[1]Both Figures I and II have been adapted from Herman M. Weisman, *Information Systems, Services and Centers* (New York: Becker and Hayes, 1972), p. 24 & 30.

[2]Ibid., pp. 14-16.

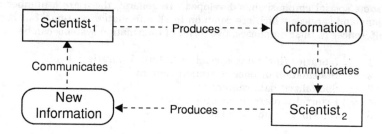

Figure I. Information transfer in a one-to-one communication mode

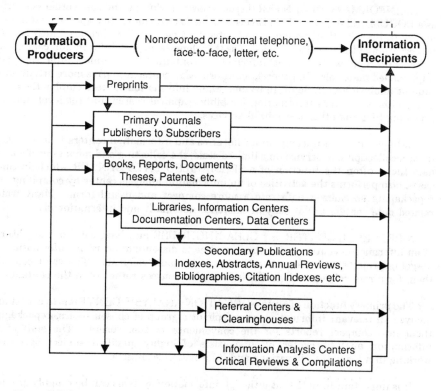

Figure II. Information transfer through a multitude of channels

with some special emphasis has developed. In general, there are a number of basic functions and services which are common to all information systems, but because of the differences in their emphases, five forms of information systems can be identified:

1. Libraries (including special or technical libraries)
2. Information or documentation centers
3. Specialized data centers
4. Referral centers or clearinghouses
5. Information analysis centers

A LIBRARY is probably the best known form of an information system. The major functions of a library consist normally of collecting, cataloging, preserving, circulating, and providing reference service. In special and technical libraries, collections may be limited to a special field with greater emphasis on unpublished materials of current value.

An INFORMATION CENTER (better known in Europe and some other countries as a DOCUMENTATION CENTER) is to some extent similar to a special or technical library in its collection emphasis and subject scope. Unlike libraries which see the preservation of the world's knowledge as their long-term goal, information centers are more concerned with current information contained in technical literature and unpublished materials. In general, an information center also pays more attention to content analysis and in-depth indexing. Many information centers employ the aid of a computer to process information for bibliographical search and retrieval, and for providing SDI and other specialized services.

Although it is not uncommon for libraries and information centers to also engage in data collection and service on a limited scale, the collecting and managing of a large data file is often the function of a SPECIALIZED DATA CENTER which in some cases, also performs the activities of an information analysis center by compiling and repackaging specialized data into a more compact and useful form. Many water related data centers are already in existence nationally and internationally.

A REFERRAL CENTER or a CLEARINGHOUSE may have some of the features of an information center, but its main task is to disseminate current information on on-going projects and research activities or to make referrals. The chief concern, then, for a referral center is in the information sources rather than the contents.

The primary function of an INFORMATION ANALYSIS CENTER is to collect and analyze all relevant information on a topic or a group of chosen topics, repackaging them into compact reports for the convenience of their users. The staff of an information analysis center often consists of highly qualified subject specialists working in a team with librarians and information scientists.

It is important to note that although information systems can be roughly grouped into the five forms, a clear distinction between each group and the others is not easy in that many of them do have overlapping functions, activities, and services. The difference among them is a matter of degree or emphasis rather than substance. Some information systems may very well by design consist of more than one of the forms described.

The National Referral Center of the Library of Congress is a good example of a library that provides referral service as a part of its total services. The National Technical Information Services (NTIS) combines the forms of a documentation center and a clearinghouse. In addition to being a depository for federally funded research and technical reports, it also indexes and abstracts them and prepares them for computer research (NTISearch), publishes a semi-monthly *Government Reports Announcements and Index* and a companion *Weekly Government Abstracts*, and sells photocopies or microfiche copies of such reports on demand. Currently, about 6,000 profiles are run daily by all organizations using the NTIS database.

Some information centers are known to be established within libraries. Vice versa some libraries may also be founded as a section of a large information center. As stated earlier, many data centers also function as information analysis centers. One of these is the National Oceanographic Data Center which performs the activities of an information analysis center in addition to being a specialized data center. An example of a clearinghouse is the Smithsonian Science Information Exchange which collects and disseminates information about ongoing or current research.

Developing an Information System

No matter in what form an information system may be, the general approach to developing an information system in an organization or an agency normally would consist of four basic phases: the background study phase, the system design phase, the development phase, and the operation phase. Each of these phases can be further divided into a number of activities which could be used as a checklist by information system planners.

I. The Background Study Phase:

    A.   The goals and mission of the "parent" organization.

    B.   The definition and characteristics of potential users.

    C.   The information needs and requirements of both the organization and users.

    D.   Existing information facilities and resources, both internal and external.

    E.   The objectives, scope, and services of the planned information system.

F. Other influencing and constraining factors:
    1. Attitude of the top management.
    2. Characteristics of the organization.
    3. Anticipated source and level of financial support.
    4. Availability of computer and telecommunication facilities.
    5. Trained library and information personnel.

II. The System Design Phase:

   A. Analysis of the findings of the background study.

   B. Decision on the form(s) of information system.

   C. Determination of the organization structure.
       1. Placement of the information system within the structure of the "parent" organization.
       2. Centralization vs. decentralization.

   D. Selection of the mode of operation.
       1. Manual vs. mechanization.
       2. Self-sufficient vs. interdependence.

   E. Definition of the scope of collection.
       1. Subject coverage.
       2. Language coverage.
       3. Geographical coverage.
       4. Medium coverage.
       5. Time coverage.

   F. Determination of resources required.
       1. Facilities.
       2. Equipment.
       3. Materials.
       4. Personnel.
       5. Cooperation and integration with existing activities.

   G. Design of system and operating procedures.
       1. System configuration.
       2. Record and data elements.
       3. Indexing and abstracting standards.
           Thesauri development.
           File structure and database format.
           Storage and retrieval considerations.
       .   Photoduplication and reproduction techniques.
       8. Interconnection with other information systems and networks.

162

H.   Cost estimates.

I.   Establishment of a time schedule for system development and implementation.

J.   Approval of the system design by the management.

III. The Development Phase:

A.   Dry run check-out of system and operating procedures.

B.   Set up pilot operation.
1.   Recruit and train staff.
2.   Acquire materials and equipment.
3.   Prepare physical facilities.
4.   Pilot operation.
5.   Provide user training.
6.   Evaluate design and procedures based on pilot operation.
7.   Revise as necessary and as feasible.

IV. The Operation Phase

A.   Implement by set stages.

B.   Check and evaluate each implemented stage and revise as necessary.

C.   Full operation of system.

D.   Periodic review.

Emerging Trend Toward National Systems and Networks

From the many papers in this session of the Conference, we are able to learn about the operating details of an assortment of information systems in water resources, some large, some small; some world-wide, some local; some in developed countries, several in developing countries. In addition, we learn about the recent trend in many countries toward the establishment of national information systems and networks in water resources.

Uncoordinated though they are, there is an abundance of information systems in water or water related fields in many of the developed countries. Giving the United States as an example, according to the 1966 *Directory of Information Resources in the United States: Water*, there were 800 non-commercial organizations that are doing

163

research or collecting data on water.[3] Many of them have their own information systems. In order to coordinate information services and data collecting activities within each country for the purpose of sharing resources and reducing unnecessary duplication, a new trend emerging in recent years is toward the establishment of national water resources information systems and networks.

Unlike that which has been the case in the United States, Canada, and some other developed countries, water resources information systems in many developing countries are understandably less well developed. The lack of needed information and data for water resources planners and others is undoubtedly a hinderance to the planning and development of sound water resources programs in these countries. Not only are the water resources information systems poorly developed, the whole of scientific information systems in many developing countries also are undernourished.

There is an encouraging sign, however, that because of the rapid economic, social and political developments in many developing countries coupled with a succession of national development plans, an awareness of the importance of library and information services in national development is increasingly seen. Through the promotion and assistance of United Nations Educational, Scientific and Cultural Organization (Unesco), attempts have been made by some countries to develop and strengthen their national information systems and infrastructures.

Similar assistance has also been provided by other international and inter-governmental organizations, private organizations and foundations, and governments of developed countries through their technical assistance programs to help developing countries establish viable information systems. The inclusion of an information transfer package as a major component of many technical assistance programs is of great significance in helping developing countries develop the capability for self reliance.

Because of this impetus, activities have begun in many developing countries to publish national bibliographies, to inventory periodical and serial holdings and to coordinate resources development and sharing among the national library, national documentation center, major academic and research libraries, public and private libraries, and special libraries. An increasing number of indigenous publications which were unknown or unaccountable before are now included in national bibliographies and periodical indexes.

Despite the many improvements, a serious problem remains in the area of unpublished materials. In the fields of development literature under which water resources is also a part, according to the recent report on the preliminary design of

---

[3]U.S. Library of Congress, National Referral Center for Science and Technology, *A Directory of Information Resources in the United States: Water* (Washington, D.C.: Government Printing Office, 1966). 248 p.

an international information system for the development sciences,[4] 60 percent of the relevant literature is unpublished material which is usually very difficult, if not impossible, to obtain. Consequently, this type of material is inadequately covered by published bibliographies and indexes. The report compares this type of material to the submerged part of an "iceberg" (Figure III). Only 40 percent of the total development literature is "visible". A majority of them are journal articles (22 percent) and books (18 percent).

To increase the accessibility to the 60 percent of invisible information requires the improvement of national information systems in each of the developing countries. The designation of a national center for water resources information and data from the existing information systems in the country is highly desirable. The national center should have the following basic responsibilities:

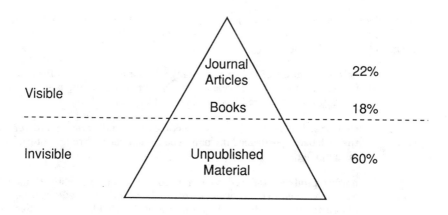

Figure III. The development literature "iceberg"

[4]*DEVSIS: The Preliminary Design of an International Information system for the Development Sciences*; prepared by the DEVSIS Study Team... (Ottawa: International development Research Centre, 1976), p. 18. (IDRC-065e).

1. coordinates the information gathering, data collection, and services of existing water resources information systems in the country;

2. creates and maintains a national bibliographical database in water resources information and data;

3. serves as a special node on water resources information in the national information network; and

4. acts as the national focal point for the exchange of water resources information with other countries and for possible future inter-connection with international information systems or networks.

International Cooperation and Networking

In the international arena there is an increasing number of information systems which have been established to serve the information needs of a worldwide user community interested in water or water-related subjects.

The first is the development of an acceptable model for the establishment of international, mission-oriented information systems based on the following principles:[5]

1. decentralization of the task of identifying and recording information as it is produced, each participating nation (or region) being responsible for reporting what is produced in its own territory;

2. centralized merging of material reported by the different input centers, the task being performed in an international agency through international financing;

3. output products tailored to the needs of advanced institutions with computer facilities, as well as printed (or microfilmed) indexes and abstracts that can be used by institutions without such facilities, and individual scientists;

4. service for photocopies or microfiches to ensure availability.

---

[5]John E. Woolston, "International Information Systems: Their Relation to Economic and social Development," paper presented at International Symposium on Information systems: Connection and Compatibility, Varna, Bulgaria, Sept. 30-Oct. 3, 1974. (IAEA-SM-189/l) pp. 1-2.

5. products available at low cost and all charges payable in local currencies;

6. international management, based on consultation with all participants;

7. engagement of governments to ensure official support and the availability and infusion of relevant government publications and reports; and

8. utilization of an internationally accepted standard bibliographical format to permit future interconnection among various international information systems.

Thus far, two operational international information systems have built on this model. They are the International Nuclear Information System (INIS) and the International Information System for the Agricultural Sciences (AGRIS). In fact, it was INIS that first developed and refined such a model. Other international information systems which will probably follow the same principles and are in the proposal and planning stages are in such fields as development sciences (DEVSIS), population and demography (IDEMIS or POPINS), science policy (SPINES), industrial technology (UNITIS), informatics (WISI), and architecture and urbanism (ARCHIS).[6] It is entirely possible that under the auspices of an appropriate UN department or agency we can add water resources (WATIS) to the list. The task of setting up an international water resources information system is not unsurmountable in that there already exist a number of well established national focal points in many countries. The extensive machine-readable database now developed by WRSIC and its collaborating agreements with many countries might easily be extended into an international system.

The second is the development of machine-readable bibliographical databases in almost all the major fields of science and technology during the last ten year. As the number and size of these databases have expanded very rapidly, there is a corresponding sharp increase in the number of searches. The increase in use coupled with the improvement made in telecommunication has resulted in a continued reduction in cost per use. This, in turn has further stimulated the use of machine-readable databases by an ever larger number of users. Several important impacts of this development have been observed:

1. more on-line terminals have been established at an increasing number of locations to facilitate the use;

2. more effective communication techniques;

3. improved standardization and cooperation among database producers;

---

[6]DEVSIS, *op. cit.*, p. 38.

167

4. expanded bibliographical services;

5. increased demand for document delivery service, interlibrary loan and photocopying service;

6. greater needs for resources sharing and networking among information systems.

The estimated number and size of databases available through Lockheed's DIALOG and the rates of both the increase in search and the decrease in cost as shown in Table I are astonishing.

Table I. The Growth of Lockheed's DIALOG[7]

Year	No. of Databases	Size of Databases	Rate of Increase in Searches	Rate of Decrease in Cost
1965	1	200,000	---	---
1970	---	---	100	100
1973	11	2,100,000	2,000	40
1975	30	8,000,000	15,000	20

The total number of on-line searches made in the U.S.A., exclusive of OCLC and MARC on-line cataloging uses, is estimated at 270,000 in 1972, 700,000 in 1974, and 1,000,000 in 1975.[8] If the current effort to lower the tariff rate for information transmission is successful, the cost of search will be even cheaper and the use will be expected to increase even more.

The third is the development of large information networks both nationally and internationally to interconnect existing information systems, databases, and computers through telecommunication linkage. Because of advances in computer and telecommunication technologies, the forming of interactive information networks becomes technically and economically feasible. Great advantages can be gained by using communication satellites to link geographically dispersed information systems into a resource-sharing network at a much reduced cost. A recent cost evaluation shows that through the use of communication satellites, the cost of long distance lines

---

[7]Lee G. Burchinal, "Bringing the American Revolution On-Line Information Science and National R & D," *Bulletin of the American Society for Information Science,* V. 2, No. 8 (March 1976), p. 27.

[8]Martha E. Williams, "The Impact of Machine-readable Data Bases on Library and Information Services," *Information Processing and Management,* V. 13, No. 2 (1977), p. 101.

has dropped dramatically. For example, in 1974, a leased voice-grade line from New York to Los Angeles cost $2,200 per month via land links: it now costs only $1,000 per month utilizing a communications satellite link.[9]

By means of information networks, extensive information resources and computer facilities became accessible to more users in wider geographical areas thereby distributing expenses for computer and database operations to a large group of users resulting in sizable cost reduction. Developing countries and some small countries that formerly could not afford to have their own computers and machine-readable databases will now be able to share such resources and facilities with developed countries without incurring high investment costs.

The large national and international information networks now in operation are ARPANET established by the Advanced Research Projects Agency of the U. S. Department of Defense and the Space Documentation Service (SDS) of the European Space Agency. Currently under planning by the Commission of the European Communities is a large multinational and multilingual information network called EURONET, or the European Network.[10] The experience gained from these networks will be very useful to the planning and design of other information networks elsewhere.

With the trend toward development of a national water resources information system in many countries and with the availability of a machine-readable database created by WRSIC, it is possible now that through the spreading of national and international information networks, one can have easy access to the water resources database from many parts of the world. The time is right also for the national water resources information systems to consider the possibility of forming a global information system on water resources based on the INIS model.

---

[9]D.M. Audsley, "One-Line Networking Between Information Centres in Europe," In NATO Advisory Group for Aerospace Research and Development, *National and International Networks of Libraries, Documentation and Information Centres*, papers presented at the Technical Information Panel Specialists' Meeting held in Brussels, Belgium, October 2-3, 1974 (Paris: Unesco, 1975). (NTIS AD-A009 426) pap. 7, p. 6.

[10]John Page, "International STI Networks: Promises and Problems." *Bulletin of the American Society for Information Science*, V. 2, No. 4 (Nov. 1975), p. 12-13.

CHALLENGES FOR THE LIBRARY AND INFORMATION PROFESSION

The thirtieth anniversary marks a major milestone for the Library Association of China. Its many important contributions to the promotion of modern library and information services in the Republic of China (ROC) deserve special recognition and applause. Without the catalyst of the Association, the recent collaboration with the National Central Library to develop a computerized Chinese MARC database and information system which encompass a wide range of programs and activities could not have been accomplished within a short four-year period. Besides the library automation project, the Association has excelled in many other areas such as: legislative action; the development of library standards; the promotion of better library services; the enhancement of library education, training, and research; consultation; international cooperation; publications; etc. This short essay on challenges for librarianship[1] in coming years, with particular reference to the Republic of China, is dedicated as a tribute to the Association on the occasion of its thirtieth anniversary.

Although the year 2000 still seems far away, it is only a short seventeen years from now. If one looks at the long history of librarianship or of our civilization, seventeen years is a brief period indeed. Moreover, with the magnitude and range of changes taking place in our society - the so called "Information Age," one can be sure that the pace and scope of change in library and information services will be even more drastic in the coming years than in the past. It will be fun in the year of 2003 to look back 20 years to see how the profession has progressed at the 50th anniversary of the Association.

The shifting of our society from an industrial base to an information base in the recent past has been depicted in some detail by John Naisbitt in his best seller, *Megatrends*. He advises that "innovations in communications and computer technology will accelerate the pace of change..."[2] One such change with major impact on the future of library and information services is electronic publishing, storage, and dissemination of information. Such a change, although still in its early stage of development, has prompted some highly respected futurists in our profession to predict the early disappearance of printed materials as well as the demise of the libraries as we know them today.

---

[1]The word, "librarianship", is used in its broadest sense to encompass the entire realm of the library and information science profession.

[2]John Naisbitt, *Megatrends: Ten New Directions Transforming Our Lives*, (New York: Warner books, 1982), p. 19.

From this scenario this essay intends to examine the current societal and technological changes that affect librarianship and to suggest a possible strategy for coping with these changes.

Unlike the predictions of Professor F. Wilfrid Lancaster in many of his publications that, with the further development of electronic publishing, the future society will be paperless and that "the library as we now know it - a building housing physical artifacts - will cease to exist...,"[3] this author has another view. It is my belief that, despite the great potential of electronic publishing which will affect our society as well as our profession, information in printed forms will continue to exist into the 21st Century. People will read more as the educational level rises, as work becomes more knowledge-based, and as the quality of life and leisure time further increase. The front page of the September 8, 1983, New York Times carried the headline - **Americans in Electronic Era Are Reading as Much as Ever** - and cited evidence to support the claim. It reported that about 50,000 book titles will be published this year, the most ever, and that book sales, bookstores, library circulation, and newspaper readership are all growing.[4]

Referring to the immortality of libraries, Dr. Richard De Gennaro feels that:

We need to lay to rest the simplistic idea that electronic technology in the hands of information entrepreneurs is going to put an end to libraries. Libraries are here to stay, but by no means are they going to stay the same. Their basic functions will remain, but the ways and means they use to perform those functions will change in varying degrees and at varying speeds for different kinds of libraries in different countries.[5]

Dr. De Gennaro's position has a large following in the profession. As living institutions, libraries adapt to societal and technological changes. "Libraries are becoming more, not less, important in our information society even though their relative share of the total information market is declining," further remarked de Gennaro.[6]

---

[3]F. Wilfrid Lancaster, "Electronic publishing: Its impact on the distribution of information," *National forum, The Phi Kappa Phi Journal*, Vol. LXIII, No. 3 (Summer 1983), p. 5.

[4]Edward Fiske, *New York Times*, 8 September 1983, p. 1.

[5]Richard De Gennaro, "Libraries, Technology, and the Information Market-place," *National Forum, The Phi Kappa Phi Journal*, Vol. LXIII, No. 3 (Summer 1983), p. 31.

[6]Ibid.

For libraries to assume this even greater role in the information society they must prepare themselves for the many challenges that lie ahead. Among these are:

1. The challenge of information explosion and pollution.
2. The challenge of new information technology.
3. The challenge of the changing roles of libraries (and information centers).
4. The challenge of new professional competencies required.
5. The challenge of global interdependence.

Each of the challenges is discussed below, as well as the associated problems and possible strategies for coping with these.

Information Explosion and Pollution

One significant characteristic of an information society is the increasing number of information occupations. According to Naisbitt, in 1950 only about 17% of American workers held information jobs. By 1982, this reached 60%. Most of these workers, be they scientists, researchers, teachers, lawyers, librarians, programmers, secretaries, bankers, clerks, accountants, stock brokers, managers, insurance agents, bureaucrats, etc., spend their time creating, processing, or distributing information. Now, more than ever before, we are experiencing the impact of the information explosion and pollution.[7] For example:

- Between 6,000 and 7,000 scientific articles are written each day.

- Scientific and technical information now increases 13% per year, which means it doubles every 5.5 years.

- But the rate will soon jump to perhaps 40% per year because of new, more powerful information systems and an increasing population of scientists. That means that data will double every 20 months.

- By 1985 the volume of information will be somewhere between 4 and 7 times what it was only a few years earlier.[8]

Such a phenomenal growth of information, unless effectively handled and organized for easy access, will soon drown us in a flood. Uncontrolled information can usefully be considered as trash which pollutes our environment.

---

[7]Naisbitt, *Megatrends*, p. 14.

[8]Ibid., p. 24.

In the case of journal publishing, there were about 1,000 journals in 1850. Today, the number has surpassed 100,000. Each day new journals are born. Managing growing, fast-changing journal publications long has been a headache for the serials librarians, not to mention users. Control of the contents of journals is an even greater problem than the management of the titles. Indexing and abstracting publications created to provide bibliographic control and access to the journal articles have in themselves become too bulky to be handled manually. To keep up with editing and publishing of these indexing and abstracting publications back in the 1960s, many of the publishers began to rely on computers for sorting, composing, and type-setting. A by-product of this was the computerized bibliographic databases which were later made searchable online and thus came the online revolution.

By searching these online databases, users can locate a large number of citations, many of which would otherwise be unknown. However, locating the bibliographic information is still much easier than actually obtaining the publication. This has substantially expanded the work of many libraries and information centers to trace needed information and obtain it for users. The rising cost of publications and limited library budgets mean that no library today can meet all of the needs of its users - especially when such needs have mushroomed through the proliferation of online databases and users who have become aware of the potentialities of new information technology. Cooperative acquisition and collection development, bibliographic control and union listing, interlibrary loan, and resource sharing are some of the necessary means currently employed by libraries in many countries to cope with this situation.

A welcome trend in document delivery in recent years has been the supplying of needed texts by database vendors and others at the time of online search. Orders can be placed online and copies of the texts can be sent by mail. Although the cost may be a little high for average users, with technological advances, it may become a cost-effective, common practice in the foreseeable future. Even online delivery, whether real time or through down loading, is finding a market. Such services, including on-demand publishing - if not, overpriced, can indeed save the libraries and information centers the cost of subscribing to and maintaining large numbers of infrequently used journals and back volumes. This, of course, poses an entirely different set of problems for journal publishers. The wave of this information explosion and pollution is now heading toward the less developed countries. Some of the experiences now sweeping through the U.S.A. will soon reach the Republic of China.

As one of the fastest developing newly industrialized nations in Asia, the Republic of China has enjoyed a high standard of living. Most of the population is educated, skilled, and industrious. Telecommunication systems are well developed. The publishing industry and the book trade are relatively active. Libraries and information centers of all types are in the process of modernization. The recent Government policy in terms of economic development is to transform the national economy from an industrial to a high technology base. Such a transition requires a strong support from the library and information profession. Already, under the leadership of the Library Association of China, in collaboration with the National Central Library, an ambitious Chinese Library Automation Planning Project was launched in 1980 with the following objectives.[9]

1. To develop the Chinese MARC format for the cataloging of Chinese materials.

2. To design an automated library and information system for the processing of library materials.

3. To create databases for Chinese materials and to bring in selected databases from abroad.

4. To establish a national information service center and a network of libraries and information centers to support the needs for national development.

To achieve these objectives is by no means simple, but with the determination, dedication, and cooperation of the library and information workers, many of these have either been realized or are well under way.

New Information Technology

In retrospect, the information explosion of the last two decades was largely responsible for the rapid development of information technology. Much of the advancement in computer technology, electronic technology, and telecommunications has found its way into the information fields through increasing market demands. The creation of large computerized databases, some of which are the by-products of computerized typesetting of indexing and abstracting publications, has made the most noticeable progress. From literature citations, to abstracts, to numeric data, and to the full text of documents; more and more databases of various types are now available for online remote access, thanks to the advancing information technology.

Two important recent developments in computerized databases are the home information service and the document delivery service.

1. Examples of home information service: **Prestel**, the pioneer of home information service in Great Britain is an interactive system made available by the British Post Office in 1979. The system enables home, library, and business users to have access through their television sets,

---

[9]National Central Library, *The Library Automation in the National Central Library, R.O.C.* (Taipei: 1983), p. 1.

modified for videotext, to a variety of computer-based information services for a fee. **CompuServe**, a private system designed for owners of home, business, and office computers is now available in many parts of the United States. CompuServe claims to serve 70,000 customers and to be adding 7,000 new users each month. It provides access to news stories of Associated Press, the Washington Post's Electronic Newsletter, price quotes and trading volume of more than 9000 stocks, Standard & Poor's descriptive and financial information on more than 3000 companies, airline schedules and fares, the Travel America service for making reservations, games, electronic mail, etc. Depending on the time of day, speed of transmission and particular database the cost of each connected hour varies from US$6 to US$15.

2.   Example of document delivery service: The Original Article Text Service (OATS) offered by the Institute for Scientific Information in the United States is one of the many commercial document fulfillment services now available. OATS enables users to order articles online through DIALOG's DIALORDER Service, SDC's ORBDOC, the ISI Search Network, and soon, BRS.

Parallel to the development of computerized databases and their online access is the quiet evolution in electronic publishing. Already many books, journals, and technical publications are typeset by computers with full text stored in disks. Two important future possibilities of electronic publishing are on-demand publishing and electronic delivery.

1.   On-demand publishing. The rising cost in publications, coupled with the information boom, have led some publishers to consider the desirability of on-demand publishing. Storing publishable materials on disks in a central facility and printing only on request is one way to slow proliferation of publications. A variation of on-demand publishing is the electronic journal described by Eugene Garfield as a personalized SDI journal.[10] Manuscripts for such a journal may be written, edited, and refereed through a computer-based network without ever producing a paper copy. The final text will be stored in disks and will be disseminated to subscribers whose interests match the subject matter of the texts.

2.   Electronic delivery. This is a logical extension of electronic publishing - electronically stored full text of any publication, either in full or in part, can be transmitted to requesters or subscribers. In a more recent

---

[10]Eugene Garfield, "ASCAmatic - The Personalized Journal," in his *Essays of an Information Scientist*, Vol. 1 (Philadelphia: ISI Press, 1977), p. 22.

article, Mr. Garfield reported other plans for electronic delivery of full texts currently under consideration:[11]

a) Article Delivery Over Network Information Service (ADONIS). This service has been proposed by a consortium of publishers, including Blackwell, Elsevier, Pergamon Press, Springer, and Academic Press to provide a user with a copy of the needed journal article stored on videodisc. The copy may be sent by mail or a telecommunications channel to a printing facility at the user's location.

b) Automated Retrieval of Text From Europe's Multinational Information Service (ARTEMIS). Proposed by the Commission of the European Communities, the service calls for storing the full text of documents on magnetic tape and transmitting them via telephone lines to computers at printing centers where the full text would be either reproduced and sent through the mail or relayed directly to the requester.

Although both of these systems, among others, are still in the early stages of planning, they point out some of the possible courses of action for electronic document delivery in the future.

In the Republic of China, applications of the new information technologies are rising since overcoming seemingly insurmountable difficulties in inputting and outputting Chinese characters and processing them by computer. The development of Chinese MARC and other computerized databases in Chinese language is well underway. What is needed is a national library and information system which will include the development of a computerized national bibliographic database and network of library and information centers to share online cataloging resources through interlibrary loan, and eventually, document delivery. Existing databases, both domestic and foreign, should be accessible online in all major cities. The development of domestic databases should be coordinated to avoid unnecessary duplication of effort and overlap of coverage. Microcomputers should be used by libraries and information centers for local applications. Care, however, should be taken to assure hardware compatibility, and both hardware and software should support common protocols, and standards[12] to facilitate future interconnection.

---

[11]Eugene Garfield, "Document Delivery-Systems in the Information Age," *National Forum, The Phi Kappa Phi Journal*, Vol. LXIII, No. 3 (Summer 1983), pp. 8-10.

[12]Such as the International Standards Organizations (ISO) open systems interconnection (OSI) - thus the ISO OSI model. A good discussion can be found in Michael Witt, "An Introduction to Layered Protocols," *Byte*, Vol. 8, No. 9 (September 1983), pp. 385-398.

Specialized or mission-oriented libraries and information centers can form their own networks to share resources.

The availability of highly reliable and efficient postal service make document delivery within the ROC by mail the most effective. Electronic mail service can be easily established also, as microcomputers and terminals are becoming widely available in offices and homes. Modern telephone service also makes this and regular telephone communication fast and easy. Telecommunication links with other countries, especially the United States via satellite, are very convenient also. These all combine to provide the ROC with advanced information services from abroad as needed.

Changing Role of Libraries and Information Centers

As dynamic institutions, the role of libraries and information centers changes with time. Change is a process in which an institution rejuvenates itself to meet new demands and challenges. Libraries and information centers, although differing in function and role, share many similarities. Libraries have existed within information centers and information centers can be established within libraries. In the information society, a library and an information center are like a person's two hands. Without being handicapped, each needs the other to do a better job. Regardless of the name, a library or an information center must be capable of performing a variety of functions to meet the wide range of user needs. Public libraries should be an integral part of their community and act as community centers to provide informational, cultural, educational, social, and recreational services. Academic and research libraries should include in their role the preservation and dissemination of scholarly information to expand the frontiers of knowledge. National and state (provincial) libraries should play leadership roles in the promotion of library cooperation and services and in the development of library and information systems and networks. School libraries should be not only the learning resources center but the center of learning. Special libraries and information centers should be providers of managerial and technical information geared to the specific needs of the parent organization. Major centers among these should serve as network and resource nodes in the national system.

In the Republic of China, the change in the roles of libraries and information centers will likely be even more drastic and necessary in the next few years as a result of social and technological transformations. Moreover, libraries and information centers have much catching up to do because of inadequate earlier modernization. The recent surge of computer applications, in varying degrees of sophistication, in many libraries and information centers has helped to shake some old concepts and practices. More and greater changes are still needed to meet the increasing informa- tion demands of a fast developing nation. The Government's policy of fostering the development of high technology in place of labor-intensive industries affords new opportunities for libraries and information centers to fill new roles.

New Professional Competencies

As a result of the information explosion and technological changes which have brought fundamental changes in the library and information profession, there has been concern in recent years about the professional competencies needed for library and information workers in the information age. To prepare future professionals, the following competencies are suggested:

1. The foundations of librarianship (including information science).
2. Subject specialization and language facility.
3. Human relations and communication.
4. Information technology and applications.
5. Management theory and practice.
6. Business knowledge and marketing.
7. Fund raising and grantsmanship.

Depending on the level and variety of responsibilities, not all these competencies need be uniformly required. For example, in large library or information center, there will be a range of positions varying in level and type. Library education should be sufficiently diversified to prepare various library and information workers needed. For top managers, advanced post-graduate, interdisciplinary programs may be needed. For middle- and upper-level professionals the program should be at the graduate level with electives for different specializations. For technical and clerical staff, four- and two-year programs at the undergraduate level should be considered as the minimum. While the emphasis of the undergraduate programs should be aimed at some degree of competency in technical skills, graduate programs focus on fundamentals (i.e., basic values) as advocated by Prof. Herbert White[13] rather than specific applications (i.e., certain skills). Because of rapid changes in technology, most of the latest applications should be given encouragement and high priority by the management. Librarianship, like engineering, cannot afford to neglect continuing education.

In addition to working in the libraries and information centers, new opportunities exist for competent professionals to work as information consultants or specialists in government agencies, business and industrial firms, and other organizations. These consultants, or specialists, can work either independently or in conjunction with other librarians to provide special information service to senior executives, decision-makers, and researchers.

Seeing the opportunity for business ventures, many entrepreneurial library and information professionals have set up private, for profit, offices to sell information

---

[13]Herbert S. White, "Defining Basic Competencies," *American Libraries*, Vol. 14, No. 8 (September 1983), p. 521.

services to institutions, business firms, or others who are in need of information.[14] The education or training of these information entrepreneurs does not differ much from those working in libraries and information centers except, perhaps, for an even greater emphasis on business and marketing.

Extending library education from the undergraduate level to graduate level and widening the curriculum to include information science and other subjects are some of the encouraging trends already underway in the Republic of China. The annual workshops for library support staff sponsored and organized by the Library Association of China have provided much needed educational opportunities for large numbers of para-professionals in library and information centers to acquire or update knowledge and skills for their work. The challenges for library education in ROC in the coming years are many. These may include continued revision of the curriculum to reflect the new emphases and needs in information science, improvement in the quality of instruction and the teaching faculty, recruitment of capable students from a variety of subject backgrounds - especially science and technology, and exploration of new frontiers in the field through interdisciplinary and multidisciplinary research. Library education in the era of information technology should be aimed at educating leaders and innovators rather than at training practitioners and followers.

One of the major obstacle to recruitment is the low status and low pay given library and information professionals. Although this may be seen as a universal problem, solutions to it must be sought from within each country. The establishment of required professional competencies may improve the professional image and attract promising people to the ranks. In the long run, the profession should strive for excellency in its services. Making library and information service indispensable is a certain way to command respect, to positively project the image, and to claim greater rewards.

Global Interdependence

"Knowledge knows no national boundary." This common belief of the scholarly world has gained new life through the development of information technology. By means of satellite communication the geographic distances among nations have shrunk. Online databases are now accessible throughout the world if one can afford the cost, which is seldom totally prohibitive. However, barriers to the free flow of information across national boundaries are still pervasive as countries seek to restrict certain information from others for reason of national security or technological competition. There are other barriers such as high telecommunications tariffs, lack of foreign exchange, inadequate telecommunication facilities, language, etc. The lack

---

[14]See Barbara B. Minor (ed.), *Information Broker/Free-Lance Librarian: - New Careers - New Library Services: Workshop Proceedings.* (Syracuse: School of Information Science, Syracuse University, 1976).

of information, particularly the information needed for national development, has been one of the characteristics of underdeveloped countries. These countries are often referred to as "information poor" countries as distinct from those which are "information rich."

In recent years, several developments have stimulated transborder information flow.

1. World-wide marketing efforts of indexing and abstracting services.

2. Broadening the coverage of many databases to include information from the Third World countries.

3. Availability of online databases from remote access via satellite, regardless of distance.

4. Increasing recognition of the importance of information for national development by developing countries.

5. Concerted efforts by many developing countries to develop a national information infrastructure, with the technical assistance of the United Nations Educational, Scientific and Cultural Organization (Unesco).

6. Development of international cooperative information systems such as the INIS (International Nuclear Information System), AGRIS (International Information System for the Agricultural Sciences and Technology), DEVSIS (Development Sciences Information System), ISDS (International Serials Data System), INDIS (Industrial Development Information System), etc. which encourages the participation of both developed and developing countries to share information among one another.[15]

7. Increasing opportunities for library and information professionals to be educated or trained abroad. International and regional conferences, seminars, short courses, etc. are being held in many parts of the world with large participation from developing countries.

---

[15]For detailed descriptions of these international systems, see *International Cooperative Information Systems: Proceedings of a Seminar Held in Vienna, Austria, 9-13 July 1979* (Ottawa: IDRC, 1980).

8. Development of international standards governing information transfer.[16]

9. Promotion of world-wide programs in Universal Bibliographic Control (UBC) and Universal Availability of Publications (UAP) by IFLA (International Federation of Library Associations and Institutions).

At the Intergovernmental Conference on Scientific and Technological Information for Development (UNISIST II) held in Paris in 1979, the following basic belief was reaffirmed:

Information, the product of the scientific and technological efforts made by the whole of humanity, is an essential resource to which all countries should have free access, and consideration should be given to the way in which scientific and technological information fits into the development process.

The more readily a society can obtain access to abundant and varied information, drawn from worldwide sources, the freer it is to make choices suited to its own style of development and to the goals that it has set.[17]

In moving from industry to high technology, the Republic of China should be strongly interested in exchanges of publications and information with other countries. Efforts by individual libraries and information centers should be encouraged and coordinated wherever appropriate to assure maximum impact. The establishment of Chinese bibliographic databases in MARC format will facilitate the exchange of bibliographic records with other countries. Special information centers should concentrate on selecting, evaluating, and repackaging suitable information for dissemination. Depending on the users, some of the information may be translated into Chinese for wider readership. Collaboration with and contributions to international information systems and major databases to expand coverage of Chinese materials will be mutually beneficial. Many of the specialized regional information resources and databases, such as those established and maintained by the Asian Institute of Technology in Bangkok, Thailand, can serve as models for developing

---

[16]See *ISO Standards Handbook 1: Information Transfer.* [texts of ISO Standards] (Geneva: International Organization for Standardization, 1977).

[17]W. Lohner, "Intergovernmental conference on Scientific and Technological Information for Development (UNISIST II): Main Issues and Results," in *International Cooperative Information Systems: Proceedings of Seminar Held in Vienna, Austria, 9-13 July 1979* (Ottawa: IDRC, 1980), p. 21.

further regional and national databases and information services.[18] Cooperation with these existing databases deserves special consideration.

Although political pressure from Communist China (the People's Republic of China - PRC) has caused many inter-governmental and international agencies to exclude the ROC from participation, Taiwan should not be discouraged by such unfair political tactics. Unofficial contacts with international organizations and participation by individual library and information professionals in international and regional conferences should be increased. The political conduct of the PRC often is self-defeating in international meetings.

****

In conclusion, the author wishes to again extend his congratulations to the Library Association of China on its thirtieth anniversary. As a life member of the Association, I share both the pride in its past accomplishments and the challenges that lie ahead. The Association can be only as good as its members. The challenges described in this essay can be effectively met with the combined wisdom and strength of the Associations membership acting in unison.

---

[18]An autonomous regional institution for postgraduate education in engineering and technology, the Asian Institute of Technology in Bangkok has established four specialized information centers to serve information needs in Asia: the Asian Information Center for Geotechnical Engineering (AGE), the International Ferrocement Information Center (IFIC), the Renewable Energy Resources Information Center (RERIC), and the Environmental Sanitation Information Center (ENSIC).

Section VI

Library Automation

The Information Technology -- New Tools and New
Possibilities for Information Storage, Retrieval
and Dissemination (1973) 187

Recent Breakthroughs in Library Automation in Taiwan (1981) 199

ALICE at One: Candid Reflections on the Adoption,
Installation, and Use of the Virginia Tech Library
System (VTLS) at Ohio University (1984) Co-authors:
K. Mulliner, E. Hoffmann-Pinther, and Hannah McCauley 211

Trends in Automation in American Academic Libraries:
Ohio University's Experiences (1989) 225

THE INFORMATION TECHNOLOGY -- NEW TOOLS AND NEW POSSIBILITIES FOR INFORMATION STORAGE, RETRIEVAL AND DISSEMINATION

Introduction

One of the most pressing problems facing the developing nations in Asia today is the inability of their libraries and information centers to respond effectively and expediently to the wide range of information needs which are required for national development.

It has been observed that there exist two types of "information gap" in Asia. One is the lack of immediate access to the growing body of knowledge accumulated because of the rapid advancement in science and technology. Another is the lack of an effective mechanism to uncover useful indigenous information, to collect it from widely scattered sources, to index it for easy retrieval, and to publicize it for and to disseminate it to the potential users. It is an unfortunate fact that even among the Asian countries themselves, there is very little cooperation and interchange of useful information between the libraries and information centers.

A great deal of human and financial resources have been wasted in Asia as a direct result of these two types of "information gap". The perpetuation of this situation has rendered the works of Asian scientists, research workers, and technical specialists both ineffective and inefficient because of the amount of unnecessary duplication of efforts.

Recognizing such a serious problem, many Asian nations already have taken steps to correct it. This is shown in the findings of a recent Unesco report:[1]

In each country visited there is active interest in the development of scientific and technical information, and plans for improvement of the present system. In Indonesia, a Ford Foundation mission recently advised on the establishment of a national network of science information centres to be coordinated by the National Scientific Documentation Centre, and the Government has requested UNDP consultant services to assist in the actual planning. In Malaysia, a mission was carried out in late 1971 under British Council sponsorship to advise on "Scientific

---

[1]*Report of Unesco Fact-Finding Mission on the Regional Information Network for Science and Technology in Southeast Asia.* 1972. 20 p. (SCP/425/2-25).

and Technical Library and Information Services in Malaysia". In Singapore, there has been no direct follow-up on the 1969 Unesco sponsored "Proposals for the Setting-up of a Scientific and Technical Information Centre", but there is active interest in revising this study to bring it in line with the changing situation in Singapore. In the Philippines, the NSDB is setting up a new National Science Information Centre which will serve as the national coordinating body and as the linkage to regional and international networks or systems. The Government has requested UNDP advisory services in planning the Centre. In Hong Kong the Committee for Scientific Co-ordination has set up a Sub-Committee on Scientific and Technical Information to consider the establishment of a "Centralized Technical Information Service". In Thailand the Thai National Documentation Centre (TNDC) which is already well established is planning further services, and the Asian Institute of Technology has advanced plans for development of a complete information service on a regional level. In all countries the value of regional linkages was recognized and the concept of regional information network in science and technology was strongly supported.[2]

For the social sciences, a comparable study was made by Mr. Erwin Kristoffersen, regional representative of the Friedrich-Ebert-Stiftung which has resulted in a well documented proposal to establish a Clearing House for Social Development in Asia as an effective measure to meet the information needs in the Social Sciences.[3] The study pointed out the serious deficiencies existing in the exchange and dissemination of indigenous information in the social sciences much of which is vital for developmental planning. The following paragraphs are quoted from the findings:

The objective need for an improvement in the exchange of information in the field of social development has often been mentioned, even in such documents as the "Jackson Report", and was discussed along with proposals for the improvement in various official and unofficial meetings.

Interviews during the course of the feasibility study of various institutions further established the fact that the exchange of information was either completely lacking or had considerable gaps within and between agencies and different government departments. Institutes and universities only in a very few cases had regular channels to receive and to disseminate information. Non-governmental agencies and organiza-

---

[2]Ibid., p. 4.

[3]Erwin Kristoffersen, *Clearing House for Social Development in Asia; Project Proposals and Report on the Findings of a Feasibility Study* (Bangkok: Friedrich-Ebert-Stiftung, Bangkok Office, 1972). 35 p.

tions were found to be almost totally excluded from the regular flow of information.

As this was found regarding "official information," a regular exchange of "unofficial information" between the mentioned institutions was not to be found at all.

In certain instances the situation was better on the international level, but worse than expected in respect to regional exchange. Compilation of information was usually undertaken on an ad hoc basis. Mailing lists for the regular dissemination of own material hardly existed.

If the premise is accepted that regional exchange of information is a condition of development promotion the objective need has clearly been established.[4]

In the light of these two studies and the important groundwork they have laid, I would like to direct my talk to the possible tools made available by recent advancements in information technology which can be applied to improve library-information services in the region.

Information Technology

Information technology is a term referring to those technologies which can be applied to library-information work. There are many such technologies available now-a-days. They generally come under one of the following three labels:

1) Reprography
2) Computers
3) Telecommunications

Each of these three actually represents a variety of applications and different degrees of sophistication. They may also work independently or together in a complex information system. Just as with other tools, not all the technologies are suitable for all situations and at all times. It is necessary that I speak only of those technologies which are considered relevant to our particular situation and requirement at the present time. As I am not a technical expert, I speak only as a librarian.

---

[4]Ibid., p. 14.

Reprography

Despite the fact that "Reprography" is a relatively new term, this technology is already under widespread use by many libraries and information centers in Southeast Asia. Unlike the newness of the name, reprography consists of many not-too-new techniques such as microfilming and various methods of copying and duplicating.

The techniques of reprography are very important for the developing countries in that:

1) they enable a wider dissemination of information some of which might not be available or accessible otherwise;

2) they have made it possible for libraries and information centers to interchange reproduced information;

3) various microforms are by far the most economic means for information storage and for dissemination to distant places by mail; and

4) the computer-output-microforms (COM) reduces the problem of storage and dissemination for the large amount of computer generated data.

Computers

Although the use of computers in library-information work has found wide acceptance throughout the world, it has just begun in Southeast Asia. The computer is a very promising tool in that it has the power and versatility to process data with high speed and precision. The main obstacles standing in the way of wider application by libraries and information centers in Asia are the factors of high cost, especially in the initial stage, and the lack of trained staff. These two obstacles can be overcome by setting up either national data processing centers within each country or multinational (or regional) data processing centers within a number of cooperating countries. The former can be affiliated with either the national library, the national documentation center, an institutional library or a special information center, whichever has the computer capability. The latter can be attached to a regional or international organization that is so equipped.

The essence of this setup is to share the costs of both owning or sharing a computer system and developing the software necessary for its support, and pooling together the trained personnel. By means of this arrangement, even small libraries and information centers can have the benefit of sharing a computer with large libraries and information centers. The work which can be best handled by such data processing centers would be:

1)   Establish and maintain a national (or regional) data bank on indigenous publications. A by-product of this data bank is the publication of national (or regional) bibliographies.

2)   Establish and maintain a national (or regional) data bank on major library collections in the country (or region). A by-product of this data bank is the publication of a national (or regional) union catalog and separate book catalogs for each participating library or information center.

3)   Establish and maintain a national (or regional) data bank on periodicals and serial publications held by major libraries and information centers in the country (or the region). A by-product of this data bank is the publication of a union list of periodicals and serials and separate lists of holdings for each participating library or information center.

4)   Establish and maintain a national (or regional) data bank for scientific and technical literature of relevance to the country (or the region). A by-product of this data bank is the publication at regular intervals of abstracting journals. A score of other services such as SDI service, current awareness service, and retrospective search of the data file can also be performed.

5)   Establish and maintain a national (or regional) data bank on such vital information as census data, demographic data, land use data, hydrological and meteorological data, inventories of communications and transportation, industrial and housing facilities, geological and natural resources, etc., and relevant economic and sociological data.

6)   Act as a national (or regional) processing center for the acquisitions, cataloging, and processing of books, journals and other materials for the libraries and information centers that want to participate in such labor-and cost-saving operations. There are a wide range of activities that can be channeled through such a central processing service.

7)   The center may also consider the possibility of acquiring the MARC (Machine-Readable Cataloging) tapes of both the U.S. Library of Congress and the British National Bibliography for local storage and manipulation.

Arrangements may also be made to obtain the machine-readable database of MEDLARS (Medical Literature Analysis and Retrieval System of the National Library of Medicine, U.S.A.), CAIN (Cataloging and Indexing System of the National Agricultural Library, U.S.A.), ERIC (Educational Resources Information Center) tapes, etc. for local storage and manipulation.

Because of the high cost of leasing some of the commercially produced databases such as the *Chemical Abstracts*, the *Engineering Index*, the *Historical Abstracts*, the *Psychological Abstracts*, etc., it may not be financially feasible for national centers to invest a large portion of their funds to acquire or lease these databases except when there is a particular need for having any one of them.

8) Develop a library of computer programs for various library-information work including programs for automatic indexing, photocomposition, etc.

9) Provide consulting services to other libraries or information centers who are interested in establishing their own computer operations.

10) Provide various computer services to individual or special library-information projects.

11) Conduct short courses, seminars and workshops for the training and up-grading of librarians and information scientists in the use of computer and other information technology for library-information work.

Telecommunications

Telecommunications is an important part of the new information technology which holds great promise for improving library-information services in Asia.

An effort has been made by the United Nations Economic Commission for Asia and the Far East (ECAFE) to make the countries of Asia into an "Asian Telecommunity". The program intends to develop in every Asian country a telecommunication network and to link the various national networks from Iran to Indonesia by a system of modern communication services provided at the most economical rates. When fully realized, it will undoubtedly accelerate the interchange of information among the libraries and information centers in the region by making possible information transmission and facsimile reproduction at high speed and at low cost. It will also facilitate the development of national library-information systems and regional library-information networks similar to those systems and networks already in operation in many parts of the world. One such example is the ESRO system which was reported in a recent article by Isotta.[5]

ESRO system is the information system for the Space Documentation Service of the European Space Research Organization located in Darmstadt, Germany. The

---

[5]N.E.C. Isotta, "International Information Networks: 1. The ESRO System." *Aslib Proceedings*, V. 24 No. 1 (January 1972) pp. 31-7.

ESRO system was designed on the concept of a centralized file maintenance and software responsibility, coupled with decentralized searching of the files by remote terminals sited in the member states. The total configuration (Figure 1) consists of the central computer facility in Darmstadt, together with its own local terminal; a single leased line to Paris where two terminals are installed; a party-line connection from Paris to St. Mary Cray in Kent where a terminal is installed at the Technology Reports Centre; a party-line connection from Paris to Bretigny, where a terminal is installed at the Centre Nationale D'Etudes Spatiale; a terminal in the ESRO establishment in Noordwijk, Holland; and another terminal in the ESRO establishment in Frascati near Rome.[6]

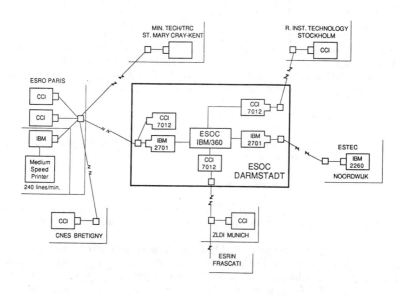

Figure 1
First European Network for the Dissemination of
Scientific and Technical Information

This type of system can be adopted in Asia if the "Asian Telecommunity" becomes a reality and the cost of telecommunications is substantially reduced.

---

[6]Ibid., p. 33.

193

Another important recent development in telecommunications which has an encouraging implication for Asia is the ability to transmit information among widely dispersed points of the world via satellites. The capability of communication satellites to transmit voice, teletype and facsimile signals to a distant place at the speed of light has a distinct advantage over other communication media for inter-continental communications. An interconnection of computers, telephones, teletypes and communication satellites can provide a most effective network of national, regional and world information systems.

A highly sophisticated network system which saw the interfacing of all these was demonstrated recently at the 35th annual meeting of the American Society for Information Science held in Washington, D.C. on October 23-26, 1972. The system demonstrated was called "International Information Retrieval Network". Through the several on-line terminals located on the conference grounds, participants of the annual meeting were able to query not just the many databases on computers located several hundred miles away in different parts of the U.S.A. but also the data files of the ESRO in Darmstadt, Germany via the INTELSAT IV communication satellite. The demonstration featured several recent innovations, including:

1)   International communications via satellite.
2)   Remote video and printing terminals.
3)   On-line, interactive retrieval systems using both natural-text and index-based techniques.
4)   Networking.
5)   Access to multiple databases.

The demonstration showed that international networks are technologically feasible, economically conceivable, and usable with minimal instruction.[7]

Another less sophisticated but operating system using only teletype machines and the INTELSAT IV F-2 satellite is the satellite linkage between John Crerar Library (JCL) in Chicago, U.S.A. and Consejo Nacional de Investigaciones Cientificas y Tecnicas (C.N.I.C.T.) in Buenos Aires, Argentina. The basis of the system consists of some fourteen technical libraries in Argentina, which are linked by Telex to each other and to C.N.I.C.T. in Buenos Aires. When an institution cannot fill its needs from its own collection, a message is sent to C.N.I.C.T. which then attempts to locate the needed item in one of the other libraries by use of the Union Lists and catalogs. If this is unsuccessful, the request is then transmitted to JCL and the latter provides

---

[7]From "A World of Information", the program of the 35th annual meeting of ASIS. p.8.

microfilm copy by return airmail. The costs of photocopies and the relay messages are borne by the National Academy of Sciences in the U.S.[8]

The JCL/C.N.I.C.T. system is a good example of what the developing countries can do to obtain the needed information from developed countries. Financial assistance of this kind is probably available from many international or foreign aid organizations.

AIT's Plans

As a regional institution for advanced engineering education and research, the Asian Institute of Technology (AIT) is deeply involved in the technical development of the Asian region and it is this involvement which has led AIT to an awareness of the urgent needs of Asian engineers for relevant information. To meet this need AIT has devoted a large portion of its resources to develop an outstanding library and information center within the Institute. Steps have been taken to expand this facility into a regional library and information center for engineering and related fields, embracing the collection, organization and dissemination of useful technical information. The recently founded Asian Information Center for Geotechnical Engineering, under the joint sponsorship of the AIT Division of Geotechnical Engineering and the Library, is an example of one such endeavor.

To improve library-information service in the region, especially in the application of the latest information technology, AIT is in a very unique position. We are now in the process of undertaking three major steps which, if successful, will undoubtedly have a far reaching effect on the development of a regional library-information network. These steps are (1) expanding computerized library-information service with a regional outlook, (2) establishing the Asian Information Center for Geotechnical Engineering, and (3) planning for an information transfer experiment via satellite between AIT and the Knowledge Availability Systems Center (KASC) of the University of Pittsburgh.

1)   Expanding computerized library-information service:

Within the next six months, a very large computer system (CDC 3600) will be installed at AIT to replace the currently overloaded IBM 1130. With the massive memory and the fast printing capabilities of a CDC computer system, we plan to greatly expand our present computerized library operations.

As a part of this plan, we have requested and received approval from the Government of the United Kingdom to provide us with a library systems

---

[8]From the letter of William S. Budington, Executive Director and Librarian of the John Crerar Library dated August 30, 1971.

analyst to help us in the planning and implementing of our expanded computer applications. This specialist is from the University of Birmingham and will join AIT Library in September. For the last six years, this specialist has been actively working with the Birmingham Libraries' Cooperative Mechanization Project which utilizes MARC records in three libraries (Aston and Birmingham Universities, and the Birmingham Public Libraries) on a cooperative basis. Work of the Project has been reported regularly in Program.[9] We hope that with the background of this specialist on library cooperative mechanization, many of our new programs will have a broader perspective and regional outlook and will tie in with the regional library-information network development.

2) Establishing the Asian Information Center for Geotechnical Engineering (AGE):

To experiment with the setting up of a regional library-information service, we have selected a very important but highly specialized field -- Geotechnical Engineering, as our pilot project. The idea of establishing AGE was conceived at the meeting of representatives of national societies of soil mechanics and foundation engineering in the Asian region which convened in Bangkok in July 1971. Through one of the resolutions of the meeting, AIT was requested to undertake the task of establishing and operating AGE for the benefit of engineers in Asia. The importance of this undertaking was recognized through a grant awarded by the International Development Research Centre of Canada to partially support the activities of the Center for the initial three-year period.

Serving as a clearing House in Asia for information on all phases of Geotechnical Engineering such as soil mechanics, foundation engineering, engineering geology, rock mechanics, earthquake engineering and other related fields. The Center will undertake the responsibility to collect all relevant information and data useful to the region, to design a computer--based information storage and retrieval system, to disseminate such information through its publications and photocopying and microfilming services, and to provide the three-R service (reference, referral and reproduction).

The detailed information concerning the data files, the publications, and the services of the Center are contained in an introductory brochure published by the Center.[10]

---

[9]Most recent report of the Project is: E.H.C. Driver, D.G.R. Buckle, S.W. Massil, D.J.Wilkins & A.R. Hall, "The Birmingham Libraries' Cooperative Mechanization Project: Progress Report, June 1970-January 1972," *Program: News of Commuters in Libraries*, V. 6, No. 2 (April 1972) pp. 120-6.

[10]*Introducing Asian Information Center for Geotechnical Engineering* (Bangkok, Asian Institute of Technology, 1973). 9 p.

3)	Planning for an information transfer experiment via satellite between AIT and the Knowledge Availability Systems Center of the University of Pittsburgh:

This experiment which is now being planned is patterned after both the ESRO system and the JCL/C.N.I.C.T. system already described. The Knowledge Availability Systems Center (KASC) is one of the six NASA Regional Dissemination Centers in the U.S. Under the directorship of Professor Allen Kent who is also the Chairman of the Department of Information Science at the University of Pittsburgh, KASC has not only the expertise in information/-computer/communications areas but also the immediate access to almost every important computerized database in science and engineering. The linkage to KASC via satellite will be a great advantage for both the AIT and the region in that we will have remote, immediate access to the many computerized databases which are vital to our information requirement and yet, too expensive for us to own. It is our plan that subsequent arrangements will be made with all parties concerned to supply information drawn from KASC through AIT to other libraries and information centers in the region. This sounds so much like a dream, but it is not far from reality.

Concluding Remarks

This paper only has scratched the surface of several recent developments which will have an important effect on the overall improvement of library-information service in the region. The advancement of information technology has definitely offered excellent possibilities for rapid improvement. It is of prime importance that the libraries and information centers in Asia will take full advantage of this development to close the "information gap" existing between the developed world and the developing world and to become a true partner in national and regional development.

Vigorous efforts should be given by all those who are concerned with the improvement of library-information service in the region to carry out the two-phase project proposed by the Unesco Fact-Finding Mission:[11]

The first phase emphasizes (1) reinforcing national centres, (2) training information specialists, (3) training users of scientific and technical information, (4) improving and extending national information services, and (5) introducing the necessary compatibility elements and links between the national information centres.

The second phase constitutes the actual establishment of formal linkages between the centres into an operational regional network.

---

[11]Unesco, *op.cit.*, p. 1.

It is felt however that the regional network to be established should not be restricted to only scientific and technical information. Instead, it should link the major libraries and information centers in all subjects including the social sciences. The libraries and information centers of the group of international organizations and agencies in the region constitute a very important resource in the social sciences. These information resources plus the proposed Clearing House for Social Development in Asia should not be left out of the regional network.

As far as AIT is concerned, as a regional institution committed to the development of Asia, we shall do whatever is possible to work for the early realization of the second phase of the project.

RECENT BREAKTHROUGHS IN
LIBRARY AUTOMATION IN TAIWAN

Introduction

The utilization of computers for bibliographical control, information database management, and other library operations in Taiwan although not begun until 1973 has made remarkable progress within a relatively short span of time. Most significant of this development is the ability now to process materials and publications in Chinese scripts along with those in Roman alphabets. This major breakthrough in Chinese library automation was revealed recently at the International Workshop on Chinese Library Automation held in Taipei from February 14 to 19, 1981. The workshop, under the joint sponsorship of the Library Association of China (Taiwan), the American Council of Learned Societies, and the Republic of China Committee for Scientific and Scholarly Cooperation with the U.S., attracted over 220 participants including 40 from such countries and territories as Australia, Belgium, Hong Kong, Japan, South Korea, Singapore, and the U.S.A. Representatives from the Library of Congress, the OCLC Online Computer Library Center, the Research Libraries Group (RLG), Washington Library Network (WLN), and several major East Asian libraries (Harvard, Hawaii, Indiana, Rutgers, Washington, and Yale) were among the American contingent.

Main Purposes of the Workshop

As stated in his opening address, His Excellency C.K. Yen, former President of the Republic of China, pointed out the three main purposes of the workshop:

1. To report and review the recent accomplishments in library automation in Taiwan.

2. to seek advice on the refinement of these initial achievements, and

3. to explore the possibility for international cooperation.

Guided by these goals, the workshop was divided into four consecutive sessions, each consisting of a number of papers.

Session I.   The Chinese Language and Computers (Chaired by Dr. Shih-Chien Yang, Dr. Ching-Chun Hsieh, Dr. Chen-Chau Yang, and Mr. Karl Lo).

Session II.   Chinese Cataloging Rules and the Chinese MARC (Chaired by Mr. James E. Agenbroad, Mr. John T. Ma, and Dr, Nelson Chou)

Session III.   Library Automation Case Studies (Chaired by Dr. Tung-Sheng Fang, Dr. Hwa-wei Lee, and Ms. Barbara Roland).

Session IV.   International Cooperation for Library Automation (Chaired by Mr. Eugene Wu, Dr, Robert M. Hayes, Ms. Margaret Chang Fung)

The following is a list of papers delivered at the workshop (papers by Taiwan participants identified by an asterisk) in the order of presentation:

*"The design of the Chinese Character Code for Information Interchange-CCCII," by C.C. Hsieh, K.T. Huang, C.T. Chang, and C.C. Yang.

*"The design of a cross-reference database for Chinese character indexing," by C.C. Yang, K.T. Huang, C.T. Chang, and C.C. Hsieh.

"Requirements definition for East Asian character support enhancements to Research Libraries Information Network," by John Haeger.

"Personal names and the Chinese Character Code for Information Interchange, volume 1 (CCCII/1) - Adequacy and implications," by James E. Agenbroad.

*"The establishment of hsing-fu-writing and consideration for the Chinese language's input method," by T.Y. Kiang and T.H. Cheng.

*"On the application of the basic component set of Chinese characters," S. Lin.

*"Discussion on the arrangement of characters used in computers from the viewpoint of Chinese character structure and evolutionary changes," by H.T. Li and C.F. Chow.

*"A survey of various forms of Chinese characters," by C.K. Pan.

*"Discussion on hsing-mu in Chinese computers," by H.H. Chin and Y.S. Ho.

*"A comparative study of Romanization systems for the Chinese language," by T.J. Liu.

*"Study on the phonetics of characters used in computers," by J.C. Lin and H. Chou.

*"An introduction to a modified system of Chinese Romanization (named Huarwern,) by Shir-Jen Jang.

"Information, computer and Chinese language," by Nelson Chou.

*"Chinese Cataloging Rules - A draft," by C.C. Lan, Working Group on Chinese Cataloging Rules.

"The use of the Chinese MARC in North American Libraries," by Karl Lo.

*"Chinese MARC: Its present status and future development," by Lucy T.C. Lee, Working Group on Chinese MARC.

"Automated library networking: Possibilities for international cooperation," by Raymond DeBuse.

"The application of computer in Chinese information systems; a general survey," by T.S. Fang.

*"The Union List of Chinese Serials in the Republic of China: A case report," by Rui-Lan Ku Wu.

*"The preliminary plan for the Index to Chinese Periodical Literature: A case report," by Rui-Lan Ku Wu.

200

*"The Agricultural Science and Technology Management System," by Wan-Jiun Wu.

*"Computer-microfilm retrieval system used for processing Chinese character criminal data in R.O.C.," by Yung-Liang Loh.

*"Freedom Council Information Abstract," by Jack K.T. Huang.

*"The Chinese Education Resources Information System," by Margaret C. Fung.

"International cooperation in library automation," by Henriette D. Avram and Lenore S. Maruyama.

"International cooperation in Chinese library automation: An American perspective," by Hideo Kaneko.

"Library automation for Chinese collections in Western Europe: Potentials and problems," by John T. Ma.

"A sketch for a computerized national library and information network," by Hwa-Wei Lee.

"The development of Japan/MARC and Chinese character sets," by Tokutaro Takahashi and Toshikazu Kanaka.

Major Accomplishments Highlighted

Most important among these papers were the ones presented by participants from Taiwan which describe in detail the following major accomplishments in Chinese library automation:

1. The development of various Chinese computer input and output devices and the design of a comprehensive cross-reference index of varying coding systems for Chinese characters.

2. The compilation of a "Chinese Character Code for Information Inter-Change" (CCCII).

3. The complete revision of the Chinese Cataloging Rules (CCR).

4. The adoption of the "Chinese MARC Format" and development of a prototype online cataloging system.

It was astonishing to note that, through the cooperative efforts of a group of determined and dedicated librarians, computer and information scientists, and philologists in Taiwan, so much was accomplished in a record time of eight months! The three working groups which were responsible for much of the success are the Chinese Character Analyses Group, the Chinese Cataloging Rules Working Group, and the Chinese MARC Working Group. All three were founded to carry out the National Library Automation Plan (NLAP) under the direction of the Library Automation Planning Committee (LAPC) which was established jointly by the Library Association of China and the National Central Library (NCL) in early 1980. The following briefly highlight the major accomplishments revealed at the workshop:

The development of various Chinese computer input and output devices and the design of a comprehensive cross-reference index of varying coding systems for Chinese characters.

Because of the complexity of the Chinese language and the large number of Chinese characters any computer system must deal with in processing, a variety of input and output devices has been developed by different organizations, computer companies, and vendors in Taiwan with the advice and assistance of many specialists in philology and computer science. Besides the several research papers focusing on the various approaches and/or problems in processing Chinese language materials that were presented at the workshop, at least 14 computer companies and vendors exhibited their Chinese input and output devices. Two of the companies: R.P.T. Intergroups International Ltd. and the Taiwan Automation Company, also displayed their prototype online Chinese MARC systems which were developed for the Chinese MARC Working Group. As observed, no attempt has been made as yet at this point of development to standardize the Chinese input and output devices since none is considered perfect. The keen competition among the computer firms in the development of a most efficient and cost-effective input and output device for the processing of Chinese language data is a very healthy thing, at least for the time being.

In coping with the various coding systems for computer input of Chinese characters, the design of a comprehensive cross reference index of these systems becomes very necessary in order to provide an effective means for identifying, finding or addressing a Chinese character by whatever coding system employed in computer input, be it based on radical, stroke count, stroke sequence, component expression (or radical expression), phonetic codes (such as kou-yu, Wade-Giles, Yale, pinyin, and Liu), telegraph code, three-corner code, four-corner code, or any one of the internal codes of various Chinese data processing systems.

Figure 1 is a block diagram of the cross-reference database for Chinese character indexing being developed by the Chinese Character Analysis Group which consists of many top philologists, librarians, and computer scientists in Taiwan. The four most active leaders of the Group are: Professors Chung-Tao Chang, Ching-Chun Hsieh, Jack Kai-Tung Huang, and Chen-Chau Yang. The database, when completed, will not only facilitate code conversions and cross-referencing but will also serve as an aid to further studies of Chinese characters.

The compilation of a "Chinese Character Code for Information Interchange"

This project which was also carried out by the Chinese Character Analysis Group is probably one of the most important undertakings in the scientific analysis of the Chinese language in recent time by a team of over 200 specialists. The task of designing CCCII consisted of two major efforts: first, to construct a code structure which can accommodate all known Chinese characters and second, to organize and

202

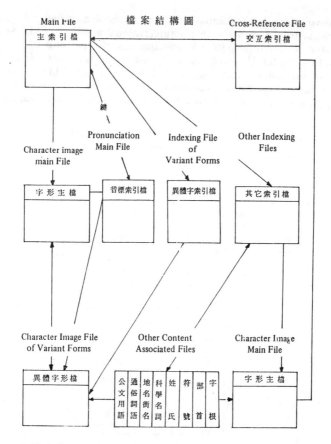

Figure 1. Block diagram of the cross-reference database for Chinese character indexing.

group them according to the code structure. So far, more than 30,000 Chinese characters, including 4,807 most commonly used ones; 16,197 less commonly used ones; and some 10,793 variant forms, have been identified, grouped and coded. It is of significance to note that the application of the Code is not confined to traditional forms of characters being used in Taiwan, Hong Kong and the overseas Chinese communities. Rather, it is also applicable to the simplified characters adopted in the Chinese mainland and Singapore and the Chinese characters in circulation in Japan and Korea. More will be added, as we were told, in the next two or three years to include languages of ethnic minorities such as Manchurian, Mongolian, Arabic and Tibetan as well as other rarely used characters. When this is done, the total number of coded Chinese characters may exceed 80,000.

To achieve international compatibility for information exchange the Code was designed in complete accordance with the international standards of ISO-646 (7-bit Coded Character Set for Information Processing Interchange) and ISO-2022 (Code Extension Techniques for Use with the ISO-7-bit Coded Character Set). Figure 2 shows the three-dimensional structure of CCCII. In it, each Chinese character is identified by a three 7-bit bytes. Vertically, the three-dimensional code structure consists of 94 planes. Horizontally, each plane has 94 sections and each section has 94 positions.

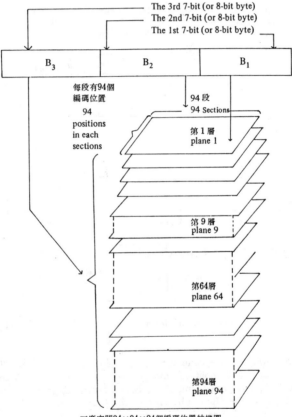

三度空間94×94×94個編碼位置結構圖
The 3-Dimensional structure of the whole 94×94×94 code

Figure 2. Three-dimensional structure of CCCII.

204

Of the first two published volumes of the Code (volume 2 is in two parts) the first volume, which represents plane one, consists of 4,807 most frequently used Chinese characters; 35 Chinese punctuation marks; 214 radicals; 41 Chinese numerical character; 37 Chinese phonetic symbols; and 4 tonal marks. The Chinese characters are arranged first according to the Kang Hsi radical sequence and then by stroke-count. Characters with the same radical sequence and stroke count are sub-arranged by stroke-order. The precedence of strokes is in descending order, is: 1) a dot; 2) a horizontal stroke; 3) a vertical stroke; 4) a stroke down to the left; and 5) a stroke down to the right.

The second volume of the Code is published in two parts. The first part consists of a revision of volume 1 with the addition of 16,197 less frequently used characters. The second part consists of 10,793 variant forms of Chinese characters.

Having variant forms is quite common to many Chinese characters. Usually many of the variant forms of a character have exactly the same pronunciation and meaning but differ in their stroke image. Although often interchangeable in writing, when used to name a person, place or thing, they are considered as different characters. In CCCII, the codes assigned to the variant forms of a character are designed to have identical two right-most bytes. In this way, the variant forms of a character are placed at the same section and same position but in different planes, below the normal form. This arrangement makes it easy to identify the variant forms of a character. An example of variant forms is shown in Figure 3.

The complete revision of the Chinese Cataloging Rules.

Taking over the work already begun by the Cataloging Committee of the Library Association of China, the Chinese Cataloging Rules Working Group, in May of 1980, began its task of revising the 1965 NCL Cataloging Rules for Books in Chinese. Under the leadership of Professor Chien-Chang Lan, the Group adopted the following guidelines for the development of the new rules:

1. The rules should be applicable to all types of publications, including print and non-print materials. The contents should range widely enough to meet the need of libraries, information centers, and any other institutions, and can be used in book catalogs, card catalogs, or machine-readable catalogs.

2. Description should based on the International Standard Bibliographic Description (ISBD).

3. The feasible part of the NCL cataloging rules should be retained; domestic circumstances and cultural tradition, be taken into consideration.

4. Merits of AACR2 (Anglo-American Cataloging Rules, second edition) and Nippon Cataloging Rules should be adopted.

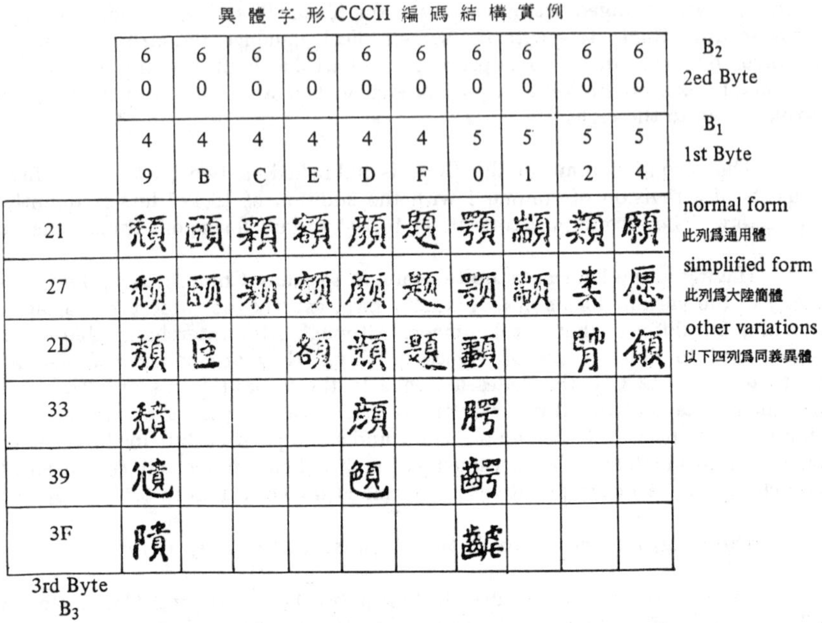

異 體 字 形 CCCII 編 碼 結 構 實 例

	6 0	6 0	6 0	6 0	6 0	6 0	6 0	6 0	6 0	6 0	B_2 2ed Byte
	4 9	4 B	4 C	4 E	4 D	4 F	5 0	5 1	5 2	5 4	B_1 1st Byte
21	頏	頤	頛	頷	顏	題	顎	顫	類	願	normal form 此列爲通用體
27	颃	颐	颎	颔	颜	题	颚	颤	类	愿	simplified form 此列爲大陸簡體
2D	頯	臣		額	顂	題	顥		臂	頌	other variations 以下四列爲同義異體
33	頹				顔		腭				
39	憤				䫫		齶				
3F	隕						齾				

3rd Byte
B_3

Figure 3. Example of the table of variant forms and associated CCCII codes.

5. UNIMARC (Universal Machine-Readable Cataloging) should be consulted to make the rules applicable to library automation.

Immediately after the guidelines were set the Group went on to translate the AACR2 and the Nippon Cataloging Rules (1978 preliminary edition) into Chinese. This was followed by a drafting of rules and collecting of examples. By the end of 1980, the Group had completed the chapters on general rules and the description of books.

The adoption of the "Chinese MARC Format' and the development of a prototype online cataloging system.

This two-pronged project which was also completed in a record time of eight months was carried out by the Chinese MARC Working Group under the leadership of Professor Lucy T.C. Lee. Aimed at facilitating international exchange and sharing of bibliographic information in machine-readable form the Chinese MARC Format follows closely the design and format of the UNIMARC and LC MARC II with only minor modifications necessary for the cataloging of Chinese materials.

In consideration of the needs of the non-Chinese speaking user and library environment, several major fields, such as title proper, statement of responsibility, physical descriptions, series, subject, etc., are designed in such a way that they can be recorded and searched in Chinese, English, or Wade-Giles romanization which is adopted as the standard transliteration. Some of the modifications and the reasons for doing so are given below:

1. Adding subfield identifier "$r" to the fields of 200, 225, and 5xx in order to make title proper and series title accessible by romanization. This provision is mainly for libraries abroad since very few libraries in Taiwan would have the need to access bibliographic records by their transliterations.

2. Adding subfield identifier "$u" to fields 3xx for libraries which use cataloging rules other than the Chinese Cataloging Rules to record notes in Chinese, English, or romanization.

3. Assigning subfield identifier "$g" to fields 600, 700, 701, and 702 to identify the dynastic era during which a Chinese individual lived either in the Ch'ing dynasty or earlier. The association of a personal name with the name of a dynasty when he lived is a ling observed tradition in Chinese bibliography and scholarship.

4. The UNIMARC undefined indicators are assigned new functions in Chinese MARC in the fields of 215 and 225. (e.g., physical description and series).

5. Field 501 (collective uniform title) and field 503 (uniform convention headings) which are not used in Chinese MARC are reserved in the Format with an asterisk * for libraries adopting cataloging rules other than the Chinese Cataloging Rules.

The published Chinese MARC Format which was distributed at the workshop consists of two parts. Part one has four sections which explain the scope, the application, the definition of terms, and the structure of the communication format. Part two includes appendices for catalog card format, tape format, character set, Wade-Giles romanization system, etc.

In the development of a prototype online cataloging system the Working Group had the cooperation and support of two computer companies: R.P.T. Intergroups International Ltd. (Wang VS Model English/Chinese Computer) and the Taiwan Automation Company (CCRT 280 System), each developed a pilot system using the same 1,100 bibliographic records selected by the Group from the Chinese National

207

Bibliography, the National Union Catalog of the Library of Congress, and the library catalog of the National Taiwan University. At the demonstration of the two online Chinese MARC systems during the workshop, the following operations were shown:

1. Computer-produced pages of the *Chinese National Bibliography*.

2. Computer-produced catalog cards.

3. Online display of Chinese bibliographic records.

4. Online query and search functions including input, update, delete, modify, search.

It was announced that beginning immediately all newly acquired titles of the National Central Library will be input into the database. This will be joined by seven large libraries later in a shared cataloging mode. The distribution of catalog cards on the new format is scheduled for October 1981 and the test tapes, in 1982. The timetable may seem ambitious, but--if the past offers any indication--nothing is impossible!

Conclusion

The workshop was a great success judging from its superior planning, organization, programming, and most important of all, its substance. Without any doubt, a great deal of effort was put into the workshop by a large number of dedicated individuals. Most important among them are Professor Chen-Ku Wang, Director of the National Central Library; Mrs. Margaret Chang Fung, Director of the National Taiwan Normal University Library; and Professor Jack Kai-Tung Huang, Director of the Department of Computer Science, Ming-Chuan College. Many foreign participants, including even those who are familiar with library development in Taiwan, were surprised and impressed by the recent accomplishments in Chinese library automation. The purposefulness, determination, and team spirit of the Chinese librarians in Taiwan, together with the cooperation and support of computer scientists and philologists, were truly admirable and applaudable. It is obvious that additional work is needed to further refine some of the accomplishments and to continue the unfinished tasks. Such efforts will bring about even greater success in the years to come.

With regard to international cooperation, the sincerity and willingness of the libraries and librarians in Taiwan to share the fruits of their labor with others deserves special mention. The continued development of Chinese computer input and output devices and the plan of the National Central Library to produce and make available Chinese MARC records, both current and retrospective, will be of great value to every library with a Chinese or East Asian collection. The prospect for international cooperation in the sharing of Chinese MARC records has drawn closer the day when one can search bibliographic records in Chinese scripts through a terminal linked to a database of a major bibliographic utility in any part of the world.

ALICE AT ONE:
CANDID REFLECTIONS ON THE ADOPTION, INSTALLATION, AND USE OF THE VIRGINIA TECH LIBRARY SYSTEM (VTLS) AT OHIO UNIVERSITY

Co-Authors: K. Mulliner, E. Hoffmann-Pinther,
And Hannah McCauley

This report presents a mixed picture. In describing the accomplishments and disappointments in using a to-be-integrated library system, we hope that our experiences will interest and benefit others who are just embarking on the treacherous path of library automation. If we focus on the problems and possibilities encountered, it is because we think that these may be of greatest value. Today numerous publications offer detailed guides as to how to acquire and implement an integrated library system. We won't recapitulate these but rather will try to shed some light on what occurs when theory meets practice or when the irresistible ideal encounters immovable realities. Despite what follows, we are very pleased with our choice of the Virginia Tech Library System (VTLS), both in terms of services provided to our library users and our relationships with the vendors.

Background

Although the activities which culminated in our present use of VTLS began in 1978, our membership dating from more than a decade before in the then Ohio College Library Center (OCLC) greatly shaped our deliberations. On August 26, 1971, Ohio University was the first member institution to input, online, a record into the OCLC database [never mind that the system immediately crashed]. Twelve years later, on October 11, 1983, Ohio University Libraries input the first record into the national online union catalog of its second ten million records (no. 10000001). As a result of this long standing commitment to entering our holdings in machine readable form and into the OCLC database, our attention was directed toward a system which would utilize these existing records.

Like many other academic libraries during the 1970s, particularly those in Ohio, we anticipated and awaited the development of subsystems by OCLC to handle acquisitions, circulation, serials control, interlibrary loans, etc. which would build on the successful online national network for shared cataloging. Although, after several delays, the highly successful interlibrary loan subsystem became a reality in 1978, the other subsystems were postponed or only partially implemented.

By 1978, the increasing capabilities and decreasing costs of minicomputers led many libraries to develop library systems at the local or regional levels which utilized the machine-readable cataloging records created for the OCLC database. It was widely recognized that circulation and online public access catalogs were prime candidates for such an undertaking. At this same time, many "turnkey" systems developed by commercial firms were introduced.

Within this environment, OCLC's failure to negotiate an agreement with GEAC and its on-again, off-again approach to developing circulation and online public access catalog subsystems induced Ohio University to explore alterative solutions. As the founders of OCLC, libraries in Ohio tended to look to OCLC for answers to automation needs. As a result, Ohio libraries (including OHIONET) have lagged behind in the development of local or regional systems in comparison with libraries in many other states.

For Ohio University, automating circulation was identified as the first priority. To explore and evaluate the possibilities, a Task Force on an Automated Circulation System was created in September 1978, consisting of library and computer center staff with representatives of the faculty and the students. The Task Force was chaired by William Betcher, then Assistant Director for Public Services and subsequently Associate Director for Services. Its charges were:

- to conduct a feasibility study for an automated circulation system in the O.U. Libraries;

- to investigate various automated circulation systems available commercially and the possibility of developing a system locally (using university computer center personnel) patterned after Ohio State University (O.S.U.) Libraries' Library Control System (LCS);

- to gather cost information on various systems for comparison, and

- to submit a report with a set of recommendations.

Although directed toward an automated circulation system, the Task Force envisioned that the selected approach should include an online public access catalog or provide for inclusion of such in the near future.

O.S.U.'s LCS was identified as a strong contender in the early phases of the investigation because: 1) O.S.U. Libraries were willing to share the LCS software with us, and 2) utilization of LCS would lead to greater cooperation with our larger sister institution to the north. The investigation revealed, however, that adoption of LCS would require considerable, costly upgrading of the university mainframe and would require substantial staff support for the computer center. Money and personnel requirements dictated the abandonment of this option.

212

Throughout 1980 and 1981, the Task Force explored all then available turnkey circulation systems. Onsite visits, demonstrations, and consultations with user-institutions of various systems were arranged. In September 1981, the Task Force visited the Virginia Polytechnic Institute and State University in Blacksburg, and, shortly thereafter, the VTLS system was selected. In December of that year, Dr. Vinod Chachra and members of the VTLS team offered a presentation and demonstration in Athens, Ohio.

The following factors were significant in the selection:

1. Provision for an integrated library system with a linkage to OCLC's online cataloging and the utilization of MARC records to create the local database.

2. Immediate availability of an automated circulation system and online public access catalog, with future expansion to include serials control, acquisitions, and management information. All of which complement the OCLC cataloging and interlibrary loan subsystems. Appendix A illustrates this interrelationship.

3. Ease of use of the system for both staff and patrons; subject search capability.

4. Reasonable costs for the software package and the annual maintenance fee compared with other available systems. (When we contracted for the software in 1982, the cost was $20,000 plus an annual maintenance fee of $3,000. The annual maintenance fee entitles us to all enhancements released during the year. Although the charges for these have risen, they are still extremely competitive.)

5. The quality and vision of the personnel on the VTLS team.

6. The degree of local control and flexibility allowed by the system, including local networking and short-form cataloging.

While the Task Force had primary responsibility for identifying systems, other staff were engaged in complementary activities before the selection of the system. Special funding was obtained from the university for a $125,000 two-year retrospective conversion project in 1979. An NEH Challenge grant provided $150,000 for cataloging the Special Collections backlog, and a $115,999 grant under Title II-C of the Higher Education Act supported cataloging of the backlog in the nationally important Southeast Asia Collection. It was also recognized that special funding would be required to acquire the system hardware and software. In 1981, $150,000 was raised from private sources to largely cover these costs.

With the selection of the system, hardware was simultaneously ordered: an HP 3000/40 minicomputer and three 404 megabyte disk drives as well as terminals, wiring, etc.

213

In planning for installation, it was decided to place the CPU and related hardware in the University Computing Services (since renamed Computing and Learning Services) because that facility, unlike the main (Vernon R. Alden) library building, had secure space and the required environmental control. Moreover, Computing Services had the trained personnel to look after the hardware for the 102 hours 7 days per week that the library is open to the public. Capitalizing on existing excellent relations, Computing Services agreed to provide a separate room for the HP3000/40 and disk drives and to provide an experienced systems analyst to be responsible for the library system in return for which a .5 FTE position was transferred to Computing Services.

During the past two and one-half years, this arrangement has worked extremely well. Augmentation of the existing expertise in the University's Computing Services has assured the necessary technical support while freeing library staff to concentrate on library aspects of the applications. Building on this basis, further agreements with Computing Services provide for maintenance of the hardware and peripherals (other than the CPU and disk drives) at about one-half the cost of external maintenance agreements and service is readily available on site, an important consideration for an installation that is 75 miles from the nearest large city. Beyond maintenance and repair support, Computing Services is able to provide loan equipment (such as a terminal or modem) while repairs are being made.

Based on our experience, if at all possible, working closely with existing computer expertise within or available to the organization is the best approach. The savings in time and personnel as well as money can be better used to provide library services.

Installation

In March 1982, installation of the HP3000/40 began. With loading of our OCLC archival tapes scheduled for July, Murphy's Law made its first of many appearances. Virginia Tech had a new program (offering a segmented rather than a single unit database) which they promised with only a three-week delay. We should have known from our OCLC experience that enhancements promised by systems people are always late. It was late August before the new program was installed and archival tape loading could begin. Loading the tapes, which contained 356,000 records, extended until the end of March 1983. At the outset, six records were loaded each minute. By the end, this had slowed to 1.5 records per minute. The rate of loading is determined by the software - under the VTLS system, each character is interrogated in loading and then passed to the buffer. When the buffer is X% full (we had set it at 80%), the buffer process then writes the record to the database and establishes the chains. We learned, belatedly, that one ought to do a super-chain process and a Syst-Dump after loading each tape. The super-chain process is the only means of speeding up the loading process.

We also learned that at the beginning of the loading of the first tape the recovery system should be tested. We lost 4-1/2 weeks of work by not doing a "Syst-Dump and restore" to ensure the correct functioning of the recovery system.

During the installation phase, circulation personnel became concerned that insufficient items would be barcoded and linked to permit implementation of the circulation system. Within our libraries, collection development and ordering is handled by professional staff serving as subject bibliographers in their areas of expertise. It was agreed that, beginning in the summer of 1982, the bibliographers - with the assistance of other staff and student employees - would barcode the volumes in that part of the LC schedule which fell within their areas of responsibility. Dual barcodes were used, with one placed in each monograph and its twin placed on the back of the shelflist card. The cataloging department could then use a light pen to scan the barcode on the shelflist and link it to the bibliographic record in the database. Linking is necessary for circulation and also to indicate the location(s) of titles.

In retrospect, this immense effort--resulting in the barcoding of 289,000 volumes-- was not needed to implement the circulation function. It proved more efficient to link each volume after it circulated. However, it permits linking of non-circulating titles (i.e., reference) and those which are yet to circulate without physically handling each volume. Linking is essential for maximum benefits from the online public catalog. This applies only to volumes in the collection before March 1983. Once the archival tapes were loaded, each addition to the collection is linked as part of the cataloging routine. One strength of the VTLS system is this interface which obviates the need to continue acquire and load OCLC tapes once the retrospective tapes have been entered.

While the barcoding was demanding of professional staff time, it served to greatly increase bibliographers' familiarity with the collection areas for which they were responsible. It also afforded the opportunity to systematically weed the collection for the first time in many years.

Inauguration and Upgrading

With the completion of tape loading, testing of the system and staff training began in earnest. Limited training had begun earlier for the circulation staff. It was evident that the system was ready for its debut, but it was also evident that the hardware and storage would soon be inadequate for our needs, not to mention meeting the needs for five years to come.

It should be stressed that, in planning and acquiring the system and the hardware configuration, we thoroughly established our wants and needs and refined these in terms of budgetary realities. Expert advice was sought and checked and double checked. But even before becoming officially available, response time problems and the need for greater database capacity and more terminals dictated the enlargement of the system.

While some library staff were preparing for the inaugural shower for our new automated system, others were in consultation with Hewlett Packard negotiating an upgrade. The inaugural cocktail party was held on July 15, 1983, to introduce the system to the campus community (and to thank the staff of the library and computer services as well as the numerous faculty and administrators who had contributed to the realization of the system). As utilized at Ohio University, the system was named ALICE. A name-that-system campaign was held among library staff which resulted in a host of acronyms. The librarian at a regional campus reminded us that the name need not be an acronym, as evident in the language Pascal. Almost synchronously, the name ALICE was suggested with allusions to the Wonderland which the system would open for library users. Clinching the argument, it was noted that in the song "White Rabbit," the Jefferson Airplane advised, "Go ask Alice, I'll think she'll know" - exactly the attitude we hoped to cultivate toward the new system.

Within the same time frame, negotiations were concluded with Hewlett-Packard to trade the HP3000/40 on the new HP3000/68 with an interim HP 3000/64 until the 68 became available. Three additional 404 MB drives were also acquired. Under a special offer then effect, an HP125 microcomputer with software was added at no additional cost. This HP125 gives us a backup to record check-ins and check-outs at circulation during times that the system is down.

After the inauguration, full implementation of the system began with the fall quarter of 1983/84. In October, the switch to the HP3000/64 was accomplished. In February 1984, this was converted to the 68 series with the addition of one extra block of main memory and disc caching.

The upgraded system has performed to our expectations. It has also greatly increased the terminal capacity. After one year, we have 9 terminals for cataloging and other exclusive staff use, 4 for circulation transactions, 3 ports for connection through the computer network or by dial access, and 25 public terminals - at least one of which is available on each of the main library's seven floors as well as in the separate music library.

This dispersal of public terminals has eliminated the central card catalog and the need for multitudinous departmental catalogs. On May 13, 1983, the main catalog was officially closed. Not only do users no longer need to check the main catalog, as a result of our cooperation with Computing and Learning Services, the library system is integrated into the intra-university computing network (diagrammed in Appendix B). Through communications controllers and a Gandalf Port Contention Controller, any of the hundreds of terminals spread across the campus (and on regional campuses) can access the library system. Moreover, the network permits dial access and thus the library system is accessible through a phone datalink for anywhere. One important impact is that the question of the number of public terminals needed is somewhat muted, virtually any terminal is a public terminal with access to the online public access catalog (including information on item availability).

Networking

With participation in the intra-university computer network, long-standing commitments to cooperation and service, the capabilities of the VTLS software, and as the only research library serving rural south and southeastern Ohio, it was probably inevitable that no sooner had ALICE become operational than explorations began for extending service to other libraries. This took two main thrusts: service to regional campuses and service to public libraries (through the regional network OVAL - Ohio Valley Area Libraries - comprised of eleven public libraries in ten counties). Complementing planning for extensions, Ohio University has been planning for a microwave system to serve regional campuses, technical colleges, and other colleges in the region. The availability of the library system has been an important addition to the planning for the interconnect system. The projected system is pictured in Appendix C.

While the microwave interconnect system will require special appropriations, planning has proceeded on extending service to the regional campuses and the public libraries, joint committees for each comprised of our staff and representatives of the participating institutions have been meeting regularly since October 1983.

As noted, dial access to ALICE on the Athens campus is currently available. Regional campuses currently utilize this facility as well as existing connections into the intra-university computer network to check our holdings for titles of interest. But planning is well underway to provide a separate but linked regional campus databases which will afford the regional campuses all of the facilities of the VTLS system. Equipment is currently being installed at the Lancaster campus as the prototype (other regional campuses are at Belmont, Chillicothe, Ironton, and Zanesville). Lancaster's retrospective OCLC tapes will be loaded into the regional campus databases (which affords all of the services of the main campus database). An existing microwave communications linkage is used, eliminating line charges.

Difficulties Encountered - Lessons Learned

Despite our general satisfaction and success in acquiring and implementing the VTLS system, the foregoing should indicate that the experience has not been without trials and tribulations. We share these with those who are contemplating or planning an integrated online system in the hope that they may be spared some grief.

1. Estimating equipment needs.

Attempting to specify the exact hardware configuration that will be needed while providing for system growth is difficult to say the least. In part this is

217

a function of the pace of change in computer technologies. There is a reluctance to acquire equipment which will soon be outdated; however, even the most careful planning is no guarantee that this will not be the case. As funds for hardware purchases are not unlimited, specification and procurement require careful estimates. Hardware vendors, to remain competitive, may recommend smaller equipment with marginal growth potential. As noted, even as the system became operational, it was obvious that greater capacity was needed. Upgrading to the HP3000/68 nearly doubled our hardware costs and our maintenance costs. At the same time, it also became evident that the initial projection that three 404 MB disk drives would be adequate for one million bibliographic records was grossly over-optimistic. With 400,000 records loaded, we discovered that three additional 404 MB drives would be needed - at a cost of $65,000. Technology contributes to this. At the June 1984 users group meeting, Hewlett Packard reported that its five-year projection is that computing power will double and cost will be halved.

2. Estimating other costs.

Cost overruns in automated systems extend well beyond hardware, although hardware is a significant factor. Recognizing the potential for overruns, we added a fudge factor of 25%. Our experience indicates that even 50% is likely insufficient. While this consideration may pose some problems for larger institutions, for smaller libraries with limited funding such overruns could be critical.

3. Loading archival tapes.

Because of the nature of the VTLS database and limited guidance in setting parameters, we found that tape loading required much longer than predicted, with a severe reduction in loading speed as the database grew. Of course, this was a function of the proportion of our collection on tape. Having participated in OCLC for more than a decade and having undertaken several retrospective conversion projects during that time, the number of records which we had on tape greatly exceeded previous VTLS users.

4. Availability of the system during loading.

An automated system which is unavailable is worse than a return to a manual system. Backlogs are created at each step of the process which then must be processed. The unavailability of the system has resulted from installation of new equipment or the installation of new versions of the VTLS software. Such down time must be scheduled for slack times; for us this is during breaks between quarters. We hope that we have made a major step toward alleviating the problem of having to fully unload and load the system each time. "Adager," a utility for H-P's IMAGE system which allows database manipulation and modification without loading and unloading, has been ordered and we hope will eliminate much of this problem.

5.   Securing the database.

In offering access to the system from many different locations in the library (several of which are uncontrolled), from any terminal on campus, and by telephone, library users have much greater access to the database. Unfortunately, this is true for experimenters or vandals as well as for the serious user. At the end of our Spring Quarter, we had a serious problem with a "Dr. Who," who was able to enter the circulation system and record 118 checkouts for books still in the library. We also had sporadic cases of other individuals, presumably computer science students, attempting to enter the system in statuses to which they were not entitled. This problem has been brought to the attention of Virginia Tech, which reports that new security measures will be available in the fall of 1984. Despite such efforts, this problem is likely to remain endemic. As people climb Mt. Everest because its there, students are likely to attempt to enter the database for the same reason. Our only solace is that, as yet, such unauthorized entries, seem prompted more by curiosity or a practical joke than malicious intent.

6.   Turnover in VTLS personnel.

Perhaps a tribute to the success of the VTLS system is the extent to which the staff have moved to other, more responsible positions. An attraction of the VTLS system was that the people engaged in development and in support were familiar with libraries, and, for us, were familiar with large academic libraries. We found them helpful and congenial. Unfortunately, the meteoric rise in installations of the system since our original contract has brought many changes. Many of the people with whom we originally worked, and who made particular commitments to us, have since left Virginia Tech for other positions. As the number of using institutions grows, the personal contacts become more tenuous, and one is forced to formal means of registering complaints and suggestions. During the past year, Virginia Tech has developed a logging system for phoned-in problems, which has largely alleviated a lack of follow-up due to changing personnel or responsibilities.

7.   Delays in developing promised subsystems.

Delays in the development and introduction of subsystems and enhancements seems intrinsic to the library automation field. Virginia Tech is no exception. Of course, different institutions have different priorities, and those responsible for selling the system will tend to emphasize what the potential purchaser wants to hear. When we first acquired the software, we were told to expect serials control and acquisitions within a year. We now have had the system operational for a year and are still told to expect these two subsystems within a year. To be fair to the VTLS organization, they have concentrated on improving and enhancing the cataloging, circulation and online public access catalog components of the system (including authority control, word search, and Boolean operators). We agree that it is important to have this core to work as well as possible before diverting staff and resources to other development efforts--as long as the delay does not become unreasonable. Conversely, when users are told that an enhancement or subsystem will be available by a certain date, much frustration could be avoided if the vendor and systems people would strive to provide realistic projections and then to achieve those targets. This situation is akin to the "revolution of rising expectations" described for the Third World. While system users have far more capacity and benefits than previously, they have been led to expect even more.

Conclusion

At the tender age of one, ALICE is a well-behaved child whose growth threatens to exceed our wildest hopes and imagination. While there are things which we would do differently (as described above), selecting the VTLS system is not among them. Perhaps our pride shows. In recent months, we have received visits and telephone calls from libraries considering integrated systems. We have responded as fully and as honestly as possible. We are aware that several of these have since joined the VTLS family. In our own evaluation of alternative systems, we found discussions with users to be extremely valuable. Institutions considering VTLS should be aware that an active users group has been formed. Information on the Group and on the results of occasional surveys of users are available from the newly elected Chair: Jack Bazuzi of the Virginia State Library. We also remain willing to show off our one-year-old ALICE.

APPENDIX A

OCLC - VTLS COMPLEMENTARITY

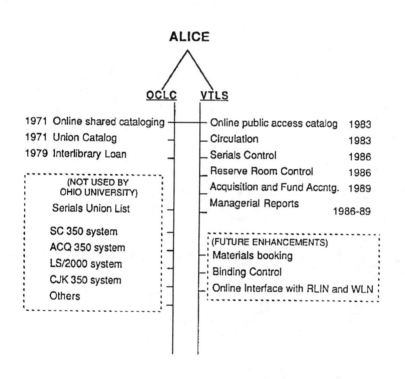

**The Development of
Local ALICE System in the 1980's**

ALICE

OCLC   **VTLS**

1971 Online shared cataloging —————— Online public access catalog   1983
1971 Union Catalog   — Circulation   1983
1979 Interlibrary Loan   — Serials Control   1986
                                      — Reserve Room Control   1986
(NOT USED BY OHIO UNIVERSITY)   — Acquisition and Fund Accntg. 1989
Serials Union List   — Managerial Reports   1986-89

SC 350 system
ACQ 350 system   (FUTURE ENHANCEMENTS)
LS/2000 system   — Materials booking
CJK 350 system   — Binding Control
Others   — Online Interface with RLIN and WLN

APPENDIX B

ALICE IN INTRA-UNIVERSITY COMPUTING NETWORK

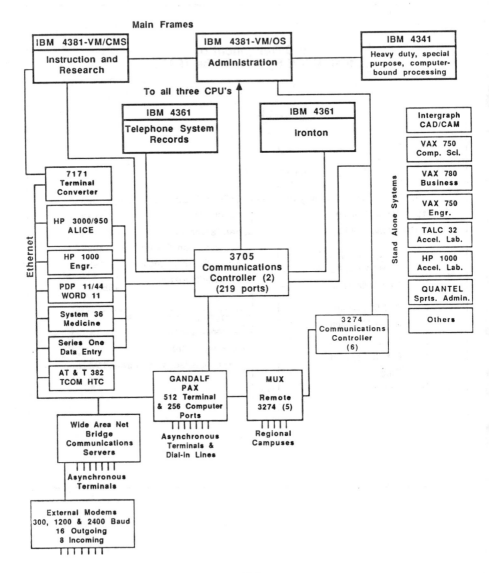

APPENDIX C

Proposed Microwave Interconnect System

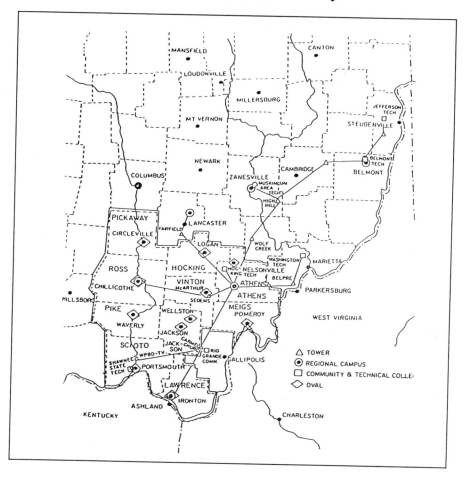

TRENDS IN AUTOMATION
IN AMERICAN ACADEMIC LIBRARIES:
OHIO UNIVERSITY'S EXPERIENCES[1]

Introduction

Historically American Libraries have been in the forefront in applying information technologies: from the origins of the Hollerith punched-card tabulating system in the latter part of the 19th century; through the growing use of micrographics in the 1930s; photocopying and data processing equipment in the 1950s; the wide-spread application of succeeding generations of computers and the accompanying developments in telecommunications in the 1960s and 1970s; to the mass storage as exemplified in optical discs in the 1980s. The pace of innovation accelerates as each new technology is adopted and refined.[2]

A comprehensive state university of 24,000 students founded in 1804, Ohio University has a main campus in Athens, Ohio, and five regional campuses in surrounding Southeastern Ohio. Just as in many American academic libraries, Ohio University Library has been in the mainstream of information technology applications and library automation. Since the beginning of OCLC under its former name, the Ohio College Library Center, back in 1967, the Ohio University Library has been an active participant and supporter. The case history of Ohio University Library in the applications of information technology and in library automation can be seen as fairly representative of academic libraries in North America. For the past three decades, despite differences in strategy, approach, and timing among academic libraries, the general trend has been comparable to that which I will describe for Ohio University.

Significant Developments in the 1960s

In the 1960s, computers (then all mainframes) were too expensive for most libraries, and library applications software was generally unavailable, yet several

---

[1]This a substantially revised and updated version of an earlier paper, Hwa-Wei Lee, "Applications of Information Technology in an American Library--The Case of Ohio University Libraries," presented at the First Pacific Conference on New Information Technologies for Library and Information Professionals, June 16-18, 1987, in Bangkok, Thailand. It appeared in the *Proceedings* (West Newton, Mass.: MicroUse Information, 1987), pp. 144-164.

[2]Stephen R. Slamon, "Library Automation." In *Encyclopedia of Library and Information Science* (New York: Marcel Dekker, 1975), V. 14, pp. 338-445.

major initiatives with far-reaching impacts on library automation were launched. These included the MEDLARS (MEDical Literature Analysis and Retrieval System) project of the National Library of Medicine, the INTREX (INformation TRansfer EXperiment) project by the Massachusetts Institute of Technology, the design and implementation of the MARC (MAchine Readable Cataloging) format by the Library of Congress, and the establishment of the Ohio College Library Center (OCLC) by a group of academic libraries in Ohio, including Ohio University. At about the same time, Stanford University initiated its BALLOTS (Bibliographic Automation of Large Library Operations using a Time-sharing System) project which evolved into the Research Libraries Information Network (RLIN). Another important trend in the 1960s was the beginning by many abstracting and indexing services to use computers in photo composition and typesetting of printed publications--making possible machine-searchable databases.

The MEDLARS Project and subsequent medical information network developed by the National Library of Medicine has benefitted immeasurably medical and health sciences libraries and the professionals whom they serve. The INTREX project, from 1965 to 1973, reaffirmed the design concept that large libraries could become information transfer systems. But, as we assess the importance of the major developments in the 1960s, the most significant and far-reaching were probably the design in 1965 of a MARC format for bibliographic data (which is machine-readable, largely interchangeable, and internationally acceptable) and the establishment in 1967 of OCLC. The beginning distribution on magnetic tapes of MARC-formatted cataloging records by the Library of Congress undoubtedly affected the design of OCLC and its first computer-based shared cataloging and union catalog system. Other than these major applications, library automation in the 1960s tended to replicate manual processes including the use of computers for the production of catalog cards, accession lists, serial holdings, and the like.

The Mushrooming of OCLC in the 1970s

The founding of OCLC in 1967 by a small number of academic library members of the Ohio College Association and the Inter-University Library Council--which consisted of library directors of state-supported universities in Ohio, followed sixteen years of study and deliberation and also involved the Ohio Library Association.[3] Only after the successful implementation of the MARC project in November 1966, cooperative, shared cataloging on a centralized computer system became practical.

Through the foresight of the Ohio academic librarians and the effective leadership of Mr. Frederic G. Kilgour, Executive Director of OCLC from its inception

---

[3]Lewis C. Branscomb and A. Robert Rogers, "The Conception and Birth Pangs of OCLC--An Account of the Struggles of the Formative Years," *College and Research Libraries*, V. 42, No.4 (July 1981), pp. 303-307.

in 1967 to his retirement in 1980, OCLC grew by leaps and bounds from a small organization of two staff members, with an initial budget of $67,000 and 54 participating libraries in Ohio to a complex organization of over 885 staff members, with a budget of $95.7 million in 1988 and a growing membership of 9,400 libraries of all types in the U.S. and 26 other countries. [Diagram I]. Initially OCLC provided a computer-based cataloging system in batch process. This was upgraded to a real-time, online, interactive mode in 1971. On August 26, 1971, Ohio University Library entered the first member-produced cataloging record online. Although the system immediately crashed, Ohio University Library ended that day with 147 titles cataloged. During the first two days an average of ten titles per terminal hour were entered.

The instant success of the OCLC shared cataloging system attracted other Ohio libraries and, soon, libraries in other states. Reflecting broader library membership and geographical distribution, OCLC in 1977 changed its name to OCLC, Inc. In 1981, with the adoption of a new governance structure, the legal name became the OCLC Online Computer Library Center, Incorporated.[4]

Most significant in OCLC's growth was the expansion of its cataloging database. From its 1971 beginning, the database reached its one millionth record in September 1974, a period of over three years. The second million records took 18 months to accumulate. As the number of members increased so did the rate of growth in the records. The most recent million records, to 19 million, in January, 1989 took only six months! This has made OCLC the largest and fastest growing bibliographic database in the world. [Diagram II]. According to OCLC, of the 19 million bibliographic records, 80 percent were contributed by OCLC members. The remaining 20 percent were provided by the Library of Congress, the National Library of Medicine, the National Agricultural Library, the National Library of Canada, the U.S. Government Printing Office, and, recently, the British Library. Benefitting from the size and currency of the database, OCLC users can locate cataloging records from OCLC for 94 percent of the items they catalog and thus need to perform original cataloging for only 6 percent of their materials.[5] This is a considerable savings in time and expense in cataloging by member libraries.

Adding to OCLC's success is its online interlibrary loan system introduced in 1979. The system is built on the shared database which includes 298 million member-location symbols. OCLC reports that in 1987/88 more than 3.78 million interlibrary loans were transacted online in one year and more than 20 million inter-library loan requests have been logged since 1979. At present, better than 90 percent of the requests can be verified online and 87 percent are filled. Facilitated by

---

[4]Kathleen L. Maciuszko, *OCLC, A Decade of Development, 1967-1977* (Littleton, Colorado: Libraries Unlimited, 1984).

[5]*OCLC Annual Report, 1987/88* (Dublin, Ohio: OCLC, 1988).

electronic library-to-library communication through the OCLC telecommunications system, interlibrary loan items are shipped by mail or UPS to borrowers within an average of four days.

Although in recent years OCLC's services have extended to many other areas including serials control, acquisitions and a decentralized, minicomputer-based local system--LS/2000, Ohio University has chosen to participate only in OCLC's online union catalog, shared cataloging, and interlibrary loan components. These, in our judgement, represent the services best offered centrally to facilitate resource sharing and take advantage of economies of scale. Other OCLC services are either less competitive or were offered too late.

While OCLC was concentrating on improving services at the national level in the late 1970s and early 1980s, many libraries were looking for local systems for local library functions. The trend in the late 1970s was to develop or purchase a local system for circulation, online public access catalog, etc., which could interface (often through tape loading) with the OCLC online union catalog and shared cataloging service. Such a system enables a library to participate in OCLC for shared cataloging and interlibrary loans while downloading the OCLC-created MARC catalog records into local computer storage to support activities in such areas as circulation, acquisitions, fund accounting, serials check-in, and online public access catalog.

The availability of the online public access catalog to replace the century-old card catalog and the COM (Computer-Output-Microform) catalog of the 1960s and 1970s is widespread in the 1980s. The OCLC online union catalog is, and will continue to be, the single most important cataloging and interlibrary loan tool, but its lack of subject access and cryptic search keys have made it unattractive as an online public access catalog, although this may be overcome with the refinements scheduled to be available late in 1989 or 1990. The declining cost and expanding power of minicomputers and microcomputers as well as the availability of software packages for library functions have lured many libraries to seek local alternatives either individually or in clusters.

The Development of the Local ALICE System in the 1980s[6]

In 1978, Ohio University opted to explore locally integrated library systems capable of interfacing with OCLC but operated independently on a dedicated

---

[6]Hwa-Wei Lee, K. Mulliner, E. Hoffmann-Pinther, and Hannah McCauley, "ALICE at One: Candid Reflections on the Adoption, Installation, and Use of the Virginia Tech Library System (VTLS) at Ohio University. **In** Second National Conference on Integrated Online Library Systems, September 13 and 14, 1984, Atlanta Georgia. *Proceedings* (Canfield, Ohio: Genaway and Associates, Inc., 1984), pp. 228-242. Included as preceding article in this compilation.

minicomputer. The result has been the successful implementation of the ALICE system which became operational in July 1983. In September 1978, a task force to explore local library systems was formed to investigate possibilities and approaches. Consisting of library and computer center staff, faculty, and students, the task force sought an integrated system which would use OCLC for shared cataloging and interlibrary loans but would support, in modular form, circulation, and online public access catalog, acquisitions, and other library functions. The system should be based on a central database created from the OCLC MARC records with added holdings and location information as well as the barcode number. The task force considered circulation and an online catalog among the first priorities. Throughout 1980 and 1981, the task force studied nearly all available systems. On-site visits and presentations by vendors to the staff were arranged. In December 1981 the Virginia Tech Library System (VTLS), designed and developed by Virginia Polytechnic Institute and State University in Blacksburg, Virginia, was selected for the following reasons:

1. Provision of an integrated library system with an online linkage to OCLC's cataloging and utilization of MARC records to create the local database.

2. Immediate availability of an automated circulation system and online public access catalog, with planned expansion to include serials control, acquisitions, and management information--all of which complement the OCLC cataloging and interlibrary loan subsystems.

3. Ease of use of the system by both staff and patrons. Searches can be by author, title, subject, call number, and, now, key words with Boolean operators.

4. Reasonable cost of the software package and the annual maintenance fee compared with other available systems. (When Ohio University contracted for the software in 1982, the cost was $20,000 plus an annual maintenance fee of $3,000. The annual maintenance entitles the library to all enhancements released during the year.)

5. The quality and vision of the personnel on the VTLS team (including a common experience in an academic environment).

6. The degree of local control and flexibility allowed by the system, including local networking and short-form cataloging.

Recognizing that an automated library system requires a database of machine-readable cataloging records, the library, in 1979, began a massive effort to convert pre-1971 cataloging records to machine-readable MARC format with grants and gifts totalling $400,000. As the first library to participate in OCLC, the Ohio University was fortunate to own a large machine-readable database for materials cataloged online since 1971. As a result of the conversion effort, when the VTLS System was installed in August 1982, nearly 400,000 catalog records--representing nearly one million volumes--were loaded from archival tapes. These comprised about 80 percent of the Library's monographs, excluding titles in governmental documents and a large portion of the microform, maps, and non-print collections which were indexed or cataloged manually.

Typical of designated depositories for U.S. government documents, the library maintains a separate collection arranged by the Superintendent of Documents (SUDOCS) classification number (based on issuing body rather than subject content) that relies on the printed *Monthly Catalog of the United States Government Publications* (and annual accumulations) augmented by Congressional Information Service indexes for access. At the same time that Ohio University was celebrating its centennial as a designated depository in 1986, we purchased retrospective cataloging records for U. S. Government documents on MARC tapes from the Government and have loaded these into the local database as an integral part of the online public access catalog. Similarly, MARC tapes available through OCLC are being acquired for major microform sets as a result of the ARL (Association of Research Libraries)-initiated Major Microforms Project.

With the signing of a contract with VTLS and the ordering and installation of a Hewlett Packard minicomputer (HP 3000/40) hardware and other peripheral equipment in the early part of 1982, a search for a name for the local system resulted in selecting ALICE, with a credit to Lewis Carroll's *Alice in Wonderland* and suggesting the wonderland which the system would open for library users. Clinching the argument, was the song, "White Rabbit", in which the Jefferson Airplane advised, "Go ask Alice, I think she'll know"--exactly the attitude we hoped to cultivate toward the new system.

With the strong support of the University's Computing and Learning Services, where the Library's HP 3000 system is housed, installation and tape loading went well. Barcoding a large portion of the library collection was time consuming, involving a majority of the library staff in 1982 and 1983. The completion of the tape loading in July 1983 enabled the library to formally inaugurate the online public access catalog and close its card catalog on July 15, 1983. Because creation of a patron file required additional preparation, the circulation function was implemented in September that year. By linking the library computer to the university-wide computer network from the beginning, the online catalog is accessible not only by library terminals located on every floor and in every service area of the main library building and the detached Music and Dance Library in the Music Building but also by terminals connected to the University network throughout the Athens campus. Dial access by microcomputers or terminals equipped with modems is also available regardless of location or distance. [Diagram in Appendix B of preceding article.] This is a feature only an online system can provide. Almost immediately, the libraries on the five regional campuses took advantage of this capability.

Because VTLS included networking in its design, the Regional Campuses located between 50 to 125 miles from Athens, have been able to network with the main library in the full use of VTLS for their library automation in a network environment. The Lancaster campus was the first to become a secondary account of VTLS, and by 1985, had every feature that is available in Athens. By sharing the central computer but maintaining a separate database, O.U.-Lancaster has its own database and holdings for its users yet, by a simple command, they can switch to our much larger database and holdings. Conversely, users in Athens can also view the Lancaster database. At the present time, we are replicating this on other campuses, some by dedicated telephone lines and others by microwave telecommunications. (See Appendix C in preceding article.)

Of course, every expansion of the local system requires the upgrading of the computer and peripheral equipment. Since the installation of a HP 3000/40 in 1982, we have upgraded to an HP 3000/64 in 1983, HP 3000/68 in 1984, HP 3000/70 in 1987, and, most recently, to an HP 3000/950 in 1989. The expansion of the CPU was accompanied by adding more and more storage capacities (from three 404 megabyte (MB) disc drives [totalling 1,212 MB] in 1982 to seven 404 MB and two 570 MB drives [totalling 3,968 MB] in 1987). The total value of the central hardware in 1989 approaches $500,000.

As the only major library in Southeastern Ohio, the Ohio University Library serves as the back-up resource library for public libraries in ten surrounding counties grouped under the Ohio Valley Area Libraries (OVAL). Through State Library funding, Ohio University Library provides reference and interlibrary loan services to OVAL libraries, amounting in 1988 to 1,912 reference responses and 6,007 loans of books or photocopies. Future interconnection of OVAL Libraries with Ohio University Libraries is feasible, based on a consultant study,[7] but depends on the wishes of the member public libraries.

The Growth of Online Database Searching

Paralleling the development of library automation since the 1960s has been the development of computerized databases by indexing and abstracting firms. Ohio University Library began online database search services in its Health Sciences Library in 1978. This was followed by a library-wide Computerized Information Retrieval Service (CIRS) inaugurated in 1979. Currently, we have online access to more than 400 databases in a variety of subject areas. In addition to those available through DIALOG, BRS, and STN, we have direct access to MEDLARS, Wilsonline,

---

[7]Jose-Marie Griffiths and Carolyn J. Goshen. *A Systems Analysis of the Ohio Valley Area Libraries (OVAL). Final Report* (Rockville, Maryland: King Research, Inc., 1985).

LEXIS/NEXIS, OhioPi (Ohio Public Information), and others. One-half of the cost for CIRS has been subsidized by the library to lessen the financial burden for students.

Our original hardware, a Texas Instruments terminal with no memory, an acoustic coupling, and 300 baud transmission speed, has been replaced by microcomputers. In 1983, the Library acquired an IBM-PC, equipped with a 1200 baud modem and Smartcom II as the communication software. This system permitted downloading of data and printing at a faster speed, and increased the cost effectiveness of searching, thus lowering patron costs. Additional hardware purchases, from 1984 to the present, have upgraded our systems to 80286-chip based IBM and Zenith machines, a Macintosh, and an IBM-XT--all with hard disks and 2400 baud modems. Further, to provide faster and better reference service, guidelines were established for the use of CIRS for ready reference service at the discretion of the reference staff, free of charge.

New and Emerging Information Technologies

In coping with the ever growing new and emerging information technologies which have flooded the market place, Ohio University Library has taken a number of steps to prepare itself for the inevitable. The future prospects are exciting and challenging. Among the steps taken are:

a. Expanding non-print collections to include many new formats.

Beginning in the 1960s the Library expanded its Microform Collection as more scholarly and research materials became available on that format. In the 1970s and 1980s, the federal government has published and distributed more and more of its publications in microfiche. To save space, money, and material, the library also decided early in 1979 to subscribe to both a paper copy and a microform copy of a number of selected journals and to discard the paper copy after the peak-use period. By 1986 the library collection in microformat exceeded that in print volumes (1,319,107 microforms vs 1,284,130 printed volumes). It is typical that in 1988 the library added 67,236 new microform units compared to 49,071 new printed volumes.

Microforms today are only one of many non-print formats: audio and video cassettes, audio and data compact discs, microcomputer floppy disks, optical discs, videodiscs, etc. To adequately service these newer formats, the Library has acquired a range of new equipment including digital image and optical character recognition (OCR) scanning equipment for conversion of print materials, image preservation, and desktop publishing.

232

b. Growing use of CD-ROM based information.

The coming of age for CD-ROM laser technology demands new knowledge, skills, and methods to handle the Read-Only-Memory (ROM) compact disc. To develop these, the Library has acquired several CD-ROM workstations which combine MS-DOS PCs and disc players. As of May 1989, 24 CD-ROM databases are offered (with more added regularly) including *ERIC, Books-in-Print Plus* and *Ulrich's Guide to Periodicals, PsycLit, Dissertation Abstracts* (from the 19th Century to the present), *MLA International Bibliography, Public Affairs Information Service (PAIS)*, a variety of Wilson Indexes and the *Academic American Encyclopedia* by Grolier. Dedicated workstations provide access to *Compact Medbase, InfoTrac*, and *NewsBank*. Offering data rather than bibliographic information on CD-ROM are *Consu/Stats I* (U.S. government-produced consumer data), *Econ/Stats I* and *StatPak* (government statistical data), and *Compact Disclosure* on corporations. Thousands of public domain software and shareware programs can be downloaded by users from *PC-SIG*. By use of the CD-ROM based information, the library hopes to develop methods and procedures for the handling of such technology to the best advantage. It is anticipated that end-user searching on CD-ROM will ease the demand for online searching (CIRS) serving increasing numbers of users without the cost of online searching; however, teaching students and faculty to use the various search software and databases effectively has proven very demanding of staff time.

c. Use of a telefacsimile machine (fax) for document delivery, reference service, and communications.

Between June 1986 and June 1987 the Health Sciences Library of Ohio University was chosen by the State Library of Ohio to operate an experimental telefacsimile network for the transmission of biomedical information in a multi-type library environment. Seventeen Ohio libraries of various types participated in the experiment. The one-year project demonstrated the need, reliability, value, and speed of using telefacsimile for document delivery of health related and biomedical interlibrary loan requests. The FAX equipment installed at the 17 sites was the Pitney Bowes 8150, which cost $2,300 each.

While the state-funded library project was underway, the Vice Provost responsible for regional campuses placed Fax equipment in the library of each regional campus. Although primarily for use in information transmission by the deans of these campuses and the Vice Provost, the libraries regularly use it for document delivery and reference queries.

After the successful experiment on the use of a FAX machine, the library has expanded its scope to cover all library areas. The FAX machine is heavily used for interlibrary loans, routine telecommunications (especially overseas), and even to share memos and materials with other offices on campus (alleviating the need for messenger deliveries). As an example, as this paper was being written, we were able to respond to a query about non-Roman scripts in libraries from the Institute of Southeast Asian Studies in Singapore.

FAX has proven an easy and efficient means of communicating at any distance, rivaling regular mail in cost and surpassing it in speed, while eliminating the ubiquitous office problem of telephone tag.

d. Providing general public computer terminals and microcomputers for students and faculty in the library.

Since 1982, in cooperation with the University's Computing and Learning Services (UCLS), the library has provided space for a computer lab--the first of many of its kind established on the Athens campus. As of May 1989, the Lab offers 25 MS-DOS microcomputers, 13 Macintosh, 9 Apple II-Es, and 33 terminals connected to the University's Wide Area Network. The terminals in these labs provide additional means to access the ALICE online catalog, as well as other mini-and mainframe computers on campus.

e. Providing microcomputers for library departments and staff.

To facilitate office automation, more than 50 microcomputers have been installed in library departments over the last seven years--about one PC for every 1.5 regular staff. Microcomputers have been in use since 1982, but initial emphasis was on sharing. Staff members have been encouraged (and given numerous professional development opportunities) to learn the use of microcomputer for data and word processing. One local area network (LAN) is in occasional use and the Library has access to the University's wide area network (WAN). Many courses and workshops in the applications of microcomputer have been offered by UCLS and the Library. Several staff struggle to remain current with the technology and serve as resident experts for other staff. Applications include calculation of the Library's acquisitions formula using SuperCalc5, specialized departmental databases, a variety of special bibliographies, a remote bulletin Board (RBBS) for Health Sciences faculty, desktop publishing in both Macintosh and MS-DOS environments, and E-Mail (using BITNET and MCI Mail--the latter also providing telex facilities).

New Development at the State Level.

The information explosion confronts academic and research libraries with new challenges and opportunities, including space (shelving print materials, storage cases for other media, and floor space for workstations and other equipment required by newer media), identification (much of the most useful information is under-repre-sented in bibliographic databases), and access (users can discover a variety of materials beyond the resources of any single institution). It was the space issue which prompted the State of Ohio to launch its first major new initiative since the founding of OCLC two decades earlier. Confronted with massive capital requests for new or

234

enlarged library buildings on state-supported university campuses, the State Legislature of Ohio created a special committee to assess the space requirements of university libraries. That committee, from its inception, recognized that space was only one dimension of the problem. The Committee emphasized:

> ... [T]he academic library of today has a threefold purpose, serving not only as a storehouse of information, but also as a gateway to information held elsewhere, and as a center for instruction about information.[8]

Following the committee's report in 1987,[9] the Board of Regents (the state-level policy agency for all state-supported post-secondary schools) established a number of task forces to begin planning for a statewide information access system, the Ohio Library Information System (OLIS).[10] That planning process is nearing fruition with a Request for Proposals (RFP) scheduled for June 15, 1989. A decision on vendor(s) is expected by December 1989, and the system is scheduled to be acquired with funding available July 1, 1990, and to become operational on July 1, 1991. The planning process has emphasized that this will be an information system for the 1990s and beyond. It is expected to join together, without replicating or replacing, local systems on the participating campuses. It will facilitate resource sharing among 15 state-supported universities and medical colleges and two private universities, including permitting users to initiate interlibrary borrowing requests without an intermediary. On a single terminal, the user will easily move from a local online public access catalog to a statewide union catalog. To make resource sharing a reality, a statewide document delivery system will bring the documents to the requester's institution in three days.

Most significant is the emphasis on information. In addition to the usual bibliographic information found in an online public access catalog (OPAC), the system will offer a variety of indexing services to transparently provide the same access to journal articles and reports as to book and periodical titles, full-text services, data, and images. The system will also provide gateways to other information services which are not available within the system. Access is expected to be through microcomputers

---

[8]Ohio Board of Regents, Library Study Committee. *Academic Libraries in Ohio: Progress through Collaboration, Storage, and Technology* (Columbus, Ohio: Ohio Board of Regents, 1987), p. vii.

[9]Ibid.

[10]Hwa-Wei Lee, "Planning Process and Considerations for a Statewide Academic Libraries Information System in Ohio," paper presented at the Second Pacific Conference on New Information Technologies for Library and Information Professionals, May 29-31, 1989, Singapore. The paper appeared in the *Proceedings* (West Newton, Mass.: MicroUse Information, 1989), pp. 203-210. Included in Section VIII of this compilation.

or, preferably, scholars workstations rather than terminals. With the anticipated innovations in the system, a phased approach is planned with attention to keeping the system open to further advances in the technology.

It would be premature to evaluate a system still in planning, but librarians, computer and telecommunications specialists, and faculty and researchers are working together to provide innovative service which may rival the earlier contributions of OCLC.

Summary and Conclusion

In reviewing library automation at Ohio University during the last three decades with particular regard to the use of computers, the picture matches nearly exactly that described by Richard DeGennaro in 1983:

> "We are well into our third decade of library automation. The first decade, the 1960s, was dominated by primitive local systems. The second decade, the 1970s, was dominated by large multitype and multipurpose library networks. The current and third decade, the 1980s, will be sophisticated multifunction turnkey systems on mini-and micro-computers; and they will have lines to a variety of library and commercial networks on large mainframe."[11]

The general trend of moving from centralization in the 1970s to the decentralization in the 1980s, according to his reasoning, has been "shaped and driven by the cost and capabilities of the computer and telecommunications technologies..." of that time period.[12]

Such has been our experience. Ohio University will seek to refine its local ALICE system and to fully implement all functions making it a completely integrated system. The exploration of the potentials and impacts of CD-ROM and other new information technologies will continue. As the cost for computers further decreases and their capacity expands, appropriate employment of new information technologies for library services is necessary to harness the changing information environment and demands in the years ahead.

If one were to add a fourth decade to De Gennaro's report, we will be serving users with greater computing power sitting on their desks than was available through

---

[11]Richard De Gennaro, "Library Automation and Networking Perspectives on Three Decades," *Library Journal*, Vol. 108, No. 7 (April 1, 1983), p. 629.

[12]Ibid.

the mainframes of the 1970s. We are preparing for a time, described by Jacques Vallee:

> "'Think about it, man,' said a young enthusiast at the San Francisco home computer fair last year [1981], 'you could have the entire Library of Congress at your fingertips.'
>
> 'What would you do if you had the entire Library of Congress at your fingertips?' I asked him.
>
> I am still waiting for an answer."[13]

Not only should we **be able** to answer the question in the next few years, we **must** answer it.

---

[13]Jacques Vallee, *The Network Revolution: Confessions of a Computer Scientist* (Berkeley: And/Or Press, 1982), p. 172.

DIAGRAM I

MUSHROOMING OF OCLC

1988

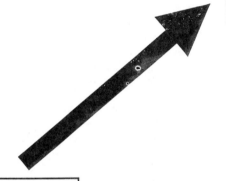

885	Staff Members
$95.7	Million Budget
9,400	Participating Libraries in U.S. and 26 Other Countries

1967

2	Staff Members
$67	Thousand Budget
54	Participating Libraries in Ohio

DIAGRAM II

GROWTH OF OCLC DATABASE

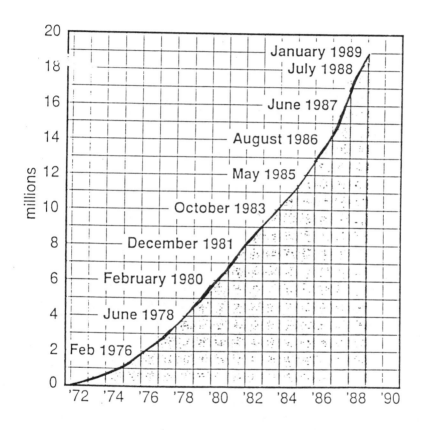

80% of the records are contributed by OCLC members and 20% by the Library of Congress, National Library of Medicine, Government Printing Office, National Library of Canada, and the British Library.

Section VII

Library Development

Fragmentation of Academic Library Resources in Thai
University Libraries (1971) 243

A New Engineering Library Emerging in Asia (1971) 257

Principles of National Library and Information
Policy (1986) 261

FRAGMENTATION OF ACADEMIC LIBRARY RESOURCES IN THAI UNIVERSITY LIBRARIES

Many of the academic institutions in the developing countries in Southeast Asia have been confronted with a serious shortage of library resources which are of vital importance for their national development. The shortage is generally blamed on the lack of adequate funds, a limited number of trained personnel, and the unavailability of suitable books and other library materials. It is true that most of the academic libraries I have visited in Southeast Asia are poorly funded as they often are not given top priority over the many competing demands which the university authorities must consider in the allocation of funds. The lack of a sufficient number of trained personnel is another factor contributing to the shortage of library resources, but this is due largely to the low pay and status of academic librarians who are generally considered inferior to their teaching colleagues.[1] The number of suitable books--especially those with academic subjects and content, published in the native languages--is far short of demand. For academic books, university libraries must rely heavily on imported foreign books for which the high cost is often prohibitive for the average reader or even the academic libraries. In order to supply a sufficient number of textbooks which students often cannot afford themselves, many academic libraries must use a large portion of their inadequate book funds to purchase multiple copies of textbooks.[2] The number of translated titles of foreign publications available is very small and frequently available only after a long delay. As a result, many academic libraries have mainly dated publications, rare and historical materials, multiple copies of textbooks, and only a small percentage of books that can be considered up-to-date and of current interest.

But this is not the most critical problem. Limited resources can be channelled into effective use. This problem of shortages in funds, personnel and books is common in the developing countries and we must learn to live with it while at the same time struggling for its improvement. The main problem lies not in the

---

[1]University librarians in Thailand generally do not have faculty status unless they also teach. It is quite common in the universities where library science courses are offered that librarians must teach in order to achieve faculty status, salary and promotion. The teaching load of an average of ten hours a week is too heavy for those who also have the responsibility of running their libraries. Consequently it is always the library service that suffers.

[2]It was reported that a library "buys as many as 50 copies of a textbook in the liberal arts because many students cannot afford to buy them." S.A. Barnett, E.L. Brown and C.W. Stone, *Developmental Book Activities and Needs in Thailand* New York: Wolf Management Services, 1967), p. 69.

shortage of library resources but in the fragmentation of the limited resources among the many faculty libraries and departmental libraries in most Thai universities. This general practice of decentralization of library resources and services coupled with the absence of effective coordination and cooperation among the many decentralized library units has further complicated the existing problems.

According to a survey of the current status of faculty libraries and departmental libraries in Thai universities which I conducted recently it was found that many of the library resources in Thai universities have been divided among the many faculty libraries and departmental libraries with little or no coordination to make the total resources within each university available to the entire university community. With only a few exceptions, most of the central libraries which do exist are very weak in resources and have no direct administrative authority over the faculty libraries. As a general rule, most of the faculties in Thai universities maintain their own faculty libraries. The university librarians (rightly these people should be called the librarians of the central libraries) often assume no responsibility in the overall planning and development of the library resources and services of their respective universities. The coordination of the various library units, using one university as an example, rests upon the office of the deputy rector for academic affairs instead of the university librarian. There is no centralized acquisition or cataloging. A union catalog of books and a union list of serials on a university-wide basis are not usually available for consultation. Many of the faculty libraries are not staffed by trained professional library staff and their materials are not properly catalogued and kept. The library hours are, in most cased, irregular and short, making them not easily accessible to the users. Because one faculty library does not know what the others are doing, unnecessary duplication in acquisition of library materials and journal subscriptions is often found on the same campus. To quote the observation of a foreign expert:

> The library situation is chaotic partly because the building and housing of collections is divided among the rival demands of faculty libraries, departmental libraries and the central library. There is great preference for faculty libraries, but no one of them is completely adequate for advanced study or research in the field. Departmental libraries tend to split up the fields which are represented in the faculty library. And the unanswered question is - What is the purpose of the central library? Sometimes the central library is referred to as though it is a place from which books may be borrowed for indefinite periods by faculty or departmental libraries, sometimes as though it is a repository for basic texts in courses.[3]

---

[3]Cited in ibid., Moody E. Prior, *Report on Graduate Education in Thailand, Bangkok*, as quoted by Barnett, Brown and Stone, p. 67.

This situation of fragmentation of library resources and services occurs not only in Thai universities, but also can be found in many of the other developing countries as well. As stated by an internationally known American librarian:

> Each of these separate libraries in a university may have its own rules and regulations, its own systems - or no system at all - of cataloging and classification, its own restrictions on use, and complete independence of any centralized administrative oversight. There is seldom cooperation among them for exchange of information, interlibrary loan, or coordinated acquisition. The role of the central library is often merely that of a dumping ground for those books which none of the other libraries wants, and it is therefore frequently the least-used by students of any of the university's libraries.[4]

The preceding observations are by no means an exaggeration of the prevailing situation. My own survey, made recently, serves to support the above statements. A summary of the data obtained from the survey is presented below.

The survey was intended to include all Thai institutions of higher learning with university standing that confer degrees but excluding military academies (some of which are considered university equivalents). There are 11 institutions of higher learning in Thailand that fall into this category:

Asian Institute of Technology
Chiangmai University
Chulalongkorn University
College of Education
Kasetsart University
Khonkaen University
Mahidol University (formerly University of Medical Sciences)
National Institute of Development Administration
Prince of Songkla University
Silapakorn University
Thammasat University

Among the 11 institutions named above: two do not have faculty libraries (Asian Institute of Technology and the National Institute of Development Administration); two did not respond to the survey (Chiangmai University and Silapakorn University, both having faculty libraries); leaving seven institutions that provided meaningful data for this study. It is of interest to note that among the seven useful replies, two do not have a central library (College of Education and Prince of

---

[4]Lester Asheim. *Librarianship in the Developing Countries*, p. 6. (Urbana: University of Illinois Press, 1966).

245

Songkla University). Other institutions varied, having from one to ten faculty libraries.

Chulalongkorn University	10 faculty libraries	(Two are off-campus)
College of Education	6 branch libraries	(The college consists of 6 branches, separately located. Each branch has its own library. There is no central library.)
Kasetsart University	4 faculty libraries	(One is off-campus.)
Khonkaen University	1 faculty library	(It is off-campus.)
Mahidol University	7 faculty libraries	(Six are off-campus.)
Prince of Songkla	3 faculty libraries	(The University consists of three faculties located on different campuses. Each has its own library. There is no central library.)
Thammasat University	5 faculty libraries	(None is off-campus.)

According to the statistical information in Appendix I, the only central library having a considerable strength over its faculty libraries is the central library of Thammasat University which has a collection over 125,000 volumes. It is followed by the central library of Chulalongkorn University, Prasarnmitr Campus of the College of Education, and the Siriraj Medical Library of the Mahidol University, each having a collection of 76,477 volumes, 62,000 volumes, and 50,000 volumes respectively. If the resources of all faculty libraries are included, Chulalongkorn University should lead all others with a combined strength of 183,561 volumes compared to the 150,136 volumes which Thammasat University has.

One serious problem, readily evident in the data in Appendix I, is the rather short library hours most of the libraries are open for service. The longest library hours were reported by the Siriraj Medical library which opens 77 hours per week in comparison to the shortest hours reported by a faculty library which opens only 20 hours per week. A compelling fact is that many of the faculty libraries are accessible only during office hours when most students are attending classes.[5]

In regard to other questions asked in the survey, only the central library of Thammasat University has an overall jurisdiction and administrative control over the faculty libraries; three central libraries, Chulalongkorn, Kasetsart, and Thammasat, are reported to have maintained or are in the process of setting up a

---

[5]I was told that some of the faculty libraries do not allow students from other faculties of the same university to use their libraries.

union catalog of all library books that are in the faculty libraries of their respective universities. Two universities, both Mahidol and Thammasat, have a union list of journals. Another one, Chulalongkorn, is in the process of setting one up. Concerning centralized library acquisition and cataloging, the central libraries of Khonkaen and Thammasat reported that they are 100% responsible for the acquisition and cataloging of library materials for their faculty libraries. The central library of Kasetsart University reported that they do the cataloging for one of their faculty libraries. The rest of the central libraries have nothing or little to do with the acquisition and cataloging of library materials for their faculty libraries.

If the faculty libraries were not under the administrative control of the central library. Librarians were asked what kind of machinery was available to coordinate the work of the various faculty libraries and the central library. Except for Thammasat where the central library does have the administrative control over its faculty libraries, most of the other institutions acknowledged having varying degrees of coordination between the central library and faculty libraries. one was by means of a library committee which consists of members from each faculty chaired by the deputy rector for academic affairs with the librarian of the central library serving as secretary. But there were others in which there were only loose coordination between the central library and the faculty libraries.

Another question put to the librarians was: "Are you generally in favor of the present setup of your library and its relationship with the faculty libraries? If your answer is a no, what will you do?" Again, except for Thammasat, most of the libraries surveyed were not in favor of the present set up of their library and their relationships with the faculty libraries, but felt it would be difficult to seek changes in the present situation especially when the administration of many institutions is decentralized.

The last question sought any special comments librarians might have concerning the question of centralized library service versus decentralized library service. Despite the fact that most Thai university libraries are decentralized, the general feeling of the librarians was definitely in favor of a centralized library service, or at least, as put this way by a university librarian, "a coordinated decentralization."[6]

---

[6]"Coordinated decentralization" is a term borrowed from the Harvard University library system where effective measures have been taken to coordinate the many autonomous library units within the University. See Douglas W. Bryant, "Centralization and Decentralization at Harvard, "Centralization and Decentralization at Harvard," *College and Research Libraries*, 3 (1961), pp. 328-334. It is of interest to note, however, that Harvard University Libraries have a combined strength of approximately 8,000,000 volumes with an annual expenditure in the neighborhood of US$8,000,000 in 1967 while the majority of libraries in Thai universities have fewer than 100,000 volumes and spend less than 20,000 US

It seems to be the consensus of the respondents that the limited library resources in Thai universities can be put to better use only through effective coordination between the central library and the various faculty libraries and departmental libraries. but, in order to do so, the position of University Librarian must first be firmly established. This position should carry with it the responsibility and appropriate authority to coordinate the library resources and services within each of the universities. Far-sighted university administrators should stand behind the university librarian and the central library to provide them with whatever support necessary to work out an effective system of coordination between the central library and the various library units.

It is also desirable that small library units in each university be consolidated into large units or be combined with the central library with the exception of those library units located off the main campus. Minimum standards must be required for the creation of new faculty libraries before they are permitted to be established and to begin functioning.

A decentralized library system without an effective means for close coordination of the fragmented resources is not suitable for the universities in developing countries. There are additional reasons for this argument.

1) The majority of academic programs in Thai universities are at the undergraduate level where a basic collection of well selected books and journals may be required by several faculties because of the overlapping needs and the interdisciplinary areas of study. Unnecessary duplication of these publications could be avoided by having them in the central library. Also the use of a well stocked central library will have the advantage over a faculty library in providing the university students with a general and broad educational experience.

2) There are many common reference books and bibliographical works which are essential to provide good library services but are too expensive to be duplicated in the faculty libraries, especially when the funds for library materials are critically inadequate.

3) If faculty libraries are to serve as a useful aid in instruction and research it will require trained library staff to man their services. This will place a great strain on the small number of trained librarians available. If untrained staff are employed, they will not be able to handle the reference, documentation and technical services expect-

---

dollars per year for books and journals. If effective co-ordination of library resources and services is necessary for Harvard it will be even more so for the university libraries in Thailand. Richard DeGennaro, "Automation in the Harvard College Library," *Harvard Library Bulletin*, 16 (1968), p. 218.

ed of them and, consequently, will reduce the usefulness of the library and make the collection inaccessible to its users.

4) It is also wasteful to require that all faculty libraries remain open for long hours and be staffed by trained librarians when a well planned central library can be kept open for service during evenings and weekends with only a skeleton of trained staff to man the key positions.

The decentralized library system, although able to be justified in a large library system where the total collection is very large and strong, is difficult to justify in a small library where the collection is both small and weak and where no effective means of coordination among the various units is available. The fragmentation of academic library resources is not only unable to meet the needs of an undergraduate education but is also inadequate to support the many graduate programs now being offered in many of the Thai universities. A recently published report, A Proposal for the establishment of the Graduate Programs in the Basic Science and Mathematics in Thailand, prepared by a team of experts appointed by the University Development Commission of the National Education Council clearly pointed out the serious deficiency of the many faculty libraries now in existence.[7]

To remedy the aforementioned deficiencies and, at the same time, to take into consideration the strong local tradition of having the academic faculties a considerable autonomy in managing their own academic affairs including the libraries, the following actions are recommended for consideration and possible adoption.

1) The position of the University Librarian (or the Director of University Libraries) should be established in each of the universities to plan and execute the overall development of library resources and services. It should be made clear that the university library consists of all the collections of books in the possession of university, wherever located.

2) The University Librarian should be vested with the responsibility of coordinating the various administratively and geographically decentralized library units so that they will be more responsive to the total needs of the university community. The University Librarian should be a member of the University Senate and have memberships in the committees which concern the academic programs so that he (or she) will be fully informed and involved in the academic development of the university.

---

[7]Thailand, University Development Commission, *A Proposal for the Establishment of the Graduate Programs in the Basic sciences and Mathematics in Thailand* (Bangkok: University Development Commission, 1968), pp. 8-9, 17, 27-28, 44.

3) The librarians of various faculty and departmental libraries should be recruited and recommended for appointment by the University Librarian in consultation with the dean of the faculty or the head of the department concerned. The librarian of the faculty or departmental library should be responsible both to the dean of the faculty or to the head of the department to which his (or her) library belongs and to the University Librarian.

4) There should be a University Libraries Administrative Council with members consisting of the university librarian, two or three senior members of the Central Library, and the librarians of the faculty libraries. The Council should meet regularly to discuss matters of concern to all library units in the university.

5) There should be a Library Advisory Committee for the University librarian consisting of one faculty member from each faculty appointed by the deans of their respective faculties and the University Librarian. The Committee should meet at least four times a year to advise the University Librarian on policy matters.

6) Although the selection of library materials for each of the faculty libraries should be the basic responsibility of the librarians in each of the faculty libraries, centralized acquisition by the central library is strongly urged to achieve economy in the operation and to avoid unnecessary duplications. Since mechanized library operations can be easily employed to obtain maximum efficiency, centralized acquisition and accounting, as well as centralized cataloging and processing should be contemplated to take advantage of modern technology. This would enable the librarians of the faculty libraries to have more free time for direct service to their readers.

7) A union catalog of books and union lists of journal holdings and serial titles should be established and maintained in the Central Library. Whenever it will be economically and technically feasible, printed book catalogs, lists of journal holdings and serial titles should be made available in the faculty and departmental libraries for the convenience of all users.

8) Even though separate library budgets for each faculty library may still be maintained, the University Librarian must see to it that all libraries have received the adequate financial support each of them will require. Careful planning and coordination by the University librarian in consultation with the university officials, deans and the librarians of the faculty libraries is necessary to ensure that the overall goals of the library development in the university will be met. The financial norm that "the annual budget should constitute from 5

to 10 per cent of the total annual university budget" as recommended by the Unesco Regional Seminar on Library Development in South Asia, 3-14 October 1960 in Delhi, India[8] should--as far as possible--be used as a guide for the budget preparation and request.

9) All professionally trained staff, whether they teach or not, should be accorded faculty status with appropriate faculty rank and salary as this will be necessary to attract the best qualified people into the academic librarianship and to enable the libraries to retain their competent staff. In order to enable the librarians to devote more time to their library work, the teaching loads for those who still work and teach should be reduced to a maximum of six hours per week with adequate time allowed for the preparation of lectures and other related instructional duties.

10) All faculty libraries should make their resources and services available not only to their own students and faculty members but also to those from other faculties within the university. Provision should be made also to enable qualified persons from outside the university to use the library collections.

11) A positive step that might be taken by the central library to reduce the number of excuses the faculties have for wanting to have their own faculty libraries is to seek immediate improvement of the resources and services of the central library by making their services more responsive to the specific needs of the faculties. Longer library hours, a more liberal loan policy for the faculty members, faster reference service and expert bibliographic assistance can all contribute to the prestige of a central library and help to earn the confidence and respect of the faculty members. The needs for faculty libraries arise when the service of the central library falls and vice versa.

12) A program of cooperative acquisition should be worked out among the library units so that each can concentrate their efforts in their fields of specialties, not competing to overlap in the subject coverage. Materials required for interdisciplinary areas should be left to the central library. In this way, a much stronger collection can be developed with minimum waste and duplication.

Just to improve the library resources and services within each of the universities is not enough. The developing countries with their limited library resources available must seek also a wider coordination and cooperation among all university

---

[8]"Regional Seminar On Library Development in South Asia," *Unesco Library Bulletin* Vol. 15, No. 4 (1961).

libraries in each of the countries and among academic libraries, governmental libraries, public libraries, special libraries, and the National Library. When the voices of professional librarians are weak in the countries where library development is not considered a priority item, leadership from higher authorities in the educational administration is urgently needed to help the librarians in their respective countries.

In Thailand, for example, the National Education Council, a coordinating body for the planning and development of all levels of education, especially higher education, can help the university librarians by establishing a committee for university libraries to review the needs of academic libraries in the universities and to make recommendations for their improvement. Appropriate legislation and minimum standards for university libraries should be drafted and promulgated to guide the development of university libraries. There is an urgent need at present to provide for the newly established universities a set of guidelines for the organization and development of their library resources and services.

Nationwide projects among the university libraries in the preparation of a union catalog of all academic libraries, a union list of journals and serial titles, interlibrary loan, expanded photocopying service, centralized technical processing, free exchange of duplicate publications, etc. could be initiated and coordinated by the National Education Council in cooperation with the National Library and the Thai National Documentation Centre.

The recommendation made by the Wolf Management services on cooperative acquisition of library materials among university libraries and the proper role of the National Education Council is well taken and should be put into operation as soon as possible:

> The National Education Council should be encouraged to coordinate acquisition of materials among college and university libraries, to help prevent future expensive duplication of high-cost resources. Looking toward expansion of graduate level studies in Thailand, it is imperative that all library resources be reviewed and regarded more or less as a common reservoir.[9]

In conclusion, the shortage of library resources in Thai universities resulting from inadequate funds, not enough trained librarians, and the lack of appropriate books, can nevertheless be improved by effective coordination and consolidation of the various library units with in each of the universities and by inter-university cooperation under the leadership of the National Education Council. The uncoordinated system of decentralization of library resources and services as those com-

---

[9]S.A. Barnett, E.L. Brown and C.W. Stone. *Developmental Book Activities and Needs in Thailand* (New York: Wolf Management Services, 1967) p. 72.

monly found in Thai universities is too luxurious for a country where most of the university libraries are considered small and inadequate in their resources. Effective measures must be taken to pool the library resources together or the programs of instruction and research in Thai universities will be retarded by the inability of their academic libraries to respond effectively to meet the needs.

APPENDIX I

Statistical survey of library resources in the institutions of higher education in Thailand as of January 1970

Except as noted in footnote 4, statistical information was obtained from survey responses from all university librarians.

Name of Institution	Cata-loged volumes	Current journals	Non-current journals	Profes-sional staff	Cleri-cal staff	Library hours per week
Asian Inst. of Tech.	23,236	714	64	3	5	72.5
Chiengmai Univ.[1]						
Chulalongkorn Univ.						
Central Library	76,477	436	200	10	16	52.0
Faculty Libraries						
Architecture	2,267	19	---	1	2	45.0
Arts	6,977	5	---	1	1	20.0
Commerce & Accountancy	4,881	68	---	1	3	44.0
Education	34,292	86	---	4	10	70.5
Engineering	18,817	23	---	1	5	37.5
Medicine[2]	18,397	245	---	3	4	64.0
Political Sci.	4,804	51	---	1	3	54.5
Science	10,300	89	---	1	9	35.0
Veterinary Science[2]	4,020	300	---	0	1	55.5
Mass Comm. & PR	2,329	35	1	1	1	68.0
College of Education[3]						
Prasarnmitr Campus	62,000	351	153	7	2	70.0
Patumwan Campus[4]	11,000	---	---	1	3	63.5
Kasetsart Univ.						
Main Library	30,325	333	474	3	20	64.0
Faculty Libraries						

Name of Institution	Cataloged volumes	Current journals	Non-current journals	Professional staff	Clerical staff	Library hours per week
Econ. & Public Administration	---	---	---	---	---	40.0
Engineering[2]	---	---	---	---	---	40.0
Fisheries	---	---	---	---	---	40.0
Forestry	---	---	---	---	---	40.0
Khonkaen Univ.						
Main Library	3,817	154	198	1	13	76.5
Faculty Libraries						
Agriculture[2]	215	7	---	---	1	35.0
Mahidol Univ.						
Siriraj Medical Library[5]	50,000	450	---	9	6	77.0
Faculty Libraries						
Dentistry[2]	2,410	77	---	1	1	40.0
Medical Tech.	2,185	21	---	0	1	40.0
Pharmacy[2]	5,468	42	---	1	2	49.3
Public Health[2]	5,000	91	33	---	4	40.0
Ramathibodhi Hospital[2]	201	280	24	2	1	70.3
Science[2]	3,000	490	---	3	5	61.5
Tropical Med.[2]	1,420	92	54	1	2	35.0
National Inst. of Development Administration	37,204	597	321	14	17	40.0
Prince of Songkla Univ.[6]						
Faculty Libraries						
Education	5,000	42	15	1	1	50.0
Engineering[2]	---	---	---	---	---	---
Science[2]	---	---	---	---	---	---
Silpakorn Univ.[1,4] Central Library	2,178	(51)		---	---	45.0
Faculty Libraries						
Archaeology	5000	---	---	(3)		35.0

Name of Institution	Cataloged volumes	Current journals	Non-current journals	Professional staff	Clerical staff	Library hours per week
Architecture	690	(8)		(2)		40.0
Painting & Sculpture	700	---	---	(2)		40.0
Tabkaew College	5,763	(53)		1	2	70.0
Thammasat Univ. Central Library	125,702	627	198	12	28	64.0
Faculty Libraries						
Commerce & Accountancy	1,530	16	11	1	3	40.0
Economics	9,404	80	---	2	7	64.0
Law	3,500	15	---	---	---	64.0
Political Science	6,000	70	---	1	---	40.0
Social Administration	4,000	53	---	1	2	64.0

1. No reply was received.

2. The faculty is located off the main campus.

3. The College has six branches, each has its own library.

4. Information obtained from *A Directory of Libraries in Bangkok* (Bangkok: Unesco Regional Office for Education in Asia, 1970).

5. It serves as central library.

6. There is no central library.

A NEW ENGINEERING LIBRARY EMERGING
IN ASIA

Today most of the Asian countries are confronted with the serious problem of a "brain drain," which has gravely hampered the speed of their national development. Unless this situation can be rectified, the gap between the developed countries and the developing countries can never be narrowed. Dependence on foreign technical assistance will not solve the development problems of the region in the long run. Rather, the best brain powers of Asia must be employed for the development of Asia. This is one of the major concerns of Asian nations that are struggling for rapid socio-political, economic, industrial, and technological development as well as for educational and cultural upsurge. Without the "brain power," nothing can be achieved or take root.

There are many factors contributing to the problem of the "brain drain." The inappropriate education and training that many of the young aspirants of Asian countries receive in the developed countries is one such factor. The overtraining and sophisticated education some of them attain constitutes a waste rather than a gain in brain power for the developing countries - this has been referred to as "brain waste."

In order to overcome the problem of a "brain drain" or, in some cases, a "brain waste," a new regional postgraduate school, the Asian Institute of Technology, (AIT) has been founded. It was first established in 1959 as the SEATO Graduate School of Engineering in Bangkok. In 1967, it became completely indepenaent of the Southeast Asia Treaty Organization (SEATO). The A.T is an autonomous, nonprofit, private, regional institution of advanced engineering education and research in Asia. It is governed by an international board òf trustees with 22 trustee members from 13 countries serving as individual members rather than as representatives of their countries. As of September 1971, the AIT Board consists of members from the following countries: Australia, Republic of China, France, Indonesia, Japan, Malaysia, New Zealand, Pakistan, the Philippines, Thailand, the United Kingdom, the United states, and South Vietnam.

AIT Program

During the 1971-1972 academic year, 215 graduate students representing 18 Asian countries were enrolled in the three types of programs - the eight-month diploma program, the twenty-month Masters degree program, and the two-year Doctoral degree program. The majority of students are enrolled in the Master's degree program under one of the six academic divisions: Environmental Engineering, Geotechnical Engineering, Structural Engineering and Mechanics, Systems Engineering and Management, Transportation Engineering, and Water Science and

257

Engineering. A new division in Agricultural Engineering will be added in January 1972, and in September 1972, another division, Electrical engineering - Power Systems is to be added.

According to the Master Plan, in 1980 AIT will become a complete institute of technology offering graduate programs in all engineering branches and related fields with a projected enrollment of 1,000. Besides the three types of programs already mentioned, the Institute will also provide in-service training and continuing education for a large number of practicing engineers, researchers, and engineering faculty of other universities through a series of seminars, workshops, conferences, and short courses. A number of short courses and conferences have already been organized and offered, but the scope of this type of continuing education will be greatly expanded in the years ahead to hasten the pace of technological development in the region by helping the engineers to keep abreast of the new knowledge available in their respective fields. The distinction of AIT's academic program, as has been demonstrated thus far, is not only to attain a quality engineering education of very high standard, which is necessary to attract the best engineering students in Asia, but also to provide an education that is relevant to the conditions and needs of the region so that its graduates can be best prepared to serve their countries.

The employment records on AIT graduates, now approaching 450, speak well of the Institute's accomplishment. Besides the 7 percent who went on for doctoral studies in the West and the 4 percent who sought employment outside Asia, the remaining 89 percent have stayed Asia to engage in various engineering works. Roughly over half, or 54 percent, of those who stay on are in government service, 24 percent work in private enterprise, and 22 percent teach in Asian universities.

AIT Library Activities

The fact that there are few adequate and up-to-date engineering libraries in Asia has prompted AIT to exert a major effort in building up a strong library resource in engineering and related subjects to serve the needs of both AIT and the region. Recent statistics reveal that the Library collection has now exceeded 35,000 books and over 1,000 journals. In addition to this conventional stock, the library also has a large number of microfiches, microfilms, technical documents and reports, maps, slides, and films. Close cooperation is maintained with other academic, research, and special libraries in Bangkok for interlibrary loan and photocopying services. For the necessary back up support, the Library has also made extensive use of the various services rendered by major libraries and documentation centers throughout the world, such as the Library of Congress, the National Library of Medicine, Linda Hall Library, and John Crerar Library in the United states and the National Lending Library for Science and Technology in Great Britain.

Although the primary function of the AIT Library is to support the instructional and research programs of the Institute, by virtue of the regional characteristics of AIT, the Library also has a regional dimension and obligation. In fact, the Board of Trustees sees the Library as a regional resource and has envisioned it as a regional library and information center in engineering and related fields. In doing so, a preliminary proposal was drawn up in February 1971 and was subsequently submitted to foundations and governmental and international agencies for financial support. Should the necessary funds be obtained, the regional library and information center concept will soon be implemented.

In preparing to assume the larger role, the Library has been actively taking part in many regional cooperative projects and activities and, at the same time, vigorously pursuing the course of expansion and innovation. Computer application in the housekeeping functions of the library was introduced in 1968. At present, it consists of the acquisitions and accounting system and the serials listing and control system.[1] Further applications are planned for the time when a larger computer system becomes available at AIT in place of the current IBM 1130.

The effective transference of scientific and technological knowledge from the developed countries to the developing countries depends to a large extent on the availability of a responsive information system or systems which have a large bibliographical database prepared both by external and internal sources. The AIT Library is currently investigating the possibility of setting up a bibliographical database using the MARC magnetic tapes and the *Engineering Index Compendex* as the major inputs.

To expedite the process of information transfer, consideration has also been given to satellite communications for linkage of national information centers in the various parts of Asia and with the major libraries in the developed countries. It is hoped that a regional network of library and information systems can be established through cooperative efforts. a preliminary discussion of such a possibility was to be held at the Conference on Scientific and Technical Information Needs for Malaysia and Singapore, in Kuala Lumpur, September 24 to 26, 1971. The Conference was jointly sponsored by the Library Association of Malaysia and the Library Association of Singapore with invited participants from other southeast Asian countries.[2]

The Asian Institute of Technology is now temporarily located on the campus of

---

[1]For a detailed description of these two systems see the article by this author, "Library Mechanization at the Asian Institute of Technology," *International Library Review*, Vol. 3, No. 3 (June 1971), pp. 257-70.

[2]By invitation, this author submitted a paper on the topic of "Regional Cooperation in Scientific and Technical Information Services."

Chulalongkorn University (the largest Thai national university) situated in the center of Bangkok. The Library of the Institute occupies a space of approximately 5,000 square feet. The rapidly growing collection and the heavy use both by AIT students and faculty and by outside patrons crowd the facility.

Fortunately, this situation will be eliminated in August 1972 when AIT will move from its present location to the new campus located 42 kilometers from Bangkok on 400 acres of land donated by the Thai Government. The new campus, now under construction, at a cost of US$20 million, when completed, will be among the best in Asia. The first phase of construction, costing more than $6.2 million, includes a major academic building - a part of which will temporarily house the library, an administration building, a campus services complex, dormitory rooms and dining facilities for 350 students, and five faculty residences. A permanent library building that will occupy 100,000 square feet of space is being planned for completion in 1974.

AIT Assistance to Other Libraries

The spirit of cooperation among libraries in Thailand and elsewhere in Asia is important for the development of better library service in the region. In pursuance of this aim, the AIT Library has been generously providing assistance to other libraries in many ways. For example, consultations were held on the establishment of the Asian Highway Technical Information Center and the reorganization plan of the Khonkaen University Library. Short training courses were conducted for library staff of the two organizations. A number of special demonstrations and lectures on computer applications were given to librarians of other libraries and to students in the several library schools in Bangkok. Exchange of duplicate books and journal files is undertaken from time to time with other libraries. Finally, the library has been actively participating in the cooperative projects of compiling a union list of serials and special bibliographies. The implementation of regional library services, if successful, will undoubtedly enhance the present role of the AIT Library to an even greater extent.

PRINCIPLES OF
NATIONAL LIBRARY AND INFORMATION POLICY

Introduction

The last quarter of this century has been described as the "information age" and our society, as an "information society." More than ever before, our world is becoming information dependent. The "information gap" between industrialized countries whose information needs have ben better served and developing countries whose information needs have been less well served is becoming wider and more serious. There is also a growing concern for the disparity in communication and information capacities among different countries. To expedite the pace of social, economic, political, cultural, scientific and technological development, it is necessary to improve library and information services to provide the information required for development. The effort to raise the level of library and information services in every country, including the Republic of China which is among the more highly developed countries of Asia, should be carefully planned and centrally coordinated at the national level to achieve maximum results.

Japan, in recent years, offers a successful model. The comprehensive National Information System for Science and Technology (NIST) plans and coordinates the information service activities of all branches and disciplines as well as the actual work done by the Japan Scientific and Technical Information Center (JICST) to collect, analyze, disseminate useful information for national development. An official white paper by the Japanese government in 1981 on the development of science and technology details the government's policies regarding scientific and technical information and compares these with other major industrialized countries. A Chinese translation is available.[1]

In planning and coordinating library and information services at the national level, every country needs to formulate a comprehensive national library and information policy targeted at supporting national development objectives. Intended as an aid to national planning for a sound library and information policy, this paper discusses the origin, definition, objectives, importance, principles and issues regarding a national library and information policy in the hope of generating further thought and discussion on this vitally important subject.

---

[1]*White Paper on the Science and Technology of Japan: Comparison of Science and Technology with other Countries and the Policy Decision of Japan.* Science and Technology Series, No. 8 (Taipei: Science and Technology Information Center of the National Science Council, 1983.) (In Chinese).

Origin

Discussion and formulation of national library and information policies, either in full or part, have been underway in some countries since the 1950s, but treatment in library literature has been sporadic and incomplete. The systematic promotion of a comprehensive national library and information policy in every country has been a major goal of the United Nations Educational, Scientific and Cultural Organization (Unesco) in the 1970s under its UNISIST program for a "world science information system." The emphasis is to provide effective coordination between the development of library and information services, especially scientific and technical information, and the information needs of national development.

A review of Unesco's activities in the promotion of library, information, documentation, and archive services in every country provides interesting insights into several major developments under the Unesco banner.[2] The UNISIST program was officially launched in 1971 after a four-year feasibility study undertaken in collaboration with the International Council of Scientific Unions (ICSU). The program administered by the Division of Scientific Documentation and Information in the science sector of Unesco emphasized scientific and technical information. To carry out the program, each country was asked to establish a national UNISIST committee and to select a national focal point. In 1974 came the NATIS (National Information System) program administered by the Department of Documentation, Libraries and Archives in the culture section of Unesco. The emphasis of NATIS was somewhat broader in scope. It encompassed library, documentation and archive services and focused on national planning and development. Both UNISIST and NATIS promoted the idea of establishing a national information policy in each country in the service of national development.

To eliminate the duplication of the two overlapping programs within Unesco, a decision was made in 1977 to incorporate NATIS into UNISIST and to place it under the administration of a new division called the General Information Programme which reports directly to the Assistant Director-General for Studies and Programming in the Unesco Secretariat.

The new division recognizes the interdependence of libraries, information centers, documentation services and archives that make up the backbone of library and information services. It seeks to harmonize on a national scale the coordination, planning and functioning of infrastructures as an important concept in developing and implementing national information policies. Such policies are best placed within the overall context of national development policies in other fields and embodied in national development plans to ensure adequate attention, publicity and support. Of

---

[2]J. Stephen Parker, *UNESCO and Library Development Planning* (London: The Library Association, 1985).

the five main themes of the General Information Programme of Unesco below, the policy consideration tops all others:

1. Promotion of the formulation of information policies and plans at national, regional, and international levels;

2. Promotion and dissemination of methods, norms, and standards for information, handling;

3. Contributions to the development of infrastructures;

4. Contributions to the development of specialized information systems in all disciplines; and

5. Promotion of the training and education of specialists in and users of information.

A number of Unesco publications have discussed national information policies in greater detail.[3]

Definition

Although the formulation of information policy and plans at the national level has been strongly promoted by Unesco under its UNISIST program, the definition of information policy is often unclear. The emphasis has been on scientific and technical information rather than on a wider context of information which include libraries and information services covering all subjects as well as publishing and other scholarly communications and information dissemination.

A national library and information policy must be broad in scope and coverage. It can be considered as a conscious attempt to direct and improve, on a long-term basis, the structure, organization, program, resources, and services of the nation's library and information systems and networks comprised of libraries, information centers, documentation services, archives, and related activities. The inclusion of publishers and information industries, both in the public and private sectors, in policy considerations is highly desirable.

---

[3]D. J. Urquhart, *National Information Policy: NATIS National Information Systems* (Paris: UNESCO, 1976). COM 76/NATIS/6.

John Gray, *Information Policy Objectives: UNISIST Proposals* (Paris: UNESCO, 1974). SC/74/WS/3.

Ines Wesley-Tanaskovic, *Guidelines on National Information Policy: Scope, Formulation and Implementation* (Paris: UNESCO, 1985). PGI-85443/14.

Put simply, national library and information policy can be defined as statements or general principles for planned and coordinated development of the nation's library and information services, including publishing and information industries, in accordance with the existing conditions in the country and its information needs for national development. The policy should address the key issues in library and information services and provide administrative guidelines for long-range management planning, decision-making, and implementation.

Objectives

In considering the formulation of a national library and information policy, several important policy objectives come to mind. These include:

1. The promotion of the free flow and use of human knowledge for the benefit of both individuals and society.

2. The requirement that information from all sources, especially from the public sector, unless classified or restricted, should be made available as a national resource.

3. The principle of free and unrestricted use of library and information services by the general public on a not-for-profit basis and for charging reasonable fees for specialized information services.

4. The provision of timely and relevant information for decision-making to decision-makers and researchers at all levels of government and in all sectors of the society.

5. The recognition of the important and mutually complementary roles played by libraries, information centers, documentation services, and archives in the selection, collection, storage, analysis, retrieval, and dissemination of information.

6. The design of appropriate administrative structures and mechanisms to effectively coordinate major programs and activities as well as to monitor and evaluate results.

7. The determination of source and level of funding to adequately support library and information services.

Besides the above policy objectives, the primary purpose of a national information policy, stated by Guinchat and Menou,[4] is to maximize the effectiveness of the national information system, and in particular:

1. To work out the information needs of different socio-professional groups;

2. to establish priorities in regard to these needs;

3. to decide how the national information systems should be organized, what services should be provided and how this is to be done;

4. to constantly monitor the capacity of the national information infrastructure (i.e., all the human, material and financial resources devoted to scientific and technical information) to cover these needs;

5. to decide what measures are needed to enable the national information system to perform its role; and

6. to decide how the national information system should be further developed.

In addition to these main guidelines, Guinchat and Menou[5] also identified a number of specific policies dealing with many aspects of scientific and technical information:

1. Development and improvement of primary publications and, more generally, of the availability of information and data;

2. expansion of document holdings and collections of data, and improved access to them;

3. access to foreign collections of documents and databases;

4. development of translation services;

5. bibliographic control, indexing and analysis of documents produced in the country;

6. development of documentation services (referral, retrospective searches, current awareness, SDI, etc) and information services;

---

[4]Clare Guinchat and Michel Menou, *General Introduction to the Techniques of Information and Documentation Work* (Paris: UNESCO, 1983), p. 314.

[5]Ibid., pp. 314-315.

7. coordination between the various information units and specialized subsystems;

8. development and standardization of equipment for the processing and communication of information;

9. standardization of information techniques and products;

10. development of specialized manpower and training facilities;

11. financing of units and the pricing of their services;

12. preparation of appropriate legislation and regulations for information activities;

13. promotion of services and user education;

14. encouragement of research and development in the information science;

15. closer cooperation with other countries and participation in international networks.

Although this list of objectives, guidelines, and specific policies is by no means complete or inclusive, it provides some excellent examples at what a national library and information policy should aim.

Importance

The preceding portion of this paper documented the need for a national library and information policy. Such a policy is important for the following reasons:

1. It calls attention to the vital roles played by library and information services in national development.

2. It provides a general statement of direction for the development of library and information services.

3. It helps the coordination of planning and implementation of library and information services at the highest levels of the government.

4. It appeals to the government for adequate funding of library and information services.

5. It makes possible integrating the policy into the national development plans.

6. It invites the participation and input in policy formulation by government leaders, planners, representative users of information, and library and information professionals.

The mere formulation of a library and information policy by a wide range of interested and concerned constituencies helps to familiarize them with the work of library and information professions and to rally their support. A national library and information policy is a way to make certain that the country's information needs, or at least its priority needs, are satisfied as far as possible and that all available resources are utilized with maximum economy and effectiveness. This can only he done through a collective effort in the preparation and implementation of policy decisions, joint actions, compromises, and the coordination of activities.

Principles

It has been said that national library and information policy should be formulated with the information needs and the specific information environment of the countries in mind. Beyond the policy objectives and guidelines already mentioned which should be taken into consideration in policy formulation, a new additional general principles should be observed.

1. **It should be based on actual situations and existing conditions of each country.**

    The information needs and the strategy for meeting them will differ in every country depending on the level of development and the infrastructure available. Often, this difference is dictated by the social, economic and political systems of the country. Allocation of priorities is necessary in countries having limited library and information resources and infrastructures.

2. **It should support the information needs in national development.**

    As much as possible, a national library and information policy should be in concert with the development goals of the country. It should consider the established priorities in the national development plans and their information requirements. For maximum impact, national library and information policy should be incorporated into the national development plans with steps for implementation.

3. **It should be formulated by a national commission at the highest government levels and be implemented by a national coordinating agency.**

    The importance of library and information services to national development should be a sufficient reason for the appointment of a national commission to formulate the national library and information policy. In the Republic of China's case, for example, the commission should have membership from the executive and legislative branches of the government, the Directors of the National Central Library and the Science and Technology Information Center of the National Science Council, representatives of the economic and cultural planning and development councils, the Library Association of China, the publishers association, and users. In addition to formulating policies, the commission may also be empowered to develop a comprehensive plan for the development of the nation's library and information services, that is, the means for implementing the policy. Such a plan may call for the establishment of a national coordinating agency to oversee and monitor the implementations of the plan.

4. **The policy should result in a well developed program for the development of the nation's library and information services and the infrastructures necessary for their provision.**

Because a national policy is considered as a statement or general principle for planned and coordinated development of the nation's library and information services, the design of a program and budget for the attainment of policy objectives should be the next step. The program may include both long and medium-terms and be implemented under the oversight and coordination of the national coordinating agency. Again, in the case of the Republic of China, such a coordinating agency may best be placed within the National Central Library which has played a leading role in the overall library development of the country. Should this be considered, the status of the National Central Library should be raised accordingly. The placing of the National Central Library, as it is now, under the Department of Social Education in the Ministry of Education is viewed by many as inappropriate and too low to fulfill its role as the national library. In policy considerations, the place of the National Central Library in the Government's hierarchy should be reviewed and, hopefully, adjusted upward.

5. **It should emphasize the interdependence of all types of library and information services.**

Although libraries, information centers, documentation services and archives have distinct purposes and functions, especially those with special missions, they also have many things in common and often can not get along without the others. To enhance the overall library and information services in a country the diversity of types should be respected and fostered while their common bonds are strengthened. Special encouragement should be given to cooperation and mutual support among libraries and information centers across the separate systems or subsystems at every level. In the development of information systems, not only scientific and technical information are important, other fields such as business, economics, industry, etc., should

268

receive equal attention. A harmonized development of all information resources and services, not just scientific and technical information, is an important reason that the national library should be considered as the national coordinating agency.

6. **It should ensure maximum availability and convenience of use for all information.**

The policy should make certain that diversified library and information resources are available to every user regardless of their location, vocation, education or wealth. A comprehensive plan for the division of responsibility in acquisitions, cataloging, analysis, indexing, abstracting, storage, and dissemination of useful information should be centrally developed and coordinated. The methods of cooperative acquisitions which have been successfully implemented in many countries should be employed at both local and national levels. In the use of information, all unnecessary restrictions and barriers should be removed to facilitate easy access to library and information services by all users.

7. **It should consider the impact of new library and information technologies.**

For effective and efficient handling of library and information resources, which are growing by leaps and bounds, to better serve the information needs of users requires the application of appropriate library and information technologies which include computers, telecommunication, micrographics, videotext, and a score of other new developments. Recent breakthroughs in computers capable of processing Chinese characters are of great importance for library and information services in the Republic of China. In planning for library automation, the successful example of OCLC (Online Computer Library Center) in the U.S.A. in the area of online shared cataloging, union catalog, interlibrary loan, etc., can serve as a model. The formulation and standardization of procedures, formats, rules, codes, systems, etc., should be established at the earliest possible stage to facilitate systems development and interconnection. In planning for library automation and networking, central coordination beginning at the earliest stage is highly desirable to maximize the cost-effectiveness of such undertakings.

8. **It should encourage active participation in international cooperation and programs.**

The recent developments in the international arena led by Unesco and other international organizations such as the International Federation of Library Associations and Institutions (IFLA), the International Council of Archives (ICA), the International Federation of Documentation (FID), etc., have expedited the growth of international cooperation in library and information services. Participation in international programs and other cooperative activities through bilateral agreements or multi-lateral arrangements should be encouraged as long as these are judged as beneficial to all parties.

The availability of remote online access via satellite of large, computerized databases in the U.S. and elsewhere in the world has opened up new opportunities as well as problems. Searches of bibliographic databases often generate large numbers of citations for which the documents are not available locally, and the costs of searches are expensive. To save communication costs, certain heavily used foreign databases can he either purchased or leased to run in local computers at major libraries and information centers which then make the databases available to local users. Creation of domestic databases, complementing but not duplicating those already available, should be initiated and the efforts coordinated.

9. **It should plan for the manpower needs in library and information services.**

Because the manpower needs are sufficiently diverse, both in terms of levels and specializations, a wide range of educational and training programs should be planned. These may include formal education at the undergraduate and graduate levels, as well as a variety of in-service training and/or continuing education programs. The policy should encourage the upgrading of library and information education at all levels and the provision of more opportunities for in-service training and continuing education. Position classifications and pay scales for library and information workers of all levels and specializations should commensurate with the qualifications required for each and with comparable professions to attract and retain talented and dedicated staff.

10. **It should promote the importance of library and information services and user education.**

The promotion of library and information services and the education of library and information users should go hand-in-hand as both will increase the rate and level of library and information use. It is generally recognized that unless the library and information resources and services are fully utilized, their true value will remain under appreciated.

11. **It should provide the basis for appropriate legislative actions pertaining to library and information services and to publishing and related activities.**

The policy should call for a review and update, if needed, of existing laws and regulations pertaining to library and information services and to publishing and related information activities. New laws should be enacted and regulations promulgated to enforce the policy and to guarantee the free and unrestricted access to public information through library and information services.

270

Issues

Beyond the major principles to be considered, some of the vital issues confronting policy makers in the Republic of China are:

(1) What should be the proper governing structure for library and information services at the national level? Which is the most preferable: centralization, decentralization or coordinated decentralization?

(2) Should the National Central Library be the coordinating agency for the planning and development of the nation's library and information services?

(3) Where should the National Central Library be in the administrative structure of the central Government?

(4) Should scientific and technical information be the only concern of a national information policy or should such policy cover the whole realm of library and information services?

(5) Should library and information services be offered free or at a fee? This issue also touches upon the question of public sector versus private sector in information services, and the debate between the advocates of free enterprise and those of free access. Is it more important for the public to have access to the information than for a private organization to profit from it?

Because each of the above issues is sufficiently major, this paper can not adequately consider the ramifications of these issues from all points of view. They are raised here to stimulate further discussions by library and government leaders as well as others concerned in the Republic of China. It is hoped, that from a careful consideration of these issues, some consensus can be reached and compromises made. The end result will be a sound policy providing administrative guidelines for long-range management planning, decision-making, and implementation for the nation's libraries, information centers, documentation services, and archives.

Section VIII

Library Networking

Proposal for the Establishment of a
National Library and Information Network
(In Chinese) (1974) 275

Sharing Information Resources Through
Computer-Assisted Systems and Network (1978) 281

A Sketch for a Computerized National Library
and Information Network (1981) 289

Planning Process and Considerations for a State-wide
Academic Libraries Information System in Ohio (1989) 297

建立全國圖書資料網芻議

一、前　　言

　　最近筆者有幸應邀回國參加第二屆國家建設會議，對國內近年來在政經建設及文教發展各方面所獲致的重大成就，有極深刻的印象；對舉國上下堅苦卓絕，努力建設的精神，尤感欽佩。在會議期間曾抽暇參觀幾所圖書館及新遷到南港隸屬國科會的科技資料中心，藉機向國內圖書館的部份同仁及先進請教，所見所聞，獲益匪淺。根據筆者愚見，深感國內的圖書館及資料中心在最近幾年來，不論在質與量方面，都有顯著的進步；但這種進步，若以當前經建發展過程中的需要來衡量，則又嫌不足。當此人類知識文化與科學技術正在突飛猛晉的時代，圖書館與資料中心的任務與使命不但大為加重，其地位亦顯然提高。愈是發展程度高的國家，對於圖書資料的需要愈為廣泛與迫切。我國經濟與科技的發展，目前已達到相當程度，對於圖書資料的需求，今後將日趨迫切。

二、圖書館的功能與使命

　　圖書館負有保存及延續人類知識與文化的使命。『保存』人類知識與文化的遺產固屬重要，但單僅保存是消極的、被動的；圖書館更重大的使命是積極的『延續』人類的知識與文化，使其發揚光大，造福人群。要想達到這種『承先啓後』、『繼往開來』的功能與使命，一方面固有賴於圖書館同仁在觀念及方法上的革新；另一方面亦有賴於社會對於圖書館的重視與支持，使之能發揮其應有的功能。

　　自從第二次世界大戰以後，由於知識的發展與科學的進步，促成了出版品的大量增加；由於出版品的劇增，有人比喻廿世紀七十年代為『資料爆炸』的時代。這種知識與資料的劇增，對於圖書館及資料中心的功能與使命產生巨大的影響。第一、在過去，學者專家們鑽研學問可以不依靠圖書館來供應圖書資料，現在已不復可能；第二、科學與技術的加速發展有賴於圖書資料的適時供應與有效支援；第三、面對浩如煙海的新知識與出版品，即使大規模的圖書館，要想盡量蒐集，亦感力不從心；第四、除了蒐集之外，對於圖書資料的整理、分類、儲藏、檢索、流通及使用等，舊的觀念與方法已不足應付。基於以上幾點改變，世界各國的圖書館都在迅速蛻變與創新，以求趕上時代，擔當起新時代中圖書館所應擔負的任務。

三、當前的趨勢

近幾年來，由於前述因素的影響，世界各國圖書館的發展有以下五點趨勢，頗值我們參考借鏡：

一、館際間分工合作的加強：圖書館館際間可以合作的項目甚多，如圖書互借，聯合目錄的設置，分類採購蒐集，及統一編目等，在國內外的圖書館間已有很多先例，其中不乏有相當成效者。當此出版品汗牛充棟且價格急遽上漲之時，欲使有限的經費、人力、與設備能發揮最大的效果，實有賴於圖書館間的密切合作，一方面互通有無，相互支援；一方面分類採購，避免重複。這種有計劃的合作是充實全國圖書資料的一項極重要的工作，亟待推廣及加強。

二、新方法及技術的採用：由於圖書館藏書不斷增加，業務加繁及人員加多，許多圖書館已紛紛採用科學的管理方式來處理一般業務。此外，由於科學技術發達，許多新穎的技術已逐漸為圖書館所採用，以擴充服務項目，增進工作效率，充分發揮圖書館的效能。此種技術目前已被使用者有微影技術、複印技術、視聽技術、電腦技術、及電訊技術等。其中有許多可值我們採用者。這些新技術若由各圖書館個別使用，也許很不經濟；但若由若干圖書館聯合使用，則不僅經濟有效，更能促進圖書館的效能。

三、特殊資料中心的設立：特殊資料中心（Specialized Information Center）的設立係由特別圖書館（Special Library）演變而來，其性質較之特別圖書館尤為專門。對於特殊資料的儲存及檢索較特別圖書館更為講究。有些資料中心還將有關資料加以精簡化，再個別的提供給某些特約的使用者。特殊資料中心有的按學科而設，有的按任務而設；有的隸屬於圖書館，有的單獨設立，情況各別。許多國家更設有全國性的科技資料中心以統籌及協調全國的科技資料及有關活動。我國國科會的科技資料中心即為一例。

四、大規模目錄及資料庫的建立：因為圖書資料的大量增加，為求有效控制，許多國家的國家圖書館已開始建立國家目錄，力求完整齊全。許多學術團體、政府及私人機構亦分別編印各種索引或摘要，以應所需。這種工作非常必要，但亦十分艱巨，因此非一般圖書館或資料中心可以個別承當。目前這種大規模的目錄及索引，如英美的 MARC (Machine-Readable Catalog) 和舉世聞名的化學摘要（Chemical Abstracts）等皆已陸續使用電腦作業，以節省人力及增廣用途。

五、圖書資料網的建立：圖書資料網的建立是館際合作的加強與具體化，其規模可大可小，其組織與性質亦按個別需要及特殊情況而定。大抵在縱的方面可按地域來分地，在橫的方面可按學科、使命或圖書館的類別來分。縱與橫之間的聯繫與合作可以逐步發展，由小而大，由簡而繁，最後達到世界性的圖書館網，以促進國際間圖書資料的自由流通。目前聯合國文教組織正為推動此一構想而努力。依我國目前的情況，我們亟應計劃及建立一個全國性的圖書資料網，使全國的圖書館及資料中心能按照國家需要做全面性的發展，使得有限的資源能發揮最大的效用；對內可促進國家的建設與發展；對外可增強國際合作與文化交流。

四、各國的先例

有關圖書資料網的建立，世界各國不乏先例。以美國之富裕及其圖書資料的完備，對圖書資料網的建立尚且不遺餘力，這種例子值得我們借鏡。美國立國的精神是以地方分權為主，加以土地面積廣大，故其圖書資料網的建立多由各州開始，目前著有成效者計有：一、新英格蘭圖書館網，二、柯羅拉多學術圖書館圖書處理中心，三、俄亥俄學院圖書館中心等。近年來全國性的圖書資料網亦逐漸分科設立，其進行已有相當成績者計有：一、以國家醫學圖書館為首的生物醫學通訊網，二、以國家農業圖書館為首的農業科學資料網及三、由國會圖書館主持的國家採購及編目計劃和全國刊物資料系統等。

除此以外，國會圖書館尚將全國圖書目錄的作業電腦化，其所創用的MARC格式，逐漸為世界各國所採用，促成了各國間國家目錄電腦作業的格式劃一。為了要進一步地促進全國各圖書館及資料中心的合作與發展，美國政府在最近還成立了一個全國圖書館及資料科學委員會，來計劃及推行全國圖書資料發展的工作。美國政府的商業部亦設立一所全國科技資料服務中心，來蒐集全國的科技研究與發展的報告，予以整理、分類、與摘要，再編入分類索引半月刊及綜合索引月刊，印發全國各地，使得有關科技的新知識資料能夠迅速而廣泛地被流傳與使用。

在英國，建立一個全國圖書資料網的計劃目前正在實施中。除了地方性的圖書館以外，政府最近尚將歷史悠久的大英博物館圖書館與其他四所國立圖書館，一同歸併入一個新的體制之中名之為大英圖書館，重新分割各圖書館的職責，將其性質重疊者予以合併或裁減，以建立一個切實有效的全國圖書資料網。

在加拿大，一九六九年頒佈的國家圖書館法授權國家圖書館館長（National Librarian）以調協全國圖書館發展之責。對於全國圖書資料網的建立發生了積極有效的作用。

在亞洲國家中，首先計劃設立全國圖書資料網者當以印尼為首。印尼政府在第一個五年發展計劃（一九六九—一九七三）中即特別強調改進科技資料供應與服務的重要性。由於圖書館界同仁的努力及國外專家的協助，一個全國圖書資料網的建立計劃經已擬定。因為印尼尚無一所國家圖書館，故有關全國圖書資料的蒐集及目錄編印等工作，將交由四所已具有規模的圖書館去分別負責，並將此四所圖書館置於一個新設置的國家圖書館長之下，由其統籌計劃及協調全國圖書資料網的發展。

五、建立圖書資料網的步驟

有鑒於當前世界趨勢及我國的國情與需要，筆者認為建立一個全國性的圖書資料網實在是當務之急，刻不容緩。為了拋磚引玉，特將個人一點淺陋的構想提出來以就教於國內圖書館同仁及學者專家。

一、在行政院下設立全國圖書資料網計劃執行委員會（以下簡稱委員會）。委員十五人，由行政院長遴聘，任期兩年，連聘得連任。

1.主任委員由現任國立中央圖書館館長兼任。

2.第一期委員中之半數，任期一年，以後每年得改聘委員會委員之半數。

3.委員之成員除國立中央圖書館館長外，應包括國科會、教育部、經濟部、國防部、交通部及科技資料中心等六單位之有關業務高級主管各一人，圖書館從業人員六人及出版界二人。

4.委員會得依實際需要設立秘書處及有關科組以掌理計劃、研究、發展、考核、及財政之責。

5.委員會之經費得由秘書處按照需要逐年編列預算呈請行政院支付。

二、本委員會應盡速擬定全國圖書館及資料中心的政策與發展計劃，包括全國圖書資料網的建立，呈請行政院核准後頒佈施行。

三、本委員會應負有督導全國圖書資料網建立與發展之責。

四、本委員會應根據實際情況及需要將全國各主要圖書館及資料中心之職責作下列重點分配，例如：

1. 國立中央圖書館應有下列各項職責：

A、本國圖書目錄中心。

B、本國期刊目錄中心。

C、本國官書目錄中心。

D、本國圖書期刊官書編目中心。

E、全國聯合圖書目錄中心。

F、國際圖書之交換與合作。

2. 科技資料中心應有下列各項職責：

A、本國科技資料之蒐集、分類、儲藏、檢索、流通、使用等。

B、本國科技資料目錄中心。

C、全國期刊聯合目錄中心。

D、國際科技資料之蒐集與交換。

3. 工業技術研究院圖書館應為全國工業技術之資料及服務中心。

4. 中山研究院應為全國國防科學及技術之圖書館及資料中心。

5. 其他各圖書館應分別著重下列各學科之圖書與期刊之蒐集：

A、臺大圖書館——自然科學、人文科學。

B、臺大醫學院——醫學、衛生。

C、臺大法學院——法律及聯合國文獻等。

D、中央研究院傅斯年圖書館——歷史、語言。

E、政大——社會科學。

F、師大——教育。

G、成大——工程。

H、清華——原子能、核子科學。

I、交通——電訊。

J、中興——農業。

K、中大——地球物理。

L、故宮博物館——古籍、珍本、檔案等。

五、本委員會應擬定全國各圖書館館際互借及資料流通之辦法。寓輔助於獎勵，應按每年出借圖書之多寡訂定經費輔助辦法。

六、本委員會應在全國各地指定若干圖書館或資料中心，設立統一採購及編目中心，其經費不敷之數得由本委員會酌予補助。

七、本委員會應在全國各地選定若干地點適中的圖書館或資料中心，協助其裝設電傳打字機以建立館際通訊網，加強館際的聯繫。

八、本委員會應考慮設立一電腦作業中心，專供各圖書館及資料中心之用。

九、本委員會應根據全國專業人才的需要，擬訂長短程圖書資料專業人員的培養與訓練計劃，協助及輔導各有關訓練機構，以加強專業人員職前教育及在職訓練。

以上各點構想仍以第一點為最重要，希望政府當局能採納實施。有了委員會的組織，則其他計劃及實行細則皆可由委員會成員集思廣益，逐項加以訂定，付諸實施。

六、結　論

加強一國的圖書館及資料中心的效能，固有賴於政府的輔導，社會的支持，以提高其地位，寬裕其經費，改善其設備，增加其圖書的蒐集與收藏；但圖書館及資料中心本身對於觀念與方法的革新，對於專業人員訓練的加強，以及館際間的合作等，亦不容忽視。除此以外，由於圖書資料的急遽增加及社會對於圖書館及資料中心的需求日漸加重，欲使有限的經費、人力、與設備，得以發揮最大的效能，有賴全國各圖書館及資料中心的同仁，秉於本身職責之艱巨，在政府輔助與督導下，設立一全國性的計劃及協調的機構，以擬定全國圖書資料長短程的發展計劃，並將全國各圖書館及資料中心納入一個整體的圖書資料網內，使得全國的圖書館及資料中心能配合國家的需要作全面的發展。

SHARING INFORMATION RESOURCES
THROUGH COMPUTER-ASSISTED
SYSTEMS AND NETWORKING

Introduction

Although information is regarded as an inexhaustible resource, making it fully available and easily accessible in meeting the diversified needs of its users requires that it be collected, organized, and shared. There is an economical reason, too, for the sharing of information resources, not only for the information "poor" countries, but also for the information "rich." With the continued rise in both the quantity and cost of publications, the shrinking of library budgets, and the constant broadening of user demands resulting from the expanding frontiers of knowledge, it becomes quite clear that finite library budgets have made it increasingly difficult to meet the infinite demands of users.

Library cooperation in sharing resources is not a new concept. In fact, many such activities have long been in existence: shared cataloging, reciprocal borrowing and photocopying, interlibrary loan, cooperative acquisitions, exchange of duplicates, cooperative storage and delivery, etc. Many of these cooperative activities have been discussed in the preceding sessions. This paper intends to discuss one of the recent developments in resources sharing: Computer-assisted information systems and networking.

Because of the introduction of computers and the rapid advancement in telecommunications technology, fast and cost-effective ways of sharing information and resources are now possible on a far greater scale than was known before. The development of computer-assisted information systems and networks is of great importance for world-wide cooperation in resources sharing involving both developed and developing countries.

The development of computer-assisted information systems and networks has three interrelated components: (1) the creation and growth of many machine-readable databases capable of on-line, interactive searching from remote terminals: (2) the development of computerized library networks connecting libraries and computer facilities and databases; and (3) the establishment of mission-oriented national and international information systems based on a well-conceived model developed for the International Nuclear Information System (INIS).

Each of these components will be discussed in some detail below. Particular attention will be given to their implications for developing countries. The future interconnection of information resources, databases, library networks, and international information systems to form a world-wide information network is a distinct possibility in the 1980s.

The Creation and Growth of Machine-Readable Databases

Because of the continued increase in the number of bibliographical records and in the cost and time required to prepare for their publication manually, many abstracting and indexing services and publishers have turned to computers for relief. The result has been a fast growth in the number and size of machine-readable databases in the last 15 years. The important by-products of these databases are their ability to provide a variety of bibliographical services such as on-line, interactive search and selective dissemination of information (SDI) service.

According to the 1976 estimate of the National Federation of Abstracting and Indexing Services, there were 2,500 indexing and abstracting services in existence world-wide; of these, about 200 were in machine-readable form, and most of these were capable of being searched from remote terminals.[1] Although most of the databases are for bibliographical information, there are others which cover news articles, full texts of legal cases and statutes, numeric data, and graphic representations.[2]

Despite their short history, machine-readable databases have become a major bibliographical and reference tool in the U.S., Canada, Europe, and some other parts of the world. To illustrate the phenomenal growth of machine-readable databases in the U.S., the experience of Lockheed Information System, a large commercial on-line database service center, is used. The table below shows that, beginning with only one database and 200,000 records in 1965, Lockheed now has nearly 30 databases containing a total of 8 million records. Using an index of 100 for 1970, in 1975 the search volume had grown to 15,000 and the cost had dropped to 20.

---

[1]Donald G. Fink, "The Impact of Technology in Library Science," *Special Libraries*, Vol. 68, no. 2 (February 1977), p. 78.

[2]Martha E. Williams, "The Impact of Machine-Readable Data Bases on Library and Information Services," *Information Processing & Management*, Vol. 13, no. 2 (1977), pp. 95-96.

Table I. The Growth of Lockheed's DIALOG[3]

Year	No. of DataBases	Size of DataBases	Rate of Increase in Searches	Rate of Decrease in Cost
1965	1	200,000	---	---
1970	---	---	100	100
1973	11	2,100,000	2,000	40
1975	30	8,000,000	15,000	20

The impact of the phenomenal growth of machine-readable databases has resulted in the following: (1) more on-line terminals established at an increasing number of locations to facilitate remote access; (2) more effective communication techniques; (3) improved standardization and cooperation among database producers; (4) expanded bibliographical services; (5) increased demand for document delivery service, interlibrary loan, and photocopying service; and (6) greater needs for resources sharing and networking among information systems.

Before leaving the discussion of databases, mention must be made of a particularly important one, the Machine-Readable Cataloging (MARC) created by the Library of Congress. The MARC format, designed to represent bibliographical data in machine-readable form, has since been adopted as the national and international standard. The MARC database has been used widely in the U.S. as a cataloging and bibliographical tool, as a source for interlibrary loan, acquisitions, and circulation, and for as many as a score of other applications. An increasing number of countries, including a few of the developing ones, are now producing their national bibliographies in MARC format. Many countries are also exchanging MARC tapes.

Because of the high costs involved in creating and maintaining machine-readable databases, it is considered impractical for most developing countries (and even some small, developed ones) to undertake such projects, except for producing their national bibliographies and periodical indexes in machine-readable format. They should, instead, make use of the large databases in developed countries, either off-line or through on-line terminals.

In recent years, Unesco and some developed countries have conducted a number of experiments or pilot projects to test the usefulness of providing SDI

---

[3]Lee G. Burchinal, "Bringing the American Revolution On-Line Information Science and National R & D," *Bulletin of the American Society for Information Science*, Vol. 2, No. 8 (March 1976), p. 27.

service to researchers in selected developing countries. The results are generally favorable.[4] However, because of the high telecommunication costs and use charges, the volume of searches to be made by developing counties may remain low unless there is a special reduced rate for users from the developing countries.

The Development of Computerized Library Networks

Another important phenomenon of recent times which facilitates the sharing of resources is the development of computerized library networks, through which machine-readable databases become a viable information resource accessible to a large number of users, both near and far.

According to the recent report by Susan K. Martin, there are twenty-five large library networks in the U.S., all relying on computers for resource sharing. If one adds the many other non-computerized library networks, there is hardly any library which does not belong to a library network. Some, in fact, belong to several networks for different purposes. Because of the proliferation of library networks, a Council of Computerized Library Networks was founded in 1973 to discuss the need for communication among networks.[5]

Of the twenty-five computerized library networks, the most successful and best known is the Ohio College Library Center (OCLC). As the name implies, OCLC was first incorporated (in 1965) as a network for academic libraries in Ohio. It became on-line in 1971. Two years later, its membership was enlarged to include out-of-state libraries. Today it has over eight hundred libraries and fifteen hundred on-line terminals, representing almost every type and size of library in forty-two states.[6] The main operation of OCLC at present is the on-line shared cataloging and processing system. Other operations currently under development by OCLC are a serials check-in subsystem, an interlibrary loan subsystem, a circulation subsystem, and an acquisitions subsystem. In cooperation with the Council on Library Resources and the Library of Congress, 200,000 serial records

---

[4]"UNISIST Pilot Projects for the Establishment of SDI Services," *UNISIST Newsletter*, Vol. 2, no. 4 (1974), p. 2; "Computer-based Information Services for Science and Technology," *NAS-CONICET (Argentina) Science Cooperation Program: Report of Activities* (Washington, D.C.: National Academy of Sciences, 1976), pp. 36-43; Charles P. Bourne, "Computer-based Reference Services as an Alternative Means to Improve Resources - Poor Local Libraries in Developing Countries," *International Library Review*, Vol. 9, no. 1 (1977), pp. 43-50.

[5]Susan K. Martin, *Library Networks 1976-77* (White Plains, N.Y.: Knowledge Industry Publications, 1976), p. 41.

[6]*OCLC Newsletter*, no. 106 (4 February 1977), pp. 1 & 4.

will soon be made available through OCLC by the Conversion of Serials Project (CONSER).

While OCLC has scored an initial success in the U.S., the development of computerized library networks in other countries, particularly the developed ones, had also made good progress. Besides the many local and national library and information networks already in existence in many countries, a number of multinational information networks have been established. Two well-known ones are ARPANET and ESRO/SDS. The former is a computer-communication system developed cooperatively by more than two dozen research and development organizations under the sponsorship of the U. S. Advanced Research Projects Agency. At present, it embraces sixty-five digital computers in forty-five locations in the U.S., and extends to Norway and London.[7] The latter, the Space Documentation Service of the European Space Agency, is a star-shaped network with its central computer facility at Frascati, Italy, connected by private leased lines to terminals located throughout most of western Europe, including Spain and Scandinavia. The network is currently operating at a level of 25,000 searches per year of some twelve databases containing around 5 million bibliographical records.[8]

Another large network, EURONET, created by the nine western countries of the European Economic Community, is in the active planning stage and should become operational in 1978. This network is being planned according to a very broad concept, concerned not merely with the provision of a modern communication network, but also with a true sharing and coordination of information resources among the member countries.[9] When established, it will have switching nodes in Frankfurt, London, Paris, and Rome and concentrators in Amsterdam, Brussels, Copenhagen, and Dublin.

For developing countries (and some small but developed ones), although local and national library and information networks have been developed largely without computers and sophisticated telecommunication systems, there is an increasing possibility that they may be connected to international networks

---

[7]J.C.R. Licklider, "A Network of Computer and Information Systems," *National and International Networks of Libraries, Documentation, and Information Centres*, AGARD Conference Proceedings, no. 158 (Paris: NATO Advisory Group for Aerospace Research and Development, 1975), p. 2.1.

[8]John Page, "International STI Networks: Promises and Problems," *Bulletin of the American Society for Information Science*, Vol. 2, no. 4 (November 1975), p. 12.

[9]Ibid., p. 13.

through a designated national node in each of their countries. A recent example of this is Morocco, which has been connected to ESRO/SDS by a leased-line.[10]

The so-called "network parasitology" concept employed successfully by Finland is another good example applicable to developing countries. Since 1971, the Helsinki University of Technology Library has been able to provide SDI and retrospective searches by using the computers and databases located at the Royal Institute of Technology Library, the Biomedical Documentation Center in Stockholm, and the Technological University of Denmark in Copenhagen. Each of the 120 SDI clients who pays about $100 for the annual subscription will receive approximately 100 SDI printouts during the year. By using telephone connections through the Tymnet link in Brussels to Palo Alto, California, the Helsinki Library can also perform on-line retrospective searches for its clients at an average cost of $30-40 per search.[11]

Other instances of networking in developing countries that are worth mentioning are the telex networks established in several Latin American countries. The best known one is the Argentine Telex Network for Scientific and Technical Information, which was initiated in 1971 under the U.S.-Argentina Science Cooperation Program. The Telex network connects the principal libraries and documentation centers in Argentina. In addition, the network center in Buenos Aires is linked to a number of cooperating libraries in the U.S. and some other countries, with the purpose of improving access to and delivery of technical information resources within Argentina as well as from the U.S., and, eventually, from other countries in Latin America and Europe.[12]

The Establishment of International Information Systems

While the development of both the machine-readable databases and the computerized networks is in progress, there is another important development being undertaken by several international and intergovernmental organizations to establish mission-oriented information systems on a global basis. The first of these is the International Nuclear Information System (INIS) established in 1970 by the

---

[10]W. A. Martin, "Maximizing the Use of an Information Service in an International Environment," *Advancement in Retrieval Technology as Related to Information Systems*, AGARD Conference Preprint, no. 207 (Paris: NATO Advisory Group for Aerospace Research and Development, 1976), p. 7.2.

[11]Elin Tornudd, "Benefits from Network 'Parasitology,'" *UNESCO Bulletin for Libraries*, Vol. 30, no. 4 (July-August 1976), pp. 206-9.

[12]"The Argentine Telex Network for Scientific and Technical Information," *NAS-CONICET (Argentina) Science Cooperation Program: Report of Activities*, pp. 1-35.

International Atomic Energy Agency as a cooperative system to handle information related to the peaceful applications of atomic energy.

During the process of planning and designing INIS, several important principles were conceived and agreed upon by its planning team. These principles, which have since been adopted as a model for several other international information systems such as the International Information System for the Agricultural Sciences and Technology (AGRIS) and the International Information System for the Development Science (DEVSIS), are: (1) decentralization of the task of identifying and recording information as it is produced, each participating nation (or region) being responsible for reporting what is produced in its own territory; (2) centralized merging of material reported by the different input centers (national focal points), the task being performed in an international agency through international financing; (3) output products tailored to the needs of advanced institutions with computer facilities, as well as printed (or microfilmed) indexes and abstracts that can be used by institutions without such facilities, and by individual scientists; (4) back-up service of photocopies or microfiches to ensure availability of texts; (5) products available at low cost and all charges payable in local currencies; (6) international management, based on consultation with all participants; (7) engagement of governments to ensure official support and the availability and infusion of relevant government publications and reports; and (8) utilization of an internationally accepted standard bibliographical format to permit future interconnection among various international information systems.[13]

The model stipulated above has many important features, some of which are of special benefit to developing countries. First, it makes each participating country responsible for reporting the relevant publications in its territory, thereby preventing duplication of effort and ensuring full coverage. Second, since each participating country is to bear the cost of initial reporting, countries with a larger volume of publication will pay more, while countries with a smaller volume will pay less. This apportionment of costs favors developing countries and therefore encourages them to participate. Third, the central processing of bibliographical records in an international center supported by international funding is more economical than for each country to attempt to process them locally. By means of central processing, bibliographical information from all participating countries can be quickly merged and made available worldwide. Furthermore, such processing helps to enforce accepted international standards in bibliographical format and reporting, and provides training opportunities for information workers in developing countries.

---

[13]John E. Woolston, "International Information Systems: Their Relation to Economic and Social Development," paper presented at the International Symposium on Information Systems: Connection and Compatibility, Varna, Bulgaria, 30 September-3 October 1974 (IAEASM-189/1), pp. 1-2.

In promoting the establishment of international mission-oriented information systems and the application of methods, norms, and standards which will maximize the inter-compatibility of all systems and facilitate their interconnections, Unesco has made a significant contribution through its UNISIST programs, whose aims are to coordinate existing trends towards cooperation and to act as a catalyst for the necessary development of a world-wide information network.

Conclusion

It is clear that a new era for resource sharing has arrived. To take advantage of machine-readable data bases and the opportunity for greater resource sharing through computerized networking and international information systems, great care must be given to standardization and system compatibility. The development of information infrastructure in each country is also a necessity for effective resource sharing.

Since knowledge has no boundaries, all countries should try to make the knowledge produced in their territories bibliographically accountable either by manual system or by computer. The imbalance of geographical and language coverage of existing machine-readable databases should be corrected to include more non-"west" publications.

While the bibliographical accessibility is bound to improve as a direct result of the development in computer-assisted systems and networks, several major impacts on library, documentation and information services in developing countries may also be expected. First is the likely increase in the demand for improved document delivery service. This has, indeed, been felt by libraries in those countries where on-line databases are used. The second is the growing language problem to be faced by libraries and their patrons because of the expanded language coverage by many databases. Both translation service and information on available translations will become necessary. The third is the need for training of database searchers and users. The fourth is the problem concerning the payment in "hard" currencies or in the form of Unesco coupons. And, finally, even though the costs for international telecommunications and the charges for database use have declined in recent years, it is still considered very expensive for researchers in developing countries. A reduced rate or some kind of subsidy for users from non-profit organizations in developing countries is highly recommended.

A SKETCH FOR A COMPUTERIZED NATIONAL LIBRARY AND INFORMATION NETWORK

Introduction

Library and information services in Taiwan, Republic of China, has entered a new era with the successful development of computer terminals and software packages which are capable of processing both Chinese characters and the Roman alphabet. Although in the past several years the use of computers for library and information work in Taiwan has been making good progress, the applications were limited to library materials in the Roman alphabet. The complexity of the Chinese language makes transliterations into Roman script inadequate and unsatisfactory. Now that both Chinese characters and the Roman alphabet can be processed by computers at the same time, coupled with the encouragement of the Chinese Government to apply computers more widely in government, business, industry, education, and research, we can foresee an accelerated use of computers in library and information work in the coming year. The holding of this international workshop on Chinese library automation is an encouraging manifestation of this movement.

Over the years I have been watching the spread of library automation in Taiwan. In a paper I wrote in 1974,[1] I proposed the formation of a National Library and Information Network. The idea was prompted by the development of national library and information services in the U.S.A., Great Britain, Canada and other countries. At that time, OCLC was still a local system and on-line search of remote databases was still in its infancy. Networking without computer and telecommunication linkage was somewhat fragile. The recent advancement of computer and telecommunication technologies and their expanded applications in library and information work have, however, greatly improved the network environment, particularly the computerized networks.

Drawing from successful experiences in computerized library and information networks in the U. S. A., this paper seeks to outline a computerized National Library and Information Network for the Republic of China in Taiwan. Since no two countries are alike and the specific network environments varies from country to country, the proposed network will be Chinese in character taking into consideration the special situation and needs in the Republic of China. Due to the shortage of time in preparing this paper, only a sketch of the proposed network is presented. It is intended for preliminary discussions only. Hopefully, through discussions and further

---

[1]Hwa-Wei Lee, "Suggestions for the Establishment of a National Library and Information Network," *Central Daily News*, 26-27 February 1974. In Chinese.

studies, more complete and refined design for a computerized National Library and Information Network may result.

Current Library Automation in Taiwan

The recent paper of Margaret C. Fung, "State of the Art: Library Automation in Taipei," offered a detailed account of the history, development and present status of library automation in Taiwan.[2] The paper also described some of the basic requirements in processing library materials in the Chinese language and the several approaches currently available for inputting.

Of all the library automation projects in Taiwan as described by Fung many have been developed by individual libraries with their particular needs in mind. Common among these are serial control systems, acquisition systems, and cataloging systems. In addition, a number of computerized databases have been built for the storage and retrieval of bibliographical and management information on some special subjects or areas.

Most important of the recent developments in library automation is the formation of the Library Automation Working Group with the aim of developing a national plan for library automation and implementing it. The Working Group, although not exactly the same as the one proposed in my 1974 paper, however, has a similar purpose in mind.

Already the group, which consists of librarians, information scientists, and computer scientists, has drawn up a Plan for a National Information Service System.[3] The plan was subsequently adopted by the National Central Library in April 1980 and is being implemented under its auspices with the assistance of the Working Group. The plan which has a completion date of 1983 consists of the following four stages:[4]

I.   Automation for Chinese library materials.

---

[2]Margaret C. Fung, "State of the Art: Library Automation in Taipei," paper presented at the 46th General Conference of the International Federation of Library Associations and Institutions, Manila, Philippines, August 18-23, 1980.

[3]National Central Library, *Plan for a National Information Service System* (Taipei: National Central Library, 1980. In Chinese.

[4]"Project for Library Automation," *National Central Library Newsletter*, Vol. 12, No. 2 (August 1980), pp. 117-119. In Chinese.

1. Research on Chinese Machine-Readable Cataloging (Chinese MARC) format:

    1.1. Revision of the cataloging rules for Chinese library materials.

    1.2. Application for use in the Republic of China of the International Standard Book Numbers (ISBN) and the International Standard Serial Numbers (ISSN).

    1.3. Compilation of a list of subject headings for Chinese library materials.

    1.4. Development of Chinese MARC format.

2. Development of a database for Chinese library materials:

    2.1. Development of Chinese MARC database.

        2.1.1. A union catalog of Chinese books.

        2.1.2. A union list of Chinese periodicals.

        2.1.3. A union catalog of other materials such as government documents, technical reports, research papers, etc.

        2.1.4. A retrieval system for Chinese library materials.

    2.2. Development of databases for Chinese library materials in various subjects.

        2.2.1. Compilation of a thesaurus.

        2.2.2. Compilation of indices and abstracts.

        2.2.3. Development of a retrieval system for subject databases.

3. Training of library and information service personnel.

II. Automation for Western library materials:

1. Development of Western MARC database:

1.1. Acquisition of the U. S. Library of Congress MARC records (LC MARC) and others.

1.2. Establishment of a database of other Western books not included in the LC MARC.

1.3. Development of a union catalog of Western books.

1.4. Making use of information retrieval systems developed by information networks abroad.

2. Development of various subject databases for Western library materials:

2.1. Acquisition of selected subject databases from abroad.

2.2. Development of subject databases locally by division of labor.

2.3. Development of an information retrieval system for subject databases in Western languages.

3. Training of library and information service personnel. (Same as I.3.)

III. Development of library management systems:

1. Acquisition.

2. Circulation.

3. Library administration.

IV. Planning for a national information network:

1. Implementation of an on-line system.

2. Selective dissemination of information (SDI) service.

The above plan, although appearing to be quite ambitious, has had a number of projects in the first stage undertaken and now near completion. The ground has thus been laid for the planning and development of the projects in the latter stages. In the light of experience gained in library automation in the U.S. it is felt that the best approach to handle most of the projects in the latter stages is to implement them through the framework of a computerized National Library and Information Network using a combination of modified OCLC and Lockheed models.

Design for a Computerized National Library and Information Network

The geographical area in Taiwan seems to favor a single, unified National Library and Information Network in order to achieve the economics of scale as well as operation efficiency in library automation. With the advent of computer and telecommunication technologies which are increasingly available in Taiwan under the Government's encouragement and the successful development of input and output devices which can process library materials and information in both Chinese and Western languages, a computerized national network is not only possible now, but is necessary to take advantage of the gigantic power these technologies can offer in information processing, storage, retrieval, and transmission.

In designing such a computerized National Library and Information Network in Taiwan one must take into consideration the specific network environment there and profit from the experience of network development in other countries. For discussion purposes a few of the basic considerations for network development are given below:

I. In the building of an on-line national union catalog, some of the successful features of the OCLC model[5] can be adapted, they are:

1. The concept of on-line shared cataloging is probably the best way to build a national union catalog by dividing labor and pooling resources. (Approximately 84% of OCLC cataloging records are contributed by participating libraries, only 16% from LC MARC)[6]

2. The concept of having one central database for all cataloged materials regardless of languages, forms, and types.

3. The concept of modulization in the systems design which enables the addition of other subsystems such as serial control, interlibrary loan,

---

[5]OCLC was founded in 1967 by the Ohio College Association and was originally called the Ohio College Library Center. As a result of its fast growth from a state network to a national network, its name was changed to OCLC, Inc. in 1977. Today OCLC operates an on-line computer network used by over 2,200 libraries in 50 states, Canada, and other countries. OCLC's database, the on-line union catalog, contains more than 6 million bibliographic records for books, serials, audiovisual materials, maps, manuscripts, scores, sound recordings, and other library materials. There are over 65 million location symbols. The database grows at a rate of about 25,000 records per week. Of these approximately 21,000 are provided by participating libraries; the remainder comes from the Library of Congress MARC records.

[6]LC MARC refers to the format of the Machine-Readable Cataloging (MARC) records of the Library of Congress.

acquisition, circulation, etc. to enhance the usage of the on-line union catalog.

4. The concept of accessibility to the on-line union catalog and affordability by all types of libraries and information centers regardless of their sizes.

5. The ability of the shared cataloging system to provide custom-printed catalog cards, and other products to participating libraries.

6. The method of sharing the cost of operations by participating libraries as determined by the number of uses made by each.

7. The concept of open communication from the participating libraries to governance, and accountability from governance to participating libraries.

II. In addition to having an on-line national union catalog, the Network should endeavor to provide on-line access to as many domestic computerized databases as possible and to selected foreign databases.

1. The development of separate, specialized, domestic, computerized databases should be encouraged but coordinated to avoid unnecessary duplication and overlap as well as to achieve the use of a standard format in input and in database structure.

2. By special arrangement and proper compensation the network should acquire the files of such domestic databases and should use the Lockheed, SDC, or BRS models[7] to make these databases available for on-line access. All databases built with a common standard format can be merged into one file to facilitate searches.

3. A cost analysis should be made to determine which of the following modes of operation for accessing foreign databases is more cost effective and efficient. Obviously, the projected volume of such searches is a major factor in the cost analysis.

    a. To subscribe or lease the tapes of selected foreign databases and store them in the network's computer for domestic access.

---

[7]Lockheed Information Systems operates one of the world's largest online information services--Dialog--which manages more than 120 databases containing a total of 40 million bibliographic citations and abstracts. Other major vendors of computerized databases in the U.S. are SDC's Orbit, BRS, etc.

b. To provide direct access via communication satellite to databases stored in Lockheed, SDC, or BRS.

c. A proper combination of 1) and 2) above.

III. Since the National Central Library in Taipei has played a prominent role in the development of library and information services in Taiwan it seems to be logical and desirable to vest the responsibility of the governance of the computerized National Library and Information Network to the National Central Library which will then he responsible for seeking the funds necessary for the operation of the network and for coordinating the activities related to the development of the network. Some of the operational considerations of the network are:

1. The National Central Library should seek the advice of a network advisory board with two-thirds of its members elected by participating libraries and the other one-third appointed by the Director of the National Central Library, all to serve a three-year staggered term.

2. The National Central Library should develop and establish the appropriate administrative office to plan, develop, manage, and evaluate the national network.

3. Whenever appropriate, the National Central Library may delegate or contract other agencies to undertake specific tasks for the network. For example, the Scientific and Technological Information Center of the National Science Council may be asked to administer the computerized databases and information search service, the Library Association of China may be contracted to organize education and training programs for staff members of network libraries, and the nation's library schools may be involved in research projects concerning the network.

4. In view of the many long-term benefits of a computerized National Library and Information Network and its impact in furthering national development, the Government should endeavor to provide adequate funding for the establishment and operation of the network. The investment in this is very small indeed if compared with other government projects, but the return will be immeasurable and the effect will be far reaching.

Conclusion

This paper has thus far touched upon a very important part of library automation, that is networking. Because of the limited time available to write this paper, many thoughts expressed therein are very sketchy. It is my firm belief, however, the need for a computerized National Library and Information Network is self evident and the timing for its initiation is just right. It is hoped that some of the suggestions made here will lead to further discussions and actions. To set the course of library automation through a well conceived plan under the framework of a National Library and Information Network will undoubtedly expedite the process of development and achieve the optimum results.

PLANNING PROCESS AND CONSIDERATIONS FOR A STATEWIDE ACADEMIC LIBRARIES INFORMATION SYSTEM IN OHIO

This article was written in the midst of the process, March 1989. As this volume is compiled, the process is nearing fruition and an "Afterword" is appended to update this report.

Ohio: The Birthplace of OCLC

Cooperation for automation and resource sharing among academic libraries, especially the state-supported university libraries, has been firmly established in Ohio since the 1960s. The most important accomplishment was the establishment of OCLC in 1967. Originally, OCLC was the abbreviation for Ohio College Library Center, an entity founded by a group of academic libraries whose institutions were members of the Ohio College Association. Under the leadership of the Inter-University Library Council (IULC), an informal organization of the library directors of state-supported universities, initial funding was obtained from the Ohio Board of Regents, the planning and coordinating agency for all state-supported institutions of higher education. OCLC's success in creating a central bibliographic database of MARC (Machine-Readable Cataloging) records to facilitate online, shared cataloging by participating libraries induced many other libraries to join. Within fifteen years, OCLC had become a multi-type library network. The membership had grown from 48 in 1967 to 2,934 in 1982, covering every state of the Union.[1] The expanding membership caused OCLC to change its name and governance. Today, OCLC stands for the Online Computer Library Center. As of June 30, 1988, OCLC had 9,400 participating libraries of all type and sizes in 50 states and 23 other countries with 17,748,222 bibliographic records, making it the world's largest bibliographic database. In 1987-88 alone, 21.9 million books and other materials were cataloged into the database, and 3.78 million transactions for interlibrary loan were handled.[2]

By the late 1970s and early 1980s, with the advances in mini-computer technologies, many libraries found it desirable to develop or acquire local library systems for other library functions not provided by OCLC. In 1988, there were 50

---

[1]Kathleen L. Maciuszko, *OCLC: A Decade of Development, 1967-1977* (Littleton, Colorado: Libraries Unlimited, 1984), pp. 17 & 219.

[2]*OCLC Annual Report, 1987/88: Furthering Access to the World's Information.* (Dublin, Ohio: OCLC Online Computer Library Center), pp. 4 & 20.

library systems vendors in the market,[3] most claiming to include a variety of integrated library functions. Additionally, many of these systems are capable of networking among a group of libraries on a local or regional basis. Even with local systems, most libraries still participate in OCLC for shared cataloging and interlibrary loans. In Ohio, for example, of the thirteen state-supported universities and two medical colleges, all of which are members of OCLC, one has a locally developed system and eight others have acquired local systems (Table I). Nearly all are capable of providing an online public access catalog (OPAC), acquisitions, fund accounting, circulation, and serials control.

Table I

AUTOMATED LIBRARY SYSTEMS IN OHIO PUBLIC UNIVERSITIES

University of Akron	Virginia Tech Library System
Ohio University	Virginia Tech Library System
Youngstown State Univ.	Virginia Tech Library System
Bowling Green State Univ.	LS/2 (quasi-orphan)
Univ. of Cincinnati	Washington Lib. Network (orphan)
Ohio State Univ.	LCS (locally developed)
Wright State Univ.	DRA (Data Research Associates)
Cleveland State Univ.	NOTIS (from Northwestern)
Kent State Univ.	NOTIS
Miami Univ.	No System (subsequently, Innovative Interfaces)
Central State Univ.	No System
Medial College of Ohio	No System
NEOUCOM	No System
Shawnee State Univ.	No System
Univ. of Toledo	No System (subsequently NOTIS)

To facilitate resource sharing, the thirteen university libraries have a reciprocal borrowing agreement allowing faculty and students at these universities to use each other's libraries. Interlibrary loan and photocopy requests among IULC libraries receive priority attention and are free of charges. Those libraries with a local system allow the other libraries remote dial-up access. Through OCLC these libraries all have access to the bibliographic records of the others; however, such records do not indicate the number of copies in a given library nor circulation status. Information on serial holdings is often incomplete or absent. Further, OCLC's massive database does not yet allow for subject, keyword, or Boolean searching. Most local systems provide these capabilities.

---

[3]Roger A. Walton & Frank R. Bridge, "Automated system marketplace 1987: Maturity and Competition," *Library Journal*, Vol. 113, no. 6 (April 1, 1988), pp. 33-44.

A New Initiative

In 1986, facing massive requests for new and enlarged library facilities on state-supported campuses, the state legislature mandated that the Ohio Board of Regents assess the need for space by the university libraries and possible alternatives. The Board created a seventeen-member Library Study Committee, chaired by Dr. Elaine Hairston, Vice Chancellor for Academic and Special Programs of the Board of Regents, consisting of a university president, a provost, two vice presidents, two deans, two library directors, a professor, and OCLC researcher, a publisher, and four additional Board of Regents senior staff officers. The Committee decided early in its deliberations that its charge would require assessment of "the role of the academic library...in its broadest contemporary sense" and that it "should consider such opportunities for improving the quality of libraries as might appear in the context of its considerations."[4]

In its published report of the year-long study, the Committee felt that:

This wider perspective is necessary because the academic library of today has a threefold purpose, serving not only as a storehouse of information, but also as a gateway to information held elsewhere, and as a center for instruction about information (p. vii).

Accordingly, the Committee's recommendation centered on three broad areas:

1) Collaboration, which encompasses a range of issues such as collaborative acquisitions, shared access, and shared storage;

2) Technology, including high density means of publication such as the existing microform and the emerging compact disk;

3) Alternative storage, including the various methods of maintaining rarely used materials in a warehouse environment.[5]

The principal recommendation for collaboration was to implement "as expeditiously as possible a statewide electronic catalog system." The project, initially the Ohio Library Access System (OLAS) was later named the Ohio Library and Information System (OLIS). Collateral recommendations included retrospective conversion of remaining paper catalog records to MARC format, the development and

---

[4]Ohio Board of Regents Library Study Committee, *Academic Libraries in Ohio: Progress Through Collaboration, Storage, and Technology. Report of the Library Study Committee* (Columbus: Library Study Committee, Ohio Board of Regents), p. vii.

[5]Ibid.

implementation of a statewide delivery system for library materials, and a plan for a cooperative preservation program.

Ohio Library Information System: The Rationale

Soon after the release of the Committee Report, the Ohio Board of Regents acted to begin planning for a statewide electronic library system. They commissioned a feasibility study[6] and an evaluation of centralized vs. distributed approaches to the statewide system,[7] established a steering committee and three task forces (one each for systems managers, librarians, and users), held a working conference featuring reports of experts on multi-campus systems from seven different states, drafted a Planning Paper and held regional hearings, and prepared a "Request for Information" (RFI) document. A chronology of events from the formation of the Library Study Committee to the issuance of the RFI is recorded in Table II and the planned implementation dates in Table III.

Table II

HISTORY OF OHIO LIBRARY AND INFORMATION SYSTEM

1986	Capital Budget Estimates for Library Buildings for Biennia 1987-1992: $121.7 million total
1986	Library Study Committee Mandated by State Legislature in Capital Budget Bill
Fall 1986	Library Study Committee Formed by Board of Regents (including Ohio University President as member)
Sept. 1987	Library Study Committee Report, *Progress Through Collaboration, Storage, and Technology*, issued. Recommendations under heading "Collaboration": 1. Five-year plan to implement statewide electronic library system 2. State funding to convert existing catalog records to machine readable format 3. Development of state distribution system for library materials
Fall 1987	Ohio Board of Regents commissions a feasibility study of statewide system from RMG Associates.

---

[6]RMG Consultants, *Alternative Approaches to Linking State University Automated Library Systems for the Ohio Board of Regents* (Chicago, IL: RMG Consultants, 1988).

[7]Bernard Hurley, *Centralization vs Decentralization for Large Library Systems in a Changing Technological Environment: A position paper for the Ohio Board of Regents* (Berkeley, California: Hurley Consulting Corp., 1988).

Winter 1988	Elaine Hairston, then Vice Chancellor of Ohio Board of Regents (since Chancellor) meets with library directors from state supported universities and Steering Committee appointed.
March 1988	Board of Regents establishes three task forces: Systems Managers, Librarians, and Users. Ohio University representatives include Kent Mulliner and Larry Buell (replaced by George Hinkle) on Systems Managers, Betty Hoffmann-Pinther on Librarians, and Dr. David Hendricker on Users.
Apr.-Aug. 1988	Task Forces work toward planning document and RFI (Request For Information) from potential systems vendors.
July 1, 1988	Board of Regents receives Capital Budget Appropriation of $2.5 million.
Summer 1988	Board of Regents commissions an evaluation of centralized vs. distributed approach to Statewide system, then known as OLAS (Ohio Library Access System)
September 1988	Working Conference in Columbus, Ohio (Videotape of Proceedings available) -- Draft of Planning Paper prepared.

Table III

OHIO LIBRARY & INFORMATION SYSTEM PROJECT PLANNING TIMETABLE

July 1, 1988	Capital Appropriation of $2.5 million available
Sept. 1988	Consultants (Library Systems--Greg Byerly of Kent State Univ. & Computer Systems--Carroll Notestine, retired from Ohio State Univ.) hired
Dec. 5-9, 1988	Regional hearings on OLIS Draft Planning Paper
Dec. 16, 1988	Final OLIS Plan and draft RFI [Request For Information] circulated to campuses
January 1989	RFI sent to vendors & meetings with vendors
March 15, 1989	Vendor Responses to RFI due
May 1, 1989	Draft RFP [Request for Proposals] circulated to campuses
June 15, 1989	RFP sent to vendors
July 1, 1989	Operating Funds for 1989-91 available
Sept. 4, 1989	RFP responses due
Sept. 15, 1989	Capital budget request for 1990-92 prepared

Sept. 22, 1989	Acting Director and initial support staff hired
Dec. 1, 1989	Vendor(s) selected
July 1, 1990	Capital budget for 1990-92 available
August 1, 1990	Operating budget request for 1991-93 prepared
July 1, 1991	Operating budget for 1991-93 available

First Phase of Implementation Begins

The Planning Paper, issued on November 2, 1988,[8] was divided into the following sections:

* Goal Statement
* Need for an Ohio Library Information System
* Assumptions
* Governance issues
* Tentative project timetable.

Because the currently installed six different local systems at the nine IULC libraries are not compatible, direct communication among them is impractical. OLIS will connect local systems at the thirteen state universities, plus the two medical colleges. OLIS is conceived as a multi-dimensional information system which will integrate traditional catalog and circulation functions for a statewide system with a document delivery service to make the information resources readily available for users from each participating university and beyond.

The Ohio Board of Regents emphasized the importance of the system by incorporating OLIS into its Selective Excellence initiatives--nationally acclaimed challenge grants to encourage outstanding programs specifically funded by the State of Ohio. Although OLIS will directly benefit the faculty, researchers and students of the state-supported universities initially, the system will be available to all citizens in Ohio and later may be expanded to include other institutions of higher learning and other types of libraries.

The Planning Paper[9] identifies the following reasons for creation of OLIS:

* Access to the diverse resources of IULC libraries
* Enhance interlibrary loan and inter-institutional borrowing

---

[8]OLAS Steering Committee, *Ohio Library Access System Planning Paper* (Columbus, Ohio: OLAS Steering Committee, Ohio Board of Regents, 1988).

[9]Ibid., pp. 4-5.

* Cooperative collection development and management
* Access to centrally maintained databases and other information resources
* Research for further improvement of information access.

Basic Assumptions for System Design

The heart of the Planning Paper treats basic assumptions,[10] which outline the bases for system design and specifications. Four categories of assumptions are identified:

* General assumptions
* Access and use assumptions,
* Functional assumptions, including:
  * Catalog creation and maintenance,
  * Document delivery and circulation,
  * Acquisitions and serials,
  * Collection development and maintenance,
  * Online public access catalog, and
* System assumptions.

Some important assumptions are summarized below:

1) A decentralized (or distributed) model with individual local systems linked to a central system is preferred. Fig. 1 shows one such model which links each local system to a central system via a Linked System Protocol (LSP) or internal protocols.

2) The System will be designed with one standard command structure for all users. It is an end-user driven system.

3) The local online catalog will serve as the first database for bibliographic searches before searching the centrally maintained database.

4) Access to circulation information in the online catalog is considered an essential element of the system. Although all Ohioans will have access to the system, users affiliated with participating institutions will be able to directly initiate request for document delivery from any of the libraries.

5) The system will have a wide variety of search capabilities including keyword and Boolean operators.

---

[10]Ibid., pp. 5-16.

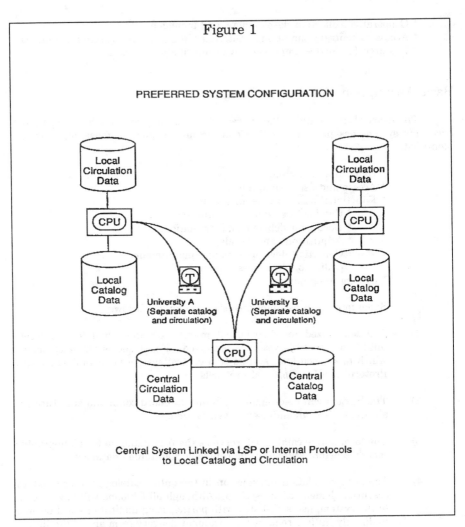

Figure 1

PREFERRED SYSTEM CONFIGURATION

Local Circulation Data

CPU

Local Catalog Data

University A
(Separate catalog
and circulation)

University B
(Separate catalog
and circulation)

Local Circulation Data

CPU

Local Catalog Data

CPU

Central Circulation Data

Central Catalog Data

Central System Linked via LSP or Internal Protocols
to Local Catalog and Circulation

6)   OLIS will not be an interlibrary loan system, but an intra-system circu-
     lation and document delivery network. A statewide circulation policy
     shall reflect this philosophy.

7)   Effective and expeditious document delivery will be provided as an inte-
     gral part of OLIS.

8)   Besides traditional bibliographic information, OLIS will provide direct

304

access to the full text of journal articles or the tables of contents of individual publications.

9) OLIS will provide capacity for collection and use analysis, cooperative collection development, preservation, etc.

10) Updates and transactions to local nodes and the central database will occur simultaneously in real time.

11) The selection of a system is neither a simple procurement process (e.g. acquire an existing system based on responses to RFP) nor an entrepreneurial development process (e.g., design a totally new system) but a combination of both: the selection of a vendor(s) to work with Ohio to design a system that will support state-of-the-art capabilities and use.

12) OLIS will move toward full implementation in stages which are governed by local constraints and interests.

13) The development process will be participatory and widely discussed.

14) Participating institutions will be involved in the governance of OLIS.

The Road Ahead

At the time of this writing (March 1989), the Request for Information (RFI) document has gone out to some 50 vendors and interested parties. The responses are due on April 15. In the meantime, the Task Forces are working on functional specifications which will be included in the Request For Proposal (RFP) document to be issued on June 15. Specialized consultative working conferences on the functional specifications are scheduled for late April and a second general working conference is scheduled on May 2-3 to consider the vendor responses to the RFI and to finalize the RFP.

Although the final shape of OLIS is still unclear, all involved in the process are encouraged by the progress thus far and remain optimistic about the future. Many questions remain, some of which will not be answered until the vendor and system have been selected and the governance structure and funding clarified.

A major question is not only what will be the system architecture, but whether there is a system that will do all that is expected. There are also concerns about whether the new system and its various components to be selected will indeed perform better than the existing local systems in all major functions. Can transition be accomplished with minimal interruption of services? Will the governance structure be able to balance central management and local will? How will OLIS be financed after the initial capital funding by the State and will there be some kind of compensation or incentives for libraries which have invested funds in their local systems? Virtually all involved are concerned that OLIS should be viewed not as a means to reduce future library funding but rather as increasing the effectiveness and richness of library resources and services to benefit all library users. Moreover, the beneficiaries should include not only users at the state-supported universities but all other Ohioans who may use them.

Document delivery, cooperative collection development, retrospective conversion, preservation, regional depository facilities for less used research materials, and the application of new technologies are all complements of the new system which, if effected correctly, will raise academic libraries in Ohio to new plateaus of excellence as they enter the 1990s.

The major academic libraries in Ohio are once again undertaking a giant step together after the success of OCLC. The results may be equally as far reaching as the first one.

Afterword -- December 1990

The statewide system is on the verge of realization. After a number of name changes [from Ohio Library Access System (OLAS) to Ohio Library & Information System (OLIS) to OhioLINK], implementation planning is underway. Because the goal is to serve academic and research users throughout Ohio, two private institutions (the University of Dayton and Case-Western Reserve University have been added to the project.

From the responses to the RFP, eight vendors were invited to present two-day demonstrations in February 1990 which were attended by steering committee, task force, and library subcommittee members as well as representatives from each institution in various functional areas (cataloging, circulation, reference, etc.). The eight vendors were: Ameritech/OCLC, CARL (Colorado Academic and Research Libraries), DRA (Digital Research), GEAC, Innovative Interfaces Inc., NOTIS, Unisys, and VTLS (Virginia Tech Library System). Following the demonstrations, the four most promising vendors were invited for further presentations and a representative expert committee made site visits to academic institutions using the four systems. These were CARL, DRA, Innovative Interfaces, and VTLS. These four were then ranked and negotiations were begun with the preferred company. [Editor's further update: In March 1991, a contract was approved with Innovative Interfaces Inc.]

It is anticipated that OhioLINK will be implemented in two phases. The first, April 1991 - June 1992, will include a number of local sites and commencement of work on the central site. In phase II, July 1992 - June 1994, the remaining sites will be installed. In addition to the local and central sites, implementation includes installing a variety of online databases (in addition to the holdings of the participating institutions),[11] a physical document-delivery service (likely through a commercial delivery service), an electronic document delivery system (using high quality transmission and recovery of fax and digital information), and ongoing research and installation of scholars work stations to take full advantage of OhioLINK's capabilities.

Throughout the planning process, emphasis focused on hardware and software selection. Only when this process was completed in mid-1990 did discussions turn to issues of governance. About one-half of the provosts (chief academic officers) of the participating institutions serve on the Governing Board, with rotating terms. Advising the Board are a Policy Advisory Committee (comprised of representative provosts, academic administrators, faculty, library directors, and library systems managers) and a Library Advisory Committee (comprised of the library directors of all participating institutions). The Library Advisory Committee is served by a number of sub-committees to provide advice on uniform policies in functional areas. An Executive Director is responsible for operations.

---

[11]Ohio Board of Regents, *Connecting People, Libraries, & Information for Ohio's Future* (Columbus: Ohio Board of Regents, 1989).

Bibliography

Below lists the professional writings of Hwa-Wei Lee in chronological order. Items marked by an asterisk "*" are the ones included in this book.

*"Africana at Duquesne University Library," *African Studies Bulletin*, Vol. VI, No. 3(October 1963), pp. 25-27.

"Africana - A Special Collection at Duquesne University," *The Catholic Library World*, Vol. XXXV, No. 4 (December 1963), pp. 209-211.

"Educational Development in Taiwan Under Nationalist Government, 1945 - 1962," (Unpublished Ph.D. dissertation, University of Pittsburgh, 1964).

"Report of the Workshop on Admission of Students from Taiwan and Hong Kong," *Chung Kuo I Chou* (China Newsweek), No. 834 (April 18, 1966), pp. 12-15. (In Chinese)

"The Recent Educational Reform in Communist China," *School and Society*, Vol. XCVI, No. 2311 (November 9, 1968), pp. 395-400.

"Computer Application in Library and Information Services: The Current AIT Experiments and Future Plans," paper presented at the First Computer Applications Symposium jointly sponsored by the Computer Science Laboratory, Chulalongkorn University and U.S. Educational Foundation in Thailand, Bangkok, June 23-25, 1969.

"Asian Institute of Technology," *The Scooper Monthly*, October 1969, pp. 76-81. (In Chinese)

"Planning for Computer Applications in the AIT Library," paper presented at the 1969 annual conference of the Thai Library Association, Bangkok, December 15-19, 1969.

*"Fragmentation of Academic Library Resources in Thai University Libraries," *International Library Review*, Vol. III, No. 2 (April 1971), pp. 155-167.

"Library Mechanization at the Asian Institute of Technology," *International Library Review*, Vol. III, No. 3 (July 1971), pp. 257-270.

*"Regional Cooperation in Scientific and Technical Information Service," *Proceedings of the Conference on Scientific and Technical Information Needs for Malaysia and Singapore*, Institiut Teknoloji Mara, Kuala Lumpur, September 24-26, 1971. Kuala Lumpur: Persatuan Perpustakaan Malaysia and Library Association of Singapore, 1972, pp. 97-105.

*"A New Engineering Library Emerging in Asia," *Libraries in International Development*, No. 41 (December 1971), pp. 103.

*"The Information Technology--New Tools and New Possibilities for Information Storage, Retrieval and Dissemination," paper presented at the Regional Seminar on Information Storage, Retrieval and Dissemination, organized by Asian Mass Communication Research and Information Centre in cooperation with the National Research Council of Thailand, Bangkok, March 26-30, 1973. 10p.

"Partner for School Library Development in Thailand," *T.L.A. Bulletin*, Vol. XVII No. 5 (September/October 1973), pp. 443-448.

*"Proposal for the Establishment of a National Library and Information Network," *Central Daily News* (Taipei), February 26-27, 1974. (In Chinese)

"Possibilities in Employing Computer and Other Information Technologies to Further Library and Information Services in Southeast Asia," *Network*, Vol. I, No. 3 (March 1974), pp. 10-12, and 24-28.

With S. W. Massil, *Library Automation at the Asian Institute of Technology-- Bangkok*. The Larc Reports, V. 7, No. 3. Peoria, Illinois: The Larc Press, 1974. 35p.

"Regional Cooperation in Scientific and Technical Information Service," In *A Survey of Automated Activities in the Libraries of Asia and the Far East*. (World Survey Series, Vol. 5). Peoria, Illinois, The Larc Press, 1974, pp. 11-17.

*"The Application of Information Technology to Close the Information Gap," paper presented at the First Conference on Asian Library cooperation, Tamsui, Taipei, August 19-22, 1974. 12 p.

*"User and Use Analysis: A Case Study of the Information Utility by Geotechnical Engineers in Asian Countries," *Information Utilities: Proceedings of the 37th Annual Conference of the American Society for Information Science, Atlanta, Georgia, October 13-17, 1974*. Edited by Pranas Zunde. Washington, D.C., 1974, V. II, pp. 133-136.

With S. W. Massil, *Proposal for Library Development at Prince of Songkla University in Southern Thailand*. Prepared at the request of the University Development Project Office, Prince of Songkla University. Bangkok: Asian Institute of Technology, 1974. 23p.

*With S. W. Massil, "Scholarly Publications: Considerations on Bibliographic Control and Dissemination," *Scholarly Publishing in Southeast Asia,* Proceedings of the Seminar on Scholarly Publishing in Southeast Asia, sponsored by the Association of Southeast Asian Institutions of Higher Learning, University of Malaya, Kuala Lumpur, January 16-18, 1975. Edited by Beda Lim. Kuala Lumpur, 1975, pp. 212-218.

*With J. C. Yang, "International Standard Numbering for Books and Serials and the Standardization of Bibliographic Descriptions," *Journals of Library and Information Science,* V. I, No. 1 (February 1975), pp. 60-66. (In Chinese).

*"The Experience of a Specialized Information Service in Asia - AGE," paper presented at the Round Table Conference on Documentation Problems in Developing Countries, Khartoum, Sudan, April 10-11, 1975 sponsored by FID/DC and FID National Member in Sudan. Published in *Journal of Library and Information Science,* V. 1, No. 2 (Oct. 1975), pp. 82-93.

"Recent Important Developments in the Library World," *Bulletin of the Library Association of China,* No. 27 (December 1975), pp. 34-36. (In Chinese)

*"Regional Cooperation for ISDS," *Proceedings of the Third Conference of Southeast Asian Librarians, Jakarta, Indonesia,* December 1-5, 1975. Edited by Luwarsih Pringgoadisurjo and Kardiati Sjahrial. Jakarta: PDIN-LIPI for Ikatan Pustakawan Indonesia (Indonesian Librarians Association), 1977, pp. 159-166.

The Possibility of Establishing a Regional Centre for the International Serials Data System in Thailand. (SC-76/WS/7), Paris: UNESCO, 1976. 43 p.

"The Third Conference of Southeast Asian Librarians," *Leads,* V. 18, No. 1 (March 1976), pp. 3-4.

"Proposal for the Establishment of an ISDS Regional Center for Southeast Asia in Thailand," *Leads,* V. 18, No. 2 (July 1976), pp. 4-5.

*"Cooperative Regional Bibliographic Projects in Southeast Asia," paper presented at the Library Seminars of the International Association of Oriental Librarians held in conjunction with the 30th International Congress of Human Sciences in Asia and North Africa, Mexico City, August 3-8, 1976. 17 p. Published in *UNESCO Bulletin for Libraries,* V. 31, No. 6 (Nov.-Dec. 1977), pp. 344-351, 370.

311

*With Marjorie Rhoades, "Approaches to Development of Water Resources Scientific Information Systems," *Water Knowledge Transfer: Proceedings of the Second International Conference on Transfer of Water Resources Knowledge*, Colorado State University, June 29-July 1, 1977. Fort Collins, Colorado: Water Resource Publications, 1978, V. 2. pp. 625-644.

*"Sharing Information Resources Through Computer-assisted Systems and Networking," *Resource Sharing of Libraries in Developing Countries* . Proceedings of the 1977 IFLA/UNESCO Pre-Session Seminar for Librarians from Developing Countries, Antwerp University, August 30-September 4, 1977. Munchen, K. G. Saur, 1979, pp. 208-216. Also published in *Journal of Library and Information Science*, V. 4, No. 1 (April 1978), pp. 14-24.

"Impacts of International Information Systems on NATIS," paper presented at Fourth Congress of Southeast Asian Librarians, Bangkok, June 5-9, 1978. Published in the *Proceedings, Regional Cooperation for the Development of National Information Services*. Bangkok: Thai Library Association, 1981, pp. 133-146.

"Online Revolution and Libraries," *Library Planning and Media Technology*. Library Workshop Proceedings, November 28-30, 1979. Taipei: National Taiwan Normal University Library, 1980, pp. 14-17. (In Chinese)

"The Current Status of Academic Library Administration in the U.S.," paper presented at the Annual Meeting of Directors of Academic and Research Libraries, Taipei, December 1, 1979. 10 p. (In Chinese)

*With K. Mulliner and Lian The-Mulliner, "International Information Exchange and Southeast Asia Collections--A View from the U.S.," presented at the 1980 Meeting of the International Association of Orientalist Librarians, Manila, August 17-23, 1980. 17 pages. Published in *Journal of Educational Media Science*, V. 18, No. 2 (Winter 1980), pp. 3-18.

*"A Sketch for a Computerized National Library and Information Network," paper presented at the International Workshop on Chinese Library Automation, Taipei, February 14-19, 1981. 11 pages.

Acquisitions From the Third World, Editor and Compiler, with K. Mulliner, special thematic issue of *Library Acquisitions: Practice and Theory*, V. 6, No. 2 (1982), pp. 79-238.

*With K. Mulliner, "Library Acquisitions from the Third World: An Introduction," *Library Acquisitions: Practice and Theory*, V. 6, No. 2 (1982), pp. 79-85.

312

*"Recent Breakthroughs in Library Automation in Taiwan," *Journal of Educational Media Science*, Vol. 19, no. 2 (Winter 1982), pp. 119-136.

*With K. Mulliner, "International Exchanges of Librarians and the Ohio University Internship Program," paper presented to the International Relations Round Table of the American Library Association at the ALA Conference in Philadelphia, July 1982. Published in *College & Research Libraries News*, V. 43, No. 10 (November 1982), pp. 345-348.

*"Challenges for the Library and Information Profession," *Bulletin of the Library Association of China*, No. 35 (1983), pp. 235-246.

*"International Library Internships: An Effective Approach to Cooperation," paper presented to the annual program of the Asian/Pacific American Librarians Association and the Chinese-American Librarians Association, in conjunction with the annual American Library Association conference, Los Angeles, June 28-29, 1983. Published in *Areas of Cooperation in Library Development in Asian and Pacific Regions*, Athens, Ohio: Chinese-American Librarians Association, 1985, pp. 21-27, and, in a revised form, in the *International Library Review*, Vol. 17, No. 1 (1985), pp. 17-25.

Areas of Cooperation in Library Development in Asia and Pacific Regions. Papers presented at the 1983 Joint Annual Program of the Asian/Pacific American Librarians Association and Chinese-American Librarians Association, June 28-29, 1983, Los Angeles, California. Editor, with Sally C. Tseng and K. Mulliner. Athens, Ohio: Chinese-American Librarians Association, 1985. 63p.

*With K. Mulliner, E. Hoffmann-Pinther, and Hannah McCauley, "ALICE at One: Candid Reflections on the Adoption, Installation, and Use of the Virginia Tech Library System (VTLS) at Ohio University," paper presented at the Integrated Online Library Systems Second National Conference, September 13-14, 1984, in Atlanta, Georgia. Published in the *Proceedings*, Canfield, Ohio: Genaway & Associates, 1984, pp. 228-242.

With M. Beckman and Jianyan Huang, "Management of Scientific and Technical Information Centres: Aspects of Planning a Course Sponsored by IDRC (Canada) and ISTIC (China)," paper presented at the International Federation for Documentation (FID) Pre-Congress Workshop on Curriculum Development in a Changing World, The Hague, September 3-4, 1984. 19p.

Lecture Notes and Suggested Readings on Modern Library Management and Automation. Athens, Ohio, 1985. 87 p.

*With K. Mulliner, "Educating for International Interdependence: The Role of the Academic Library--Ohio University and Malaysia," at the First Annual Tun Abdul Razak Conference in Malaysia, Athens, Ohio, May 10, 1985. 9p.

*With K. Mulliner, "Funding for the Southeast Asia Collection and Research Resources at Ohio University," paper presented at the Annual Meeting of the Association for Asian Studies in Chicago, Illinois, March 21, 1986.

"International Exchanges and Internships for Librarians," paper presented at the LACUNY [Library Association of the City University of New York] Institute '86, New York City, April 4, 1986.

"Current Status and Trends of American Libraries," *Newsletter of the Library Society of Fujian Province,* No. 25 (1986), pp. 14-38.

*"Principles and Issues on National Library and Information Policy," *Papers of the Library Cooperation and Development Seminar, August 17-18, 1986.* Taipei: National Central Library, 1987, pp. 5.1-5.22. Also published in *Journal of Library and Information Science,* V.13, No. 1 (April 1987), pp. 1-16.

"Applications of Information Technology in An American Library--The Case of Ohio University Libraries," published in First Pacific Conference On New Information Technology for Library and Information Professionals, June 16-18, 1987, Bangkok, *Proceedings.* Edited by Ching-Chih Chen and David I. Raitt. West Newton, MA: MicroUse Information, 1987, pp. 155-164.

"Library Automation at Ohio University Library: Past, Present and Future." In *Collection of Essays Honoring Chiang Wei-Tang on His Ninetieth Birthday.* Taipei, Library Association of China, 1987. pp. 47-72.

*"Trends in Automation in American Academic Libraries: Ohio University's Experience," by Educational Resources Information Center, ED 315 081, ERIC Clearinghouse, May 1989. 20 pp.

"Major Milestones in American Library Automation Since the 1960s," *National Central Library News Bulletin,* Vol. 11, No. 4 (Nov. 1989), pp. 4-7. (Speech delivered at the National Central Library in Taipei on June 2, 1989). (In Chinese)

*"Planning Process and Considerations for a State-Wide Academic Libraries Information System in Ohio," Second Pacific Conference on New Information Technology for Library and Information Professionals and Educational Media Specialists and Technologists, Singapore, May 29-31, 1989. Published in *Proceedings,* edited by Ching-chih Chen and David I. Raitt. West Newton, MA: MicroUse Information, 1989, 203-210. Also

published in *Journal of Educational Media & Library Sciences*, V.27, No. 2 (Winter 1990). pp. 127-138.

New Concepts and New Technology in Library Services. Library Lecture Series., No. 10. Kaohsiung, Taiwan: National Sun Yat-Sen University, 1989. 25 pp. (In Chinese)

Final Report of the INNERTAP Project Review. Consultant Report on the Information Network on New and Renewable Energy Resources and Technologies for Asia and the Pacific, commissioned by the International Development Research Centre. Ottawa, Canada: IDRC, 1990. 33 pp.

INDEX

AACR2 (Anglo-American Cataloging Rules, 2nd Edition) 40, 205, 206

Abstract/s 6, 53, 71, 84, 87, 105, 114, 120, 128, 132-135, 150, 151, 161, 166, 175, 192, 233, 287, 291, 294

Abstracting journals 140, 191

Academic and research libraries 82, 84, 89, 167, 178, 234, 306

Academic librarians 226, 243

Academic library/ies 12, 75, 101, 105, 146, 185, 211, 219, 225, 226, 235, 241, 243, 249, 252, 253, 273, 284, 297, 299, 306

Access 7, 22, 23, 28, 40-43, 67, 81, 88, 103, 104, 120, 135, 137, 140, 141, 143, 146, 157, 169, 173-176, 181, 182, 187, 194, 197, 207, 212, 213, 216, 217, 219, 220, 228-231, 233-235, 265, 269-271, 283, 286, 294, 295, 297-299, 301-303, 305, 306

Accessibility 9, 11, 22, 39 165, 288, 294

Accountability 294

Acquisition/s 1, 4, 6, 9, 19-28, 31-36, 35-38, 41, 42, 52, 69, 87, 88, 103, 104, 141, 144, 155, 174, 191, 211, 213, 219, 228, 229, 234, 244, 245, 247, 250-252, 259, 269, 281, 283, 284, 290, 292, 294, 298, 299, 303

ADONIS (Article Delivery Over Network Information Service) 177

Advanced Research Projects Agency 169, 285

Affordability 294

AGE. SEE Asian Information Center for Geotechnical Engineering.

Agency for International Development 105, 112, 118

Agricultural Information Bank for Asia (AIBA) 63, 74

AGRIS. SEE International Information System for the Agricultural Sciences.

AIBA. SEE Agricultural Information Bank for Asia.

AIT. SEE Asian Institute of Technology.

ALICE (Ohio University Library System) 24, 104, 185, 211, 216, 217, 220, 222, 228-230, 234, 236

American Council of Learned Societies (ACLS) 112, 199

American National Standards Institute (ANSI) 57

Amsterdam 285

Anglo-American Cataloging Rules, 2nd Edition. SEE AACR2.

Applications Technology Satellite (ATS) 88

Appropriate information technology 141

Arabic 4, 5, 25, 203

Archival tapes 214, 215, 218, 230

Argentina 67, 93, 143, 194, 284, 286

ARL. SEE Association of Research Libraries.

ARPANET (Advanced Research Projects Agency Network) 169, 285

ARTEMIS (Automated Retrieval of Text from Europe's Multinational Information Service) 177

ASAIHL. SEE Association of Southeast Asian Institutions of Higher Learning.

ASEAN. SEE Association of Southeast Asian Nations.

Asia Foundation 30, 105

Asian and Pacific Council (ASPAC) 89

Asian Development Bank 112

Asian Geotechnical Engineering. SEE Asian Information Center for Geotechnical Engineering.

Asian Information Center for Geotechnical Engineering (AGE) 11, 70-72, 125, 127-130, 133-136, 144, 145, 149-156, 171, 177, 179, 183, 195, 196, 220, 233, 261

Asian Institute of Technology (AIT) 70, 84-87, 88, 89, 95, 99, 118, 127, 138, 143-145, 149, 152, 182, 183, 188, 195-198, 245, 257-260

Asian librarians 9, 10, 64, 65, 95, 99, 102, 103, 113

Asian Mass Communication Research and Information Centre (AMIC) 63, 68-70, 74, 137

Asian Telecommunity 141, 142, 192, 193

ASPAC. SEE Asian and Pacific Council.

Association for Asian Studies (AAS) 106

Association of Research Libraries (ARL) 230

Association of Southeast Asian Institutions of Higher Learning (ASAIHL) 89

Association of Southeast Asian Nations (ASEAN) 13, 30, 32, 63, 66, 73, 105, 106

ATS. SEE Applications Technology Satellite.

Audio 43, 232

Australia 9, 21, 43, 50, 52, 67, 72, 88, 93, 102, 117, 130, 144, 146, 151, 199, 257

Automated circulation system 104, 212, 213, 229

Automated Retrieval of Text from Europe's Multinational Information Service. SEE ARTEMIS.

Automation 13, 24, 171, 175, 185, 199-202, 206-208, 211, 212, 219, 225, 226, 231, 234, 236, 248, 269, 289-293, 295-297

Availability 23, 32, 41, 116, 144, 146, 152, 154, 158, 162, 166, 167, 169, 178, 181, 182, 195, 197, 213, 217, 218, 228, 229, 259, 265, 269, 270, 287

Availability of Publications 182

BALLOTS (Bibliographic Automation of Large Library Operations on a Time-sharing System) 226

Barcoding 215, 230

Barriers 80, 81, 140, 180, 269

Baud 232

Bibliographic centers 83

Bibliographic control 47, 49, 51-53, 64, 91, 95-97, 152-154, 174, 182, 199, 265

Bibliographic data 79, 82-84, 86, 87, 139, 203

Bibliographic database 177, 227, 297

Bibliographic projects 10, 47, 63, 69, 73, 74,

Bibliographic services 168, 282, 283

Biomedical Documentation Center 286

Birmingham Libraries' Cooperative Mechanization Project 144, 196

Boolean operators 220, 229, 303

Bowker, R. R. 50

Brain drain 12, 257

Britain 19, 49-52, 117, 175, 258, 289

British Council 138, 187

British Library 20, 23, 227

BRS (Bibliographic Retrieval Services, Inc.) 120, 176, 231, 294, 295

Brunei 9, 32, 33, 35, 43, 52, 65, 105, 106

Budget/s 3, 28, 31, 33-36, 40, 96, 97, 227, 250, 251, 268, 300-302

Burma 8, 9, 65, 130

C.N.I.C.T. SEE Consejo Nacional de Investigaciones Cientificas y Tecnicas.

318

California Library Authority for Systems and Services (CLASS) 11, 107, 127

Canada 19, 66, 67, 93, 127, 145, 150, 164, 196, 227, 282, 289, 293

Cataloging 9, 33, 35, 40, 42, 51, 87, 103, 104, 114, 116, 120, 141, 146, 160, 168, 175, 177, 191, 199-201, 205-208, 211-213, 215, 216, 220, 226-230, 244, 245, 247, 250, 269, 281, 283, 284, 290, 291, 293, 294, 297, 298, 306

Cataloging database 227

Cataloguing In Publication 52

CCCII. SEE Chinese Character Code for Information Inter-Change.

CD-ROM (Compact Disc--Read-Only Memory) 233, 236

Central library 171, 175, 201, 208, 244-251, 254-256, 268, 271, 290, 295

Centralization 162, 236, 247, 271, 300

Centralized processing center 141

Chemical Abstracts 84, 87, 105, 114, 120, 192

Chinese bibliographic databases 182

Chinese Cataloging Rules 199-201, 205, 207

Chinese Character Code for Information Inter-Change (CCCII) 201, 200-202, 204-206

Chinese characters 177, 200-203, 205, 269, 289

Chinese language 177, 199, 200, 202, 289, 290

Chinese MARC 171, 175, 177, 199-202, 206-208, 291

Chinese materials 175, 182, 207

Chulalongkorn University 12, 113, 245, 246, 260

CIP. SEE Cataloguing In Publication.

Circulation 104, 120, 172, 203, 211-213, 215, 216, 219, 220, 228-230, 283, 284, 292, 294, 298, 302-304, 306

CIRS (Computerized Information Retrieval Service) 231-233

Citations 21, 32, 53, 174, 175, 270, 294

CLASS. SEE California Library Authority for Systems and Services.

Clearing House for Social Development in Asia 138, 188, 198

Clearing-houses/clearinghouse/s 81, 83, 97, 160, 161

CLR. SEE Council on Library Resources.

CMEA. SEE Council for Mutual Economic Assistance

Coding systems 201, 202

Collection/s 1, 3-7, 9-15, 23, 24, 26-39, 41-44, 46, 52, 65, 70, 71, 86, 87 101-103, 105-108, 113, 114, 118, 123, 127, 128, 140, 143, 144, 146, 150-153, 160, 162, 166, 174, 191, 194, 195, 201, 208, 213, 215, 218, 230, 232, 244, 246, 248, 249, 251, 258, 260, 264, 265, 303, 305, 306

COM. SEE Computer-output microforms.

Commission of the European Communities 169, 177

Committee Z39 57

Communication linkage 82, 88

Communication satellites 80, 142, 168, 194

Communication/s 11, 13, 14, 22, 44, 50, 63, 68, 69, 74, 79, 80, 82, 83, 88, 98, 112, 137, 141-143, 146, 158, 167-169, 171, 178-180, 191, 192, 194, 197, 207, 216, 217, 228, 232, 233, 259, 261, 263, 266, 270, 283-285, 294, 295, 302

Compact discs 232

Compatibility 81, 166, 177, 197, 204, 287, 288

CompuServe 176

Computer applications 88, 104, 178, 196, 260

Computer-based data banks 93

Computer-output microforms (COM) 91, 92, 139, 190, 228, 263

Computer technology 79, 171, 175

Computerization 114
Computerized bibliographic databases 174
Computerized cataloging 104
Computerized database 146, 197
Computerized Information Retrieval Service. SEE CIRS.
Computerized library system 88
Computerized online cataloging 120
Computerized system 97, 98
Computers 79, 139, 140, 142-144, 168, 169, 174, 176, 177, 189, 190, 194, 199, 200, 225, 226, 234, 236, 269, 270, 281, 282, 284-286, 289
Computing network 216, 222
Conference/Congress of Southeast Asian Librarians 10, 64-66, 74, 95, 102, 103
CONSAL. SEE Conference/Congress of Southeast Asian Librarians.
Consejo Nacional de Investigaciones Cientificas y Tecnicas (C.N.I.C.T.) 143, 146, 194, 195, 197
Consultating services 83, 141, 192
Continuing education 102, 179, 258, 270
Cooperation 7, 8, 10, 11, 13, 19, 21, 23, 24, 26-28, 39, 40, 43, 46, 49, 63, 64, 66, 67, 72, 74, 75, 77, 78, 80-84, 86, 89, 91, 94, 96-99, 104, 109, 113, 116-118, 121-124, 137, 154, 157, 162, 166, 167, 171, 175, 178, 183, 187, 199-201, 207, 208, 212, 216, 217, 234, 244, 245, 251, 252, 258-260, 266, 268, 269, 281, 283, 284, 286, 287, 297
Cooperative acquisitions 9, 24, 27, 31, 35, 269, 281
Coordinating 78, 83, 89, 115, 121, 188, 249, 252, 261, 267-269, 271, 295, 297
Coordinating agency 267-269, 271, 297
Coordination 32, 54, 82, 87, 93, 244, 247-252, 262, 266-269, 285
Copying 80, 139, 190

Cost/s 7, 14, 16, 21, 31, 33-36, 38, 40, 87, 88, 98, 105, 108, 115, 121-123, 128, 140-142, 143, 151, 155, 163, 167-169, 174, 176, 180, 190-193, 195, 202, 212-214, 213, 216, 218, 228, 229, 232-234, 236, 243, 252, 260, 269, 270, 281-284, 286 287, 288, 294
Cost analysis 294
Council for Mutual Economic Assistance (CMEA) 78
Council on Library Resources 11, 284
Currency 20, 152, 155, 227
Current awareness service 71, 128, 134, 135, 140, 150, 191
79-84, 86, 87, 93-95, 107, 128, 129, 133-135, 139-141, 143-146, 154, 157, 158, 160-162, 164-166, 168, 173, 175, 181, 190, 191, 194, 196, 201, 202, 225, 226, 232-235, 245, 246, 265, 282, 283, 288, 298

Data bank 68, 86, 87, 94, 95, 140, 141, 191
Data center 84, 160, 161
Data processing centers 190
Database/s 22, 24, 42, 74, 82, 84, 87, 120,, 141, 143, 146, 158, 167-169, 174-177, 180-183, 192, 194, 197, 217, 226, 231, 233, 234, 265, 270, 276, 281-286, 288-292, 294, 295, 303, 306
Database searches 114
Decentralization 162, 166, 236, 244, 247, 252, 271, 287, 300
Decision-making 264, 271
Departmental libraries 244, 248, 250
Deposit 39, 49, 51, 52
Depository laws 52, 154
Design 84, 88, 93, 128, 133, 134, 144, 145, 151, 154, 157, 161-165, 169, 175, 196, 200-202, 207, 226, 231, 264, 268, 286, 290, 293, 303, 305
Desktop 232, 234

320

Developing countries 13, 19, 23, 66, 70, 74, 77, 79, 84, 89, 92, 113, 127, 136, 139, 143, 149, 152-157, 163-165, 169, 181, 190, 195, 243, 245, 248, 251, 257, 259, 261, 281, 283-288

Development 10, 13, 14, 19, 22, 23, 22-24, 29, 30, 32, 33, 35, 40, 42, 43, 49, 52, 63, 65, 66, 70, 72-74, 77-81, 83, 85-87, 89, 91, 92, 97, 99, 101-103, 105-108, 112, 114, 117, 118, 122-124, 125, 127, 137, 138, 142-145, 147, 150, 152, 155-157, 161-169, 171, 172, 174-178, 180-182, 187-189, 192, 194-202, 205-208, 211, 212, 215, 219, 220, 227, 228, 231, 234, 241, 243-245, 249-252, 255, 257, 258, 260-269, 271, 281, 284-297, 299, 300, 303, 305, 306

Development literature 22, 164, 165

Development sciences 74, 165, 167, 181

Development Sciences Information System (DEVSIS) 74, 154, 165, 167, 181, 287

DEVSIS. SEE Development Sciences Information System.

Dial-up access 298

Dialog 120, 168, 176, 231, 283, 294

Disks 176, 232

Dissemination 80, 83, 87, 127, 137-139, 144, 146, 158, 171, 178, 182, 185, 187-190, 193, 195, 197, 263, 264, 269, 282, 292

Document delivery 22, 24, 70, 168, 174-178, 233, 235, 283, 288, 302-304, 306, 307

Documentalists 68, 74, 79, 82, 83, 152, 154

Documentation 5, 49, 66, 69-71, 77, 78, 81-84, 87-89, 91, 92, 137, 138, 142, 149, 151-156, 160, 161, 164, 169, 187, 188, 190, 192, 248, 252, 258, 262-265, 268, 269, 271, 285, 286, 288

Documentation center/s 66, 77, 82-84, 87-89, 154, 155, 160, 161, 164, 190, 258, 286

Documentation services 49, 71, 151, 152, 156, 262-265, 268, 271

Domestic databases 177, 270, 294

Downloading 228, 232

Duplication 25, 84, 87, 164, 177, 187, 244, 248, 251, 252, 262, 287, 294

E-Mail. SEE Electronic Mail.

ECAFE. SEE Economic Commission for Asia and the Far East.

Economic Commission for Asia and the Far East (ECAFE) [later ESCAP, Economic and Social Commission for Asia and the Pacific] 141, 192

Economic development 70, 73, 101, 102, 107, 150, 174

Educating leaders 180

Education 3, 11, 12, 14, 28, 31, 32, 34, 39-41, 46, 69, 85, 88, 89, 101, 102, 105, 107, 113, 116-119, 122, 127, 131, 143, 171, 179, 180, 183, 195, 201, 213, 244-246, 249, 252, 254, 255, 257, 258, 263, 266, 268-270, 289, 295, 297

Electronic journal 176

Electronic mail 176, 178, 234

Electronic publishing 171, 172, 176

Engineering 15, 63, 70, 71, 74, 85-87, 107, 127-129, 131-135, 143-146, 149-154, 156, 179, 183, 192, 195-197, 241, 254, 257-259

Engineering libraries 258

English proficiency 123

ESRO. SEE European Space Research Organization.

ESRO/SDS (European Space Research Organization / Space Documentation Service) 285

ESRO system 142, 146, 192, 193, 197

EURONET (European Network) 169, 285

European Economic Community 285

European Space Agency 169, 285
European Space Research Organization (ESRO) 142, 143, 146, 192-194, 197, 285
Evaluation 81, 122, 123, 133, 168, 220, 300, 301
Exchange of publications 83

Facilities 12, 14, 64, 71, 81, 82, 131-133, 135, 140, 141, 151, 161-163, 166, 169, 180, 191, 217, 234, 260, 266, 281, 287, 299, 306
Facsimile 14, 80, 82, 88, 142, 192, 194
Faculty libraries 244-251, 254-256
Faculty status 243, 251, 243
FES. SEE Friedrich Ebert Stiftung.
FID. SEE International Federation for Documentation.
FID/CAO (Commission for Asia and Oceania of the International Federation for Documentation) 89
Films 39, 107, 258
Flexibility 122, 123, 213, 229
Ford Foundation 137, 187
Foreign books 20, 243
Foreign exchange 155, 180
Foundation engineering 70, 127, 128, 145, 149, 196
Fragmentation 241, 243-245, 249
French Government 67, 93
Friedrich-Ebert-Stiftung (FES) 69, 72-74, 138, 188
Fulbright Exchange Program 112
Full-text 235
Fund/ing 1, 3, 4, 10, 23, 28-38, 40-42, 46, 66, 73, 74, 94, 97, 98, 108, 113, 115, 116, 118, 120-123, 213, 218, 231, 235, 264, 266, 287, 295, 297, 300, 305, 306
Funding Sources 36, 97, 98, 118, 122
Funds 82, 93, 98, 122, 146, 192, 218, 243, 248, 252, 259, 295, 301, 306

Gateway 235, 299

Geotechnical engineering 63, 70, 71, 74, 86, 127, 128, 132, 134, 135, 144, 145, 149-153, 156, 183, 195, 196, 257
Global information system 157, 169
Goals 28, 86, 114, 161, 182, 199, 250, 267
Governance 227, 294, 295, 297, 302, 305, 307
Government 87, 88, 93, 95, 101, 106, 108, 112, 114, 122, 131, 137, 138, 154, 155, 161, 164, 167, 174, 178, 179, 187, 188, 195, 227, 230, 232, 233, 258, 260, 261, 264, 266-268, 271, 287, 289, 291, 293, 295

Hardware 79, 177, 213-215, 217, 218, 230-232, 307
Harvard University 247
Hawaii 7, 8, 11, 8, 88, 199
Health sciences 226, 231, 233, 234
Helsinki University of Technology 286
Hewlett Packard 216, 218, 230
High technology 174, 178, 182
Hoffmann-Pinther, Elizabeth 104, 185, 211, 228, 301
Home information service 175
Hong Kong 69, 113, 130, 138, 188, 199, 203
Hours 214, 243, 244, 246, 249, 251, 254
Human resources management 120

ICA. SEE International Council of Archives.
ICSU. SEE International Council of Scientific Unions.
IDRC. SEE International Development Research Centre.
IFIP. SEE International Federation for Information Processing.
IFLA. SEE International Federation of Library Associations and Institutions
Images 235

Imbalance 288
Implementation 40, 49, 64, 89, 93, 115, 163, 215, 216, 226, 229, 260, 263, 264, 266, 267, 271, 292, 300, 302, 305, 306
In-service training 83, 97, 258, 270
Indexes 104, 134, 153-155, 161, 164-166, 230, 233, 283, 287
India 19, 63, 69, 130, 251
Indigenous material 153
Indigenous publications 140, 154, 164, 191
INDIS. SEE Industrial Development Information System.
Indonesia 8, 9, 26, 29, 31, 32, 35, 52, 63-65, 68, 69, 73, 77, 84, 89, 94, 95, 98, 106, 113, 118, 119, 129, 130, 137, 142, 187, 192, 257
Industrial Development Information System (INDIS) 181
Information 1, 5-11, 13-15, 22, 23, 22-24, 27, 28, 35, 39-43, 49-54, 63-74, 75, 77-89, 91-93, 95-97, 101-105, 107, 112, 113, 115-123, 125, 127-129, 131-147, 149-152, 154-158, 160-169, 171-183, 185, 187-202, 204, 205, 207, 212, 213, 217, 220, 225, 226, 229-236, 241, 245, 246, 254, 259-271, 273, 281-307
Information age 11, 171, 177, 179, 261
Information analysis center 160, 161
Information center/s 49-54, 63-74, 85, 95, 118, 120, 127, 138, 140, 144, 145, 149, 152, 156, 160, 161, 178, 179, 183, 190, 191, 195, 196, 259-261, 268, 276, 295
Information consciousness 152, 156
Information explosion 15, 53, 79, 173-175, 179, 234
Information gap 54, 125, 137, 143, 147, 187, 197, 261
Information industries 263, 264
Information infrastructure 181, 265, 288

Information needs 77, 83, 85, 89, 129, 133, 135-138, 158, 161, 166, 183, 187, 188, 259, 261, 262, 264, 265, 267, 269
Information network 14, 27, 137, 138, 144, 145, 166, 169, 187, 188, 195, 196, 200, 201, 226, 273, 282, 287, 289, 290, 292, 293, 295, 296
Information policy 261-268, 271
Information processing 78, 79, 81, 140, 168, 204, 282, 293
Information processing centers 140
Information resources 35, 67, 71, 81, 82, 84, 85, 89, 151, 163, 164, 169, 182, 198, 267, 269, 270, 273, 281, 285, 286, 302, 303
Information service/s 70, 72, 75, 77-79, 81, 83, 87, 92, 105, 119, 120, 123, 125, 127, 128, 138, 139, 141, 144, 145, 147, 149, 150, 155, 156, 161, 164, 168, 171, 175, 176, 178-180, 183, 188, 189, 192, 195-197, 230, 233, 235, 259, 261-271, 282, 284, 285, 288, 289-92, 294, 295
Information sharing 28, 116
Information society 172, 173, 178, 261
Information specialists 24, 79, 82, 83, 197
Information system 74, 78-80, 82, 91, 92, 141, 142, 157, 158, 160-162, 165, 167, 169, 171, 175, 177, 181, 189, 192, 201, 235, 259, 261, 262, 265, 273, 281, 282, 286, 287, 297, 299-302, 306
Information technology 13, 28, 103, 105, 125, 139, 141, 144, 147, 173-175, 179, 180, 185, 187, 189, 192, 195, 197, 225
Information transfer 49, 78, 79, 87, 91, 92, 96, 144, 146, 158, 164, 182, 195, 197, 226, 259
Information transmission 142, 168, 192, 233
Information utility 72, 125, 127, 135, 151

Infrastructures 74, 91, 92, 154, 156, 164, 262, 263, 267, 268

INIS. SEE International Nuclear Information System.

Institute of Scientific and Technical Information of China (ISTIC) 113

Integrated system 229, 236

INTELSAT 14-17, 143, 194

Inter-compatibility 287

Inter-continental communications 142, 194

Inter-institutional cooperation 116, 123

Inter-University Library Council (IULC) 226, 297, 298, 302

Interconnection 67, 71, 88, 91, 92, 151, 157, 162, 167, 177, 194, 231, 269, 281, 287

Interdisciplinary 157, 179, 180, 248, 251

Interlibrary loan/s 10, 23, 38, 83, 114, 120, 168, 174, 177, 211, 213, 227-229, 231, 233, 245, 252, 258, 269, 281, 283, 284, 293, 297, 298, 302, 304

International 1, 5, 7-15, 21, 22, 24, 27-32, 34, 40-43, 45, 46, 47, 49-51, 63, 64, 66-70, 73, 74, 75, 77-85, 87-89, 91-93, 95-98, 101-106, 109, 111, 112, 114-118, 121-123, 127, 138, 142-146, 150, 153, 154, 157, 164-167, 169, 171, 177, 181, 182, 183, 188-190, 192, 194-196, 198-202, 204, 205, 207, 208, 233, 257, 259, 262, 263, 266, 269, 281-291

International Communication Agency 112

International cooperation 11, 24, 28, 43, 75, 78, 80, 82, 91, 98, 116, 121 154, 166, 171, 199-201, 208, 269

International Council of Scientific Unions (ICSU) 78, 80, 84, 91-93, 262

International Council of Archives (ICA) 91, 269

International Development Research Centre (IDRC) 22, 24, 26, 28, 66, 68, 72-74, 127, 145, 150, 151, 155, 165, 181, 182, 196

International exchange 9, 14, 15, 40, 80, 102, 109, 111, 121, 207

International Federation for Documentation (FID) 70, 78, 89, 91, 149, 154, 269

International Federation for Information Processing (IFIP) 78.

International Federation of Library Associations and Institutions (IFLA) 7, 13, 23, 28, 51, 55, 91, 111, 146, 182, 269, 290

International Geotechnical Classification System 70, 150

International information systems 74, 154, 157, 166, 167, 182, 281, 282, 286-288

International Information Retrieval Network 142, 194

International Information System for the Agricultural Sciences (AGRIS) 74, 154, 167, 181, 286, 287

International interdependence 75

International internship program 102, 105

International ISBN Agency 50, 56

International Nuclear Information System (INIS) 74, 87, 154, 167, 169, 181, 201, 281, 286

International Organization for Standardization 182

International Serials Data Systems (ISDS) 50

International Standard Bibliographic Description (ISBD) 8, 91, 154, 205

International Standard Bibliographic Description for Monographs (ISBD [M]) 8, 55, 58

International Standard Bibliographic Description for Serials (ISBD [S]) 55, 60

International Standard Book Number/s (ISBN) 49-52, 55, 56, 91, 291

International Standard Serial Number/s (ISSN) 50-53, 55, 57, 67, 68, 93, 95, 97, 291
International standards 49, 177, 182, 204, 287
International Standards Organization (ISO) 49, 78, 177, 182, 202, 204
International Studies 22, 29, 31, 32, 34, 104, 106
Internships 40, 102, 109, 113, 114, 116-119, 121-123
INTREX (Information Transfer Experiment) 87, 226
Iran 130, 142, 192
ISBD. SEE International Standard Bibliographic Description
ISBN. SEE International Standard Book Number.
ISDS Bulletin 50, 67, 93
ISDS International Centre 50, 95
ISO. SEE International Standards Organization.
ISO-646 204
ISSN SEE International Standard Serial Number.
ISTIC. SEE Institute of Scientific and Technical Information of China.

Japan 19, 67, 93, 130, 199, 201, 203, 257, 261
Japan Scientific and Technical Information Center (JICST) 261
John Crerar Library 143, 194, 195, 258
Journal articles 87, 165, 174, 235, 305
Journal literature 153

KASC. SEE Knowledge Availability Systems Center.
Key words 153, 229
Knowledge 4, 10, 13, 15, 46, 49, 52, 67, 78, 79, 85, 93, 103, 107, 113, 119, 123, 137, 144, 146, 154, 158, 160, 172, 178-180, 187, 195, 197, 233, 258, 259, 264, 281, 284, 288
Knowledge Availability Systems Center (KASC) 144, 146, 195, 197
Korea 69, 130, 199, 203

LAN. SEE Local Area Network.
Language differences 152
Latin America 21, 286
Laws 51, 52, 154, 270
LC MARC II 207
Leadership 30, 45, 175, 178, 205, 206, 226, 252, 297
Leased-line 285
Legislation 51, 252, 266
LEXIS/NEXIS 232
Librarian/s 7-12, 15, 20, 22-24, 27, 28, 32, 35, 39, 40, 46, 53, 64, 65, 68, 74, 79, 82, 83, 94, 95, 99, 101-103, 105, 109, 111-113, 115-118, 121, 141, 160, 173, 174, 179, 192, 201, 202, 208, 226, 236, 243, 244, 247-252, 254, 260, 290, 300, 301
Library Association of China 171, 175, 180, 183, 189, 201, 205, 268, 295
Library buildings 235, 300
Library development 40, 99, 114, 117, 118, 208, 241, 250-252, 262, 268
Library education 113, 117-119, 171, 179, 180
Library facilities 71, 82, 131-133, 135, 151, 299
Library-information service 144, 145, 147, 195-197
Library management 114, 292
Library networks 10, 236, 277, 281, 284, 285
Library professionals 117
Library schools 9, 12, 97, 114, 117, 119, 120, 260, 295
Library science 40, 102, 103, 112, 113, 116, 243, 282
Library science faculty 40, 103, 113
Linked Systems Project (LSP) 11, 42, 303

Local area network (LAN) 8, 200, 205, 234
Local system/s 228, 230, 231, 289, 298, 303
Lockheed 168, 282, 283, 292, 294, 295
Long-range 86, 92, 98, 264, 271
LSP. SEE Linked Systems Project.

Machine-readable 15, 40, 70, 82, 87, 94, 141, 150, 167-169, 191, 205-207, 212, 226, 229, 281-284, 286, 288, 291, 293, 297
Machine-readable database/s 70, 150, 167, 169, 191, 229, 281-284, 286, 288
Machine Readable Cataloging 87, 146, 226
Magnetic tape 93, 139, 177
Major Microforms Project 230
Malaysia 8, 9, 14, 22, 30-35, 37-39, 43, 45, 46, 52, 63, 65, 68, 69, 72, 75, 77, 84, 89, 95, 98, 101, 102, 105-108, 113, 114, 118, 119, 130, 137, 138, 146, 187, 188, 257, 259
Malaysian materials 106, 108
Malaysian Resource Center 39, 43, 101, 102, 104-108
Malaysian students 30, 38, 39, 107, 108
Management 14, 86, 103, 113, 114, 116, 119, 120, 157, 162, 163, 167, 168, 174, 179, 199, 201, 213, 229, 243, 252, 257, 264, 271, 282, 287, 290, 292, 303, 305
Management personnel 113
Manpower 11, 67, 92, 94, 117, 266, 270
MARA Institute of Technology 30, 102
MARC 87, 141, 144, 146, 168, 171, 175, 177, 182, 191, 196, 199-202, 206-208, 213, 226, 228-230, 259, 283, 291-293, 297, 299
MARC format 146, 182, 201, 206, 207, 226, 229, 299

MARC records 144, 196, 208, 229, 292, 293
MARC tapes 146, 230
Marketing 136, 179-181
Mass communication/s 63, 68, 69, 74, 137
Massachusetts Institute of Technology 226
Massil, Stephen W. 47, 49, 144, 146, 196
McCauley, Hannah V. 104, 185, 211, 228
Media Asia 69
Medical information network 226
MEDLARS 87, 191, 226, 231
MEDLINE 120
Methods 80, 139, 140, 158, 190, 233, 263, 269, 287, 299
Microcomputers 42, 104, 177, 178, 228, 230, 232, 234, 235
Microfilming 24, 64, 65, 80, 139, 145, 190, 196
Microform 21, 27, 35, 40, 64-66, 228, 230, 232, 299
Migration 73
Minicomputers 212, 228
Mission-oriented 157, 166, 178, 281, 286, 287
Modernization 174, 178
Modulization 293
Mongolian 203
Morocco 285
Mulliner, K. 1, 7, 8, 19, 29, 38, 40, 43, 75, 101-104, 109, 111, 121, 185, 211, 228, 301
Multifunction 236

NASA. SEE National Aeronautics and Space Administration.
National Academy of Sciences 112, 143, 195, 284
National Aeronautics and Space Administration (NASA) 87, 88, 146, 197
National Agricultural Library 87, 191, 227

National bibliographic services 50-52
National bibliography/ies 5, 52, 83, 141, 146, 153, 154, 164, 208, 283
National Central Library (Taiwan) 171, 175, 201, 208, 268, 271, 290, 295
National development 49, 52, 77, 117, 137, 156, 164, 175, 181, 187, 243, 257, 261, 262, 264, 266, 267, 295
National development plans 164, 262, 266, 267
National documentation center/s 77, 88, 154, 155, 164, 190
National focal points 167, 287
National information centres 197
National information policies 262, 263
National Information System (NATIS) 92, 261, 262, 263, 265
National Information System for Science and Technology 263
National library/ies 8, 10, 49-52, 54, 66-68, 74, 77, 82-84, 87, 89 96, 98, 106, 117, 138, 142, 144, 146, 154, 164, 177, 190-192, 201, 226, 227, 241, 252, 258, 261-264, 266-269, 273, 285, 289, 290, 292, 293, 295, 296
National library-information systems 142, 192
National library and information network 138, 201, 273, 289, 290, 292, 293, 295, 296
National Library of Australia 8, 50, 52, 144, 146
National Library of Canada 227
National Library of Thailand 67, 68, 98
National MARC database 146
National Oceanographic Data Center 161
National Referral Center 161, 164
National Research Council of Thailand 72, 137, 138, 261, 268, 295
National Technical Information Services (NTIS) 155, 161, 169

National union catalog 6, 208, 293, 294
NATIS. SEE National Information System.
Nepal 69, 129, 130
Network parasitology 286
Networking 13, 104, 114, 116, 120, 143, 157, 166, 168, 169, 194, 200, 213, 217, 229, 231, 236, 269, 273, 275, 278, 281, 283, 286, 288, 289, 295, 298
New serial titles 68, 94, 97
Nippon Cataloging Rules 205, 206
NIST (National Information System for Science and Technology) 261
Non-print 205, 230, 232
Non-Roman languages 140
NORDFORSK (Scandinavian Council for Applied Research) 78
NORDinfo (Scandinavian Committee for Technical Information Services) 78
Norms 263, 287
Norway 72, 78, 285
NTIS. SEE National Technical Information Services.
NTISearch 161
Numeric data 175, 282

Objectives 85, 86, 92, 95, 120, 161, 175, 261, 263-268
OCLC. SEE OCLC Online Computer Library Center.
OCLC database 14, 211, 212
OCLC Online Computer Library Center 10, 11, 14, 28, 34, 40, 42, 104, 105, 107, 114, 120, 168, 199, 211-215, 217, 218, 221, 225-230, 234, 236, 269, 284, 285, 289, 292, 293, 297-299, 306
OCR (Optical Character Recognition) 232
OECD. SEE Organization for Economic and Cooperative Development.
OECD Macrothesaurus 73

Office automation 234
Ohio 1, 7, 11, 12, 14, 22, 29-46, 75,
    101-109, 111, 113-116, 118, 120-124,
    185, 211-213, 216, 217, 225-236,
    273, 284, 293, 297-302, 305-307
Ohio Board of Regents 235, 297, 299-
    302, 307
Ohio College Association 226, 293,
    297
Ohio College Library Center (cf.
    OCLC Online Computer Library
    Center) 104, 211, 225, 226, 284,
    293, 297
Ohio Library Information System
    (OLIS; later OhioLINK, q.v.) 235,
    299-302, 304-306
Ohio University 1, 11, 12, 22, 29-46,
    75, 101-108, 111, 113-116, 118, 121-
    124, 185, 211, 212, 216, 217, 225-
    233, 236, 298, 300, 301
Ohio Valley Area Libraries (OVAL)
    217, 231
OhioLINK 306, 307
OhioPi 232
OLIS. SEE Ohio Library Information
    System AND OhioLINK.
On-demand publishing 174, 176
Online database search 231
Online access 40, 176, 231, 270
Online databases 42, 174, 180, 181,
    306
Online delivery 174
Online information services 105, 294
Online public access catalog/s (OPAC)
    104, 120, 212, 213, 217, 220, 228-
    230, 235, 298, 303
Online revolution 174
Online search 174
OPAC. SEE Online public access
    catalog/s.
Operation/s 8, 13, 40, 50, 67, 69-71,
    78, 88, 92-95, 97, 102, 127, 138, 140,
    142, 149, 154, 161-163, 169, 192,
    250, 252, 284, 293-295
Optical character recognition 232
Optical discs 225, 232

Organization 8, 19, 24, 27, 28, 49, 74,
    78, 81, 84, 85, 89, 91, 95, 96, 98,
    103, 112, 120, 122, 127, 142, 144,
    151, 158, 161, 162, 164, 178, 181,
    182, 190, 192, 195, 208, 214, 220,
    227, 252, 257, 262, 263, 271, 297
Organization for Economic Co-opera-
    tion and Development (OECD) 19,
    73, 78
Outreach program 106
OVAL. SEE Ohio Valley Area Librar-
    ies.

Pakistan 69, 130, 257
Papua New Guinea 65, 105
Para-professionals 180
Peace Corps 9, 112
PEACESAT (PanPacific Education
    and Communication Experiment by
    Satellite) 88
People's Republic of China 25, 105,
    112, 119, 183
Personnel 12, 104, 113, 117, 140, 162,
    190, 212-215, 219, 229, 243, 291,
    292
Philippines 7-9, 32, 63, 65, 68, 69, 72,
    73, 77, 84, 89, 94, 95, 98, 106, 117,
    119, 130, 138, 188, 257, 290
Photocopying 115, 121, 145, 153, 168,
    196, 225, 252, 258, 281, 283
Photoduplication 24, 35, 162
Planning 9, 52, 64, 73, 81, 84, 89, 91,
    92, 94, 98, 123, 137, 138, 144, 146,
    152, 154, 157, 164, 167, 169, 175,
    177, 187, 188, 195-197, 201, 208,
    214, 215, 217, 218, 235, 236, 244,
    250, 252, 261, 262, 264, 266, 268,
    269, 271, 273, 285, 286, 292, 297,
    300-303, 306, 307
Plans 24, 28, 73, 77, 87, 89, 95, 137,
    138, 143, 144, 164, 177, 187, 188,
    195, 261-263, 266, 267
Policy 19, 32, 33, 43, 71, 72, 78, 93,
    96, 106, 127, 129, 130, 157, 167,
    174, 178, 235, 241, 250, 251, 261-
    271, 304, 307

Practical experience 103, 113, 118, 120
Practitioners 124, 180
Prestel 175
Pricing 266
Priorities 83, 219, 229, 265, 267
Private sector 271
Professional competencies 173, 179, 180
Professional education 102
Promotion 69, 74, 80, 81, 164, 171, 178, 182, 189, 243, 262-264, 266, 270
Public sector 264, 271
Publishers 22, 49-54, 97, 174, 176, 177, 263, 268, 282
Publishing 8, 22, 26, 52-54, 108, 171, 172, 174, 176, 232, 234, 263, 264, 270

Ready reference 232
Reciprocal borrowing 281, 298
Reference 4, 7, 8, 71, 83, 97, 98, 103, 128, 134, 145, 151, 160, 171, 196, 200-203, 215, 231-233, 248, 251, 282, 284, 306
Referral 71, 83, 128, 135, 145, 151, 160, 161, 164, 196, 265
Referral services 83
Referral center/re/s 63, 67, 68, 74, 93-98, 160, 161, 164
Regional Centre for ISDS 98
Regional clearing-house 68, 72
Regional conferences 83, 181, 183
Regional cooperation 10, 11, 63, 64, 67, 74, 75, 77, 78, 81-84, 86, 89, 91, 99, 259
Regional information center/s, 82, 84, 85, 127, 152
Regional library-information networks 142, 192
Regulations 33, 155, 245, 266, 270
Remote access 175, 181, 283
Report literature 154
Reproduction 81, 83, 128, 134, 142, 145, 162, 192, 196

Reprography 71, 79, 139, 151, 189, 190
Republic of China (ROC; cf. Taiwan) 25, 105, 112, 119, 130, 138, 171, 174, 177, 178, 180, 182, 183, 199, 200, 257, 261, 268, 269, 271, 289, 291
Request for Information (RFI) 300, 301, 305
Request for Proposal/s (RFP) 235, 301, 305, 306
Research 1, 5, 7-11, 13, 14, 20-24, 27-35, 37-42, 44, 46, 49, 63-66, 68-74, 78, 82, 84, 85, 87, 89, 102, 105-108, 111, 112, 116, 121, 127, 128, 131, 134, 135, 137, 142, 143, 145, 150, 151, 154, 155, 160, 161, 164, 165, 169, 171, 178, 180, 187, 192, 195, 196, 199, 200, 202, 217, 226, 230-232, 234, 244, 247, 248, 253, 257-259, 266, 285, 286, 289, 291, 295, 298, 303, 306, 307
Resource sharing 13, 22, 23, 106, 174, 228, 235, 284, 288, 297, 298
Retraining 117
Retrieval 13, 40, 70, 87, 128, 133, 137, 142, 143, 145, 150, 160, 162, 177, 185, 187, 191, 194, 196, 201, 226, 231, 264, 285, 290-293
Retrospective search 140, 191
RFI. SEE Request for Information.
RFP. SEE Request for Proposals.
Rhoades, Marjorie H. 125, 157
RLIN (Research Library Information Network) 10, 11, 27, 28, 34, 40, 42, 226
ROC. SEE Republic of China.
Royal Institute of Technology 286
Royal Thai Government 95

SARBICA (Southeast Asia Branch of the International Council on Archives) 10, 64-66, 74
Satellite/s 13-16, 80, 82, 88, 142-144, 146, 168, 169, 178, 180, 181, 194, 195, 197, 259, 270, 295

Satellite communications 13, 80, 82, 259

Saudi Arabia 105, 119

SAULNET (Southeast Asia University Library Network) 13

Scandinavia 285

Scandinavian Committee for Technical Information Services. SEE NORDinfo.

Scandinavian Council for Applied Research. SEE NORDFORSK.

Scanning 232

Scholarly Publications 53, 67, 68

Science information policies 78, 92

Scientific and technical information 77, 78, 83, 85, 88, 89, 92, 113, 137, 138, 173, 187, 188, 193, 197, 198, 259, 261-263, 265, 268, 269, 271, 286

Scientific and technical information services 77, 259

Scientific and Technological Information Center 295

Scientific information 80, 81, 92, 125, 157, 158, 164, 176

SDS. SEE Space Documentation Service.

SDI (selective dissemination of information) service 140, 150, 191, 283

SEAMEO. SEE South East Asian Ministers of Education Organization.

SEATO. SEE Southeast Asia Treaty Organization.

Seminars 9, 73, 86, 97, 117, 120, 131, 132, 141, 181, 192, 258

Serial data bank 94

Serial publications 53, 67, 68, 91, 93-97, 140, 153, 191

Serial record 94

Serials 23, 47, 50-53, 67, 68, 83, 91, 93, 95, 97, 104, 139, 140, 144-146, 174, 181, 191, 200, 211, 213, 219, 228, 229, 244, 259, 260, 284, 293, 298, 303

Serials control 104, 211, 213, 219, 228, 229, 298

Shared cataloging 208, 211, 226-229, 269, 281, 284, 293, 294, 297, 298

Short courses 83, 97, 117, 141, 181, 192, 258

Simmons College 113

Social Development 63, 72-74, 138, 166, 188, 198, 287

Social Science Research Council 112

Soil mechanics 70, 127, 128, 132, 145, 149, 150, 196

Soil Mechanics Thesaurus 70, 150

South East Asian Ministers of Education Organization (SEAMEO) 89

Southeast Asia 1, 7-15, 25, 29-36, 35-44, 46, 53, 63-65, 68, 74, 77, 79, 82, 84, 89, 94, 95, 98, 101-103, 105-108, 112-116, 118, 119, 123, 137, 140, 146, 187, 190, 213, 243, 257

Southeast Asia Collection 1, 12, 29, 31, 33-39, 43, 101-103, 105-108, 113, 114, 118, 123, 213

Southeast Asia Treaty Organization (SEATO) 85, 257

Space Documentation Service (SDS) 120, 142, 169, 176 192, 285, 294, 295

Spain 285

Specifications 93, 157, 303, 305

Sri Lanka 69, 130

Staff 4, 12, 24, 25, 29, 41, 72, 83, 96-98, 103, 104, 113-115, 118-124, 140, 160, 163, 179, 180, 190, 212-217, 219, 220, 227, 229, 230, 232-234, 244, 248, 249, 251, 254, 260, 270, 295, 299, 302

Standard format 74, 294

Standardization 8, 47, 78, 91, 116, 154, 167, 182, 266, 269, 283, 288

Standards 8, 49, 51, 53, 81, 83, 93, 113, 162, 171, 177, 182, 204, 248, 252, 263, 287

Stanford University 226

State Library of Ohio 233

330

STN (Scientific and Technical Information Network) 231
Subject headings 291
SUDOCS (Superintendent of Documents) 230
System design 93, 161-163, 303

Tables of contents 305
Taiwan (cf. Republic of China) 12, 25, 105, 113, 115, 118, 119, 183, 185, 199-203, 207, 208, 289, 290, 293, 295
TALINET. SEE Telefax Library Information Network.
Tape loading 214, 215, 218, 228, 230
Tapes 4, 43, 84, 87, 88, 97, 107, 141, 146, 191, 208, 214, 215, 217, 218, 226, 230, 259, 283, 294
Technical assistance 122, 164, 181
Technical information 71, 75, 77, 78, 83, 85, 86, 88, 89, 92, 113, 127, 131-135, 137, 138, 144, 151, 154, 155, 161, 169, 173, 178, 187, 188, 193, 195, 197, 198, 259-263, 265, 268, 269, 271, 286
Technical papers 153
Technological application 120
Technological University of Denmark 286
Technologies 79, 114, 117, 120, 139, 157, 168, 177, 189, 218, 225, 232, 235, 236, 269, 289, 293, 297, 306
Telecommunication linkage 168, 289
Telecommunications 79, 80, 139, 141, 142, 175, 177, 180, 189, 192-194, 225, 228, 231, 233, 236, 281, 288,
Telefacsimile (cf. Facsimile) 233
Telefax Library Information Network (TALINET) 14
Telephone 14, 39, 80, 82, 115, 177, 178, 219, 220, 231, 234, 286
Teletype/s 80, 82, 88, 142, 143, 194
Telex networks 286
Textbooks 121, 243
Thesaurus 70, 150, 291

Third World nations 21, 22, 24, 26, 28, 101, 116
Tibetan 203
Training 4, 68, 69, 74, 83, 94, 97, 105, 113-124, 141, 163, 171, 180, 192, 197, 215, 257, 258, 260, 263, 266, 270, 287, 288, 291, 292, 295
Training coordinator 119, 122
Training program 69, 114
Transborder information flow 181
Translation 73, 261, 265, 288
Transliteration 207
Tun Abdul Razak Chair 33, 38, 45, 46, 106, 114
Tymnet 286

U.S. Information Agency 112
U.S. Government Printing Office 227
U.S./U.S.A. SEE United States.
UAP. SEE Universal Availability of Publications.
UBC. SEE Universal Bibliographic Control.
Ulrich's International Periodicals Directory 50
Ulrich's Irregular Serials and Annuals 50
UNDP SEE United Nations Development Programme.
Unesco (United Nations Educational, Scientific and Cultural Organization) 10, 12, 13, 22, 23, 28, 40, 49, 50, 53, 55, 63, 67-69, 74, 77, 78, 80, 81, 89, 91-93, 95, 97, 98, 105, 112, 113, 115, 116, 118, 122, 137, 138, 145, 154, 155, 164, 169, 181, 187, 188, 197, 251, 254, 262, 263, 265, 269, 283, 286-288
Unesco coupons 155, 288
UNIMARC (Universal MARC) 206, 207
Union catalog/s 6, 10, 83, 140, 146, 191, 208, 211, 226, 228, 235, 244, 247, 250, 252, 269, 291, 294
Union list of journals 247, 252
Union list of periodicals 140, 191

331

Union list of serials 83, 144-146, 244, 260

UNISIST 13, 50, 57, 67, 74, 78-81, 84, 91-93, 98, 145, 182, 262, 263, 284, 287

United Kingdom 20, 67, 195, 257

United Nations Development Programme (UNDP) 97, 137, 138, 187, 188

United Nations Economic Commission for Asia and the Far East. SEE Economic Commission for Asia and the Far East.

United Nations Educational, Scientific, and Cultural Organization. SEE Unesco.

United States (U.S./U.S.A.) 3, 7-11, 19, 24, 27-31, 46, 52, 67, 72, 88, 93, 101, 114, 130, 143, 163, 164, 168, 174, 176, 178 199,, 230, 257, 258, 269, 289

Universal Availability of Publications (UAP) 23, 182

Universal Bibliographic Control (UBC) 49, 50, 91, 154, 182

Universities 9, 11, 23, 30, 31, 35, 39, 41, 49, 69, 101, 106, 107, 112, 115, 131, 144, 188, 196, 226, 235, 243-245, 247-249, 251-253, 258, 297, 298, 301, 302, 306

University librarian 244, 247-250

University libraries 20, 101, 111, 114-116, 211, 225, 231, 235, 241, 243, 247-253, 297-299

University of Hawaii 8, 11, 88

University of Pittsburgh 105,144, 146, 195, 197

Use 32, 34, 40, 42, 43, 49, 53, 64, 68, 69, 72, 80, 81, 87, 88, 93, 94, 97, 104, 108, 116125, 127, 129, 131-133, 135, 136, 139-141, 143, 146, 151, 154-156, 167, 168, 172, 185, 190-192, 194, 200, 204, 207, 211, 213, 215, 216, 225, 226, 228, 229, 231, 232-234, 236, 243, 245, 246, 248, 251, 258, 260, 264, 269, 270, 283-285, 288, 289, 291, 292, 294, 298, 303, 305, 306

User Analysis 129

User education 266, 270

Users 9, 24, 34, 42, 49, 71, 104, 106, 127, 128, 135, 136, 151, 155-157, 160, 161, 167, 169, 174-176, 182, 187, 197, 211, 216, 218-220, 227, 230, 231, 233-236, 244, 249, 250, 263, 267-270, 281, 284, 288, 300-303, 306

Video 43, 143, 194, 232

Videodisc/s 177, 232

Vietnam 8, 29, 257

Virginia Tech Library System (VTLS) 104, 185, 211, 213-215, 217-221, 228-231, 298, 306

VTLS. SEE Virginia Tech Library System.

Wade-Giles romanization 207

WAN. SEE Wide area network/s.

Washington Library Network (WLN; subsequently Western Library Network) 11, 199

Water resources 125, 157, 163-167, 169

Water resources information systems 157, 164, 166, 169

Wide area network/s 201, 234

Wilsonline 231

WLN. SEE Washington Library Network.

Women 73

Word processing 234

Workshops 97, 114, 115, 117, 120, 121, 131, 132, 141, 180, 192, 234, 258

Workstations 233, 234, 236

World Health Organization 112

World Science Information System 78, 80, 91, 262

WRSIC (Water Resources Scientific Information Centre) 167, 169

國立中央圖書館出版品預行編目資料

圖書館學的世界觀：1963-1989論文選集 = Librarianship
in world perspective : selected writings, 1963-
1989/ 李華偉著．-- 初版．-- 臺北市：臺灣學生，民
80
　　面；　　公分
參考書目：面
含索引
ISBN 957-15-0255-3（精裝）． -- ISBN 957-15-
0256-1（平裝）
1. 圖書館學 - 論文，講詞等
020.7　　　　　　　　　　　　　　　　80002771

圖書館學的世界觀（全一冊）

著　作　者：李　　　華　　　偉
出　版　者：臺　灣　學　生　書　局
發　行　人：丁　　　文　　　治
發　行　所：臺　灣　學　生　書　局
臺北市和平東路一段一九八號
郵政劃撥帳號〇〇〇二四六六八號
電　話：3 6 3 4 1 5 6
FAX：3 6 3 6 3 3 4
本書局登記
記　證　字　號：行政院新聞局局版臺業字第一一〇〇號
印　刷　所：淵　明　印　刷　有　限　公　司
地　址：永和市成功路一段43巷五號
電　話：9 2 8 7 1 4 5
香港總經銷：藝　文　圖　書　公　司
地址：九龍偉業街99號連順大厦五字
樓及七字樓　電話：7959595
定價　精裝新台幣三一〇元
　　　平裝新台幣二六〇元

中　華　民　國　八　十　年　九　月　初　版

02010
ISBN 957-15-0255-3（精裝）
ISBN 957-15-0256-1（平裝）